Little Charley Ross

BOOKS BY NORMAN ZIEROLD

THE CHILD STARS

LITTLE CHARLEY ROSS
America's First Kidnapping for Ransom

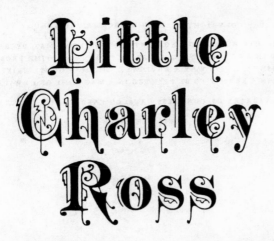

Little Charley Ross

America's First Kidnapping for Ransom

by NORMAN ZIEROLD

WITH ILLUSTRATIONS

LITTLE, BROWN AND COMPANY · BOSTON · TORONTO

Published simultaneously in Canada
by Little, Brown & Company (Canada) Limited

PRINTED IN THE UNITED STATES OF AMERICA

For My Family

Illustrations

Book One

Charles Brewster Ross

1

THE TEMPERATURE in Philadelphia on July 1, 1874, hovered comfortably in the seventies. The sky was clear, bright, and sunny, giving the inhabitants one more reason to be joyful at the approaching weekend. The Fourth of July was the national holiday most closely identified with Philadelphia's colorful early history, and this year it would be celebrated with redoubled spirits. The city already had been chosen as the site for the Centennial Exposition, scheduled to open in time to celebrate the one hundredth anniversary of the nation's independence. The Centennial Board of Finance had just awarded contracts for the Memorial building and the main Exposition building, which would cover eighteen acres.

Overlying the general optimism were two ceremonies specifically planned for the Fourth, both symbols of municipal progress. At one end of the city, the new Girard Avenue Bridge, a thousand feet long and one hundred feet wide — the widest bridge in the world — was to be formally opened for travel across the Schuylkill River. The span was to be the principal avenue to the newly opened Zoological Gardens in Fairmount Park, sixteen acres of aviaries, monkey houses, bear pits, prairie dog villages, and deer parks. A display of fireworks which promised to be "an unusually brilliant one" was scheduled for Fairmount Park in the presence of the City Council.

At Penn Square the cornerstone was to be laid for the new City Hall, an enormous structure with an elaborate French

Renaissance exterior and a sweeping tower capped by a statue of the city's founder, William Penn. Pennsylvania's Governor John Frederick Hartranft and President Ulysses S. Grant had been invited for the ceremonies, but by reason of engagements previously made had said they would be unable to appear. Philadelphia Mayor William S. Stokley's speech thus took on added importance, and as he prepared it his civic pride rose to remarkable heights.

"I have seen and lived in most all of the capitals of Europe and I have read of all of the great cities of the world," he wrote, "but I have never seen or read of such a city as this is. There is no town in the world of its dimension and population, and there never has been one that possesses such accommodations for its people. Artisans, even laborers, live with us as they have never lived before. Men whose daily earnings in other cities will hardly sustain life and provide a shelter for themselves and their families except in the most rude, coarse, scanty, and crowded way, are here the occupants of single and comfortable dwellings, and thousands of them the owners of their own houses.

"The effect of this upon the mental and moral condition of the citizens is evident even to transient visitors. We have no such class here as the poor working man; our city is filled with workmen, independent, prosperous freemen, who bring up families of boys with habits of thrift and industry to go out in life prepared and resolved to earn homes because they have enjoyed them in their happy childhood."

To document his case, the mayor contrasted his city with New York. At the beginning of 1873 Philadelphia had 134,740 buildings, of which 124,302 were dwelling houses, some 60,000 more than New York. And this despite the fact that the population of Philadelphia was less than 800,000, while New York's was more than 1,000,000.

Philadelphia's citizens lived in a comfortably sprawling

area of 12 square miles crisscrossed by more than 900 miles of streets and roads, more than 500 of them paved. The city boasted 10,000 gas lamps; more than 1600 schoolteachers and more than 80,000 pupils; more than 34,000 bathrooms, most of them supplied with hot water; and more than 400 places of public worship. The Quaker City's well-stocked houses of prostitution were understandably omitted from the tabulation.

"Of all the cities in this nation, Philadelphia is pre-eminently American," the mayor continued after inditing these figures. "Its characteristics and customs, the habits and peculiarities of the people are essentially American. If a foreigner were to ask me where will I find a real man untouched in his character and nationality by the ever-drifting tide of emigration, domestic and foreign, and with no taint of provincial narrowness, I would say go to Philadelphia, and there you will find just such men and women by the hundreds of thousands."

Having prepared this eulogy to the city, Mayor Stokley made his plans to get out of it. Shortly after the Fourth he would leave for Long Branch, a fashionable watering place on the coast north of Atlantic City. The mayor would spend the entire month there and return to the city only for brief visits to attend to urgent business.

At that safe distance he would probably read in the papers an account of the Total Abstinence Beneficial Societies, who planned to turn out in full force on the Fourth, singing and praying in front of saloons; and of the meeting at Independence Square of Temperance Blessing, a group which had scheduled, in addition to a reading of the Declaration of Independence, the recitation by two young children of poems entitled "The Inebriate's Ladder" and "The Drunkard's Tomb."

He was also likely to note an advertisement which the advocates of prohibition frequently inserted in the *Public*

Ledger, a newspaper run by the mayor's friend William V. McKean. It drew attention to "Buttermilk, the great summer drink," and provided an address where that refreshing beverage could be obtained.

The mayor had been mildly surprised recently when the *Ledger* took issue with a different type of prohibition, that against bathing in the city's rivers. Only a few days earlier, when city police arrested twenty-one persons in the Schuylkill, the paper had come to their defense, stating that bathing and swimming were good exercise and that there ought to be as little hindrance to them as possible, especially as the authorities had failed to provide the means for those who had no facilities at home. The *Ledger* editorial contended that a dip in the river could not be technically prohibited if there were no "exposure of the person," and advised that "a first-rate bathing dress" could be made by taking an old pair of pantaloons and cutting the legs off a little above the knees.

In the same issue, the *Ledger* printed a notice from Police Chief Kennard H. Jones in which he declared that the ordinance prohibiting the firing of crackers, rockets, and other fireworks would be rigidly enforced during the holiday weekend. Parents and guardians were earnestly requested to see that those under their control obeyed the ordinance.

These were minor dampers on the buoyant mood which prevailed. Despite the police chief's notice, crackers and rockets were on sale throughout the day. At Fairmount Park, moreover, the schedule provided for a Grand Oriental Illumination and a Grand Balloon Ascension, as well as a Grand Fourth of July Picnic.

The city's regular entertainments would be open to the public. At Mortimer's Varieties the "gifted, sensational actress and daring equestrian" Miss Kate Raymond was appearing in the extravagant spectacle *Mazeppa.* Her celebrated Arabian thoroughbred Dreadnaught was billed as "the most beautiful and best-trained horse on the American stage.'' At Colonel Wood's Museum there was a Grand Harlequinade, as well as a Mysterious Turk and the Christy Minstrels. At the Grand Central Variety Theatre a ''celebrated, sensational'' drama entitled *Ins and Outs; or, I'm There* was on the same bill with a ''champion ballet troupe, comprising 40 beautiful ladies.'' And at Fox's New American Theatre, at Chestnut above 10th, the ''great serio-comic'' Mademoiselle Zitella opened a program that included the first local appearance on stage of ''LIVE INDIANS!'' and ended with an ''exciting drama'' entitled *Gettysburg; or, The Struggles of the Border,* produced at ''an immense expense with new scenery, effects, and costumes.''

On Wednesday, July 1, a local correspondent found ample justification for advising the New York *Herald* that ''the Fourth will be celebrated with universal spirit here.'' By Saturday, however, the weather had turned around, rain forced cancellation of the fireworks, and angry gusts of wind swept the subdued Centennial City. Still, it was not the wind or the rain which dampened the spirits of the populace. On July 1 a little boy had been stolen from his home and was not yet recovered. His name was Charley Ross and his plight had suddenly become the overwhelming obsession of the entire city. Soon that obsession would spread to the nation, and far beyond.

2

CHRISTIAN K. ROSS, little Charley's father, lived with his family in Germantown, a fashionable, somewhat sleepy quarter within the corporate limits of Philadelphia but about seven miles from the city's heart. Settled in 1683 by German immigrants whose beliefs were akin to those of the English Quakers, the area abounded in reminders of the historic past. Near the Rosses' was the Chew House, from which Lord Howe, the British Commander, repulsed General Washington during the second year of the American Revolution. And on a ridge close by perched the oldest American "White House" still standing, inhabited by President Washington in 1793 and 1794.

The Ross house was on the north side of Washington Lane, which ran northeasterly from Main Street past the Chestnut Hill railroad station, a commuter line. It was only the eighth residence from Main Street, almost half a mile distant. The station lay across from the ninth. Each of the houses on both sides of Washington Lane was set well back from the broad roadway and enclosed in from one to ten acres of richly landscaped grounds. The abundant shrubbery and trees provided a good deal of privacy. Gardens and stables were in the rear. So imposing were these homes that they were often described as villas.

The Ross residence, on rising ground, was a handsome old-fashioned house built of white stone, three stories crowned with a cupola, and a broad porch on three sides. To the east, across from the commuter depot, lived the nearest neighbors, the McDowells. To the west, between the Rosses' house and the next, owned by a family named Kidder, a three-acre lot was overgrown with trees and bushes. Due to the dense foliage, neither the Kidders nor the Rosses could see much of the street in front of this area. Here the Ross children liked to play.

Their father at this time was fifty years old. He was born on November 6, 1823, in Middletown, Pennsylvania, and attended private schools in Middletown and nearby Carlisle. In 1838 he came to Philadelphia to secure employment in a wholesale dry goods firm, and eventually he set up his own business. In 1862 he had married Sarah Ann Lewis from Brookline, Massachusetts, who was of a similarly well-to-do background and, at twenty-eight, ten years younger than he. Their firstborn child died in 1863. Thereafter, however, seven youngsters entered the household in rapid succession, four boys and three girls. While raising this large family, Christian and Sarah found time to take an active part in community affairs. Sarah served on various charitable committees and Christian gave of his energies to his political party (Republican) and to his church (Methodist), for which he taught a Bible class. The Rosses were "well thought of."

Now in 1874, the family had already begun dispersing for the summer. On Friday, June 26, the two eldest boys, Stoughton and Harry, had left to spend the summer vacation with their paternal grandmother in Middletown. On the same day Mrs. Ross, in delicate health, which had been lately further impaired by worry over her husband's recent business reverses, left for Atlantic City accompanied by her eldest daughter Sophia. She had promised her youngest sons Walter and Charley that in two weeks she would send Sophia home and have them come to join her at the seaside.

On Wednesday, July 1, the boys were at home, along with the family's two younger daughters, Marian Kimball and Anne Christine. Also about the house were Bridget and Sarah Kerr, in charge of the children; Mary, the cook; and Tom Foley, the gardener. Before the father left for his business at 304 Market Street in downtown Philadelphia, the children asked him for money to buy firecrackers for the Fourth. So anxious were they to be well prepared in advance that Christian Ross promised he would get a carload of seashore sand that very day. The crackers could then be fired into the sand, meeting Police Chief Jones's ordinance against them halfway, and eliminating worries about setting fire to the house.

After Ross left to wrestle with the affairs of his dry goods concern, Ross, Schott, and Company, the household settled into cheerful anticipation of the forthcoming holiday. In the middle of the afternoon the children were given their baths. The two little girls and Walter, a boy of almost six, slight, with light brown hair and clear, intelligent eyes, needed little help in dressing. Charley, the youngest, who had just celebrated his fourth birthday on May 4, wore a common uniform of the day, a brown linen suit with a short, full pleated skirt and overpants of the same length. Sarah Kerr helped him with it, and into a pair of blue and white stockings and black laced shoes, size seven. Because it was a bright sunny day, she handed him a broad-brimmed straw hat with a decorative band of ribbon.

The family was amused by little Charley's desire to be neat and trim, but this was only one of the reasons he was a household favorite. He was a beautiful child, straight and well formed, with prettily dimpled hands, a sturdy neck, and a comely rounded face, with another dimple highlighting the chin. The eyes were brown, with very light eyebrows under a broad forehead. Silky flaxen hair curled easily in ringlets and was worn long, forming a cowlick on the left side when parted. Clear white skin testified to a good constitution — little Charley had seldom been sick after six months of age. The boy's beauty was complemented by a depending, confiding nature. After they had finished dressing, Charley took Walter's hand as the two ran out into the lane. Like his older brothers, Walter was always eager to please Charley, to play with him when he stood waiting for them as they returned from school, or to have him sleep in the same room. Walter knew, too, that Charley was sensitive, that a harsh word could cause the tears to gather in his eyes and easily overflow. Perhaps most endearing was a certain quaintness about the young boy. While he spoke plainly, he was shy and retiring, his walk and manner often so deliberate and old-fashioned that the family called him ''little William Penn.'' Above all, he was uneasy with strangers and had the habit of using a hand to shield his eyes when approached by an unfamiliar figure.

3

Now, in the drowsy late afternoon of July 1, little Charley Ross paused to raise his arm in the characteristic gesture. A horse and buggy had drawn up to the deserted area where the boys were playing. When one of the two men inside began to engage in idle banter, Charley relaxed. He recognized them. The previous Saturday they had come down the lane and given the boys candy. Walter had told his father about the incident and shown him a four-inch chunk he was keeping for Charley. Ross had been very firm, telling Walter that under no circumstances should he accept candy from strangers.

The next day on their way to Sunday school the boys saw the men on foot across the street, where one paused to shout a friendly hello. By Monday the effect of Ross's injunction had worn off, and when the men came by in their buggy, a one-seater with a collapsible top, Walter and Charley, playing store in front of the house, chatted with them and helped themselves to more candy. Almost directly opposite, workmen were putting up a house for the Boutilliers, one of several under construction nearby during the summer. Like the others, the Boutillier house was set some fifty feet in from the lane, and the workmen, absorbed in their activity, paid little attention to passersby they could barely see through the trees and shrubbery. Daniel Pruddy, a handyman working for the Boutilliers, heard snatches of conversation in the street as he went about his tasks. Through the foliage he several times caught a vague glimpse of the men as they offered the boys candy. Peter Callahan, the Boutilliers' young Irish gardener, also noticed them, especially the younger of the two as he sat in the buggy one afternoon, his head held down.

The dark wagon, with red stripes painted on the small front wheels and the larger rear wheels, was a familiar sight to the boys when it drew up again on Tuesday. Walter had become intrigued by the bay which drew it. His harness was old, the silver plating of the mountings almost worn off. He had a white mark on the forehead, and sometimes when he opened his mouth and turned his head Walter had the peculiar sensation that the horse was laughing at him.

By Wednesday the boys were looking forward to the appearance of the generous strangers when they pulled up to a leisurely halt, apparently to fix a part of the harness. With an eye for glitter, Walter and Charley were aware that the younger man carried an open-faced gold watch with a gold vest chain, while his partner sported two gold rings on one of his middle fingers, one plain and the other set with a red stone.

As they occupied themselves with the harness, the men asked the boys casual questions about the Ross household — Was their mother pretty? Was their daddy a rich man? Did he go to work every day? When did he return home? In the way of children, the boys tended to speak somewhat boastfully of their family. The men gave them candy, a sweetmeat of the barley-sugar variety and said, inaccurately, that they had heard crackers shooting off in the yard. Didn't the boys want to go buy some more?

Charley, his natural reserve melted away, said he would like very much to ride in the wagon and go buy crackers. The men promised that later they would grant him his wish. They started away, driving west on the flat past the Kidder house and on up the sloping hill which led toward Main Street. At the top of the hill they appeared to hesitate and then came slowly back. As the wagon drew to a halt, the younger man got out and lifted Charley up onto the back of the seat. Walter clambered up on his own and sat on the knee of the older, who gave instructions to his partner to get going. Walter suggested driving to Main Street for the crackers. "No, we will take you to Aunt Susie's, who keeps a store, and will give you a pocketful for five cents," the older man told him. Disturbed by his rasping voice, Charley, as was his wont, lifted his arm to shield his eyes from him. The man, replying with a weird salute of his own, raised his hand and with a handkerchief shrouded his face to hide a marked deformity of the nose.

The wagon took on speed as it wheeled away from the direction of Main Street to head toward the Limekiln Pike which bounded Washington Lane on the east. A lap cover was drawn up which largely obscured both boys from view, and most residents who heard the clatter of the horse's hoofs pass by their house were totally unaware that in broad daylight kidnappers were carrying Walter and little Charley Ross away.

4

AFTER A difficult day at his office, Christian Ross came home shortly after six o'clock, bringing the cartload of sand he had promised his children. Not seeing the boys, he made inquiry of the servants, who said that since their bath they had been playing outside. The father walked down to the gate. The street was empty. Concerned, but expecting the boys' return at any moment, Ross read the evening paper. When an hour had passed with still no sign of the boys, he began to feel uneasy. Once more he went to the gate and called their names. There was no answer. After walking about the immediate area, he ordered his two little daughters to make a search around the railroad station, while he went off in the direction of Main Street. He was returning, alone, when Mary Kidder called from her porch. Through the bushes of the neighboring lot she had heard Walter and Charley talking to two strange men, she said, and later she thought she had seen them pass by her house in a wagon.

Night was falling as the suddenly alarmed Ross hurried home to find the boys still gone. Mr. Kidder had joined him, and together the two started up the hill toward Main Street and the police station in the town hall. A wave of relief swept over Ross as in the dusk of evening he saw little Walter in the distance. He was accompanied by a man. When the two parties met, Walter was in an agitated state, almost too frightened to speak. His companion, a Mr. Henry Peacock, explained that he had found Walter crying on the corner of Palmer and Richmond streets in Kensington, a district some eight miles away in the northern part of the city.

"Where is Charley?" Ross anxiously asked his boy.

"Why, he's all right. He's in the wagon," Walter replied, clearly under the impression that it was he who had been lost.

Taking him by the hand, Ross, along with Kidder, walked briskly to the police station, which immediately sent a message to Philadelphia asking the headquarters office to telegraph all district station houses to see if Charley was in one of them. A half hour later the reply came back; no such boy had been found. Ross was told to see the captain of detectives, William Heins, at headquarters.

A little after nine-thirty, Ross delivered a sleepy Walter into the hands of his nurse. After seeing Kidder home, he went to the nearby house of Joseph Lewis, one of his wife's brothers, and told the family the whole story. His nephew, Frank D. Lewis, then accompanied him to the Central Police Station at Fifth and Chestnut streets. It was eleven o'clock when they arrived, and they were told that Captain Heins had just gone home. Detective Joyce, in charge, suggested that the two strangers had picked up the boys in a drunken frolic and that when they sobered up they would take little Charley home.

For the anxious father the theory was momentarily comforting but inadequate. With his nephew he went directly to Kensington, the area where Walter was found. At the closest district station house they learned that no clues had been uncovered. Despite the late hour, they went to the house of Henry Peacock on Eustin Street and roused him from his sleep. Peacock, a railroad company employee, told how he had come upon Walter on the curbstone. The boy was holding several packs of firecrackers and a torpedo and was looking frantically up and down Palmer Street. Two women were speaking to him and he had begun to jump and scream, complaining that a man had put him out of a wagon and gone off and left him. When Peacock asked where he lived he burst into tears, but eventually calmed down sufficiently to speak of his home on Washington Lane. Skipping supper, Peacock decided to take Walter by train and streetcar to Germantown. The boy was so frightened that he said nothing during the trip about his brother's still being in the wagon. Indeed, Walter's only mention was of "a man," never of two men.

Peacock declared he had discovered no further clue to the lost boy. He took Ross and Lewis to the corner where he had found Walter. After the three had explored the area for several hours without result, it was decided to give up for the night. Peacock walked home. Since it was three in the morning, Ross and Lewis could not take a streetcar. They made several efforts but at that hour could find no one to take them on the long journey to Germantown. After walking for some distance they finally managed to hire a horse and buggy, and at five o'clock, with a new day breaking, they reached home.

Although he was desperately exhausted, Ross, taking to his
bed in the silent house, lay wide awake.

5

AFTER AN HOUR of tossing and turning, Ross arose and went to
the kitchen where the cook had already prepared breakfast.
He had no appetite. The day — it was now Thursday, July 2
— promised to be hot and humid. Ross looked out at the
street from which his boy had disappeared. In the early morning it looked peaceful and empty. Shortly there would be a
flurry of activity as businessmen made their way to the railroad station or the streetcar line for the journey downtown.
The street would then be silent until the men returned in the
late afternoon, carrying satchels of unfinished work.

At seven-thirty the father woke little Walter, who still appeared pale and nervous, and saw to it that he ate an un-
troubled breakfast. Afterwards he took him to the house of
Joseph Lewis. In the presence of his uncle, Walter told the
story of his abduction, which he had been too incoherent to
relate the night before. He described the horse and buggy,
and gave his impressions of the two kidnappers. The driver
appeared to him to be about the same medium size and height
as his father. He wore glasses and was rather red in the face.
He sported a sandy-red mustache. The other man, the older
and more solidly built of the two, had sandy whiskers which
flowed down from his cheeks and chin to form an impressive
beard. He wore large spectacles or goggles, and had what
Walter called "a monkey nose."

Walter recalled how, as the journey began, the older man
had placed him on his knee and pulled a shabby lap shawl in
front of them. From time to time he had given instructions

to the driver, telling him to speed up or slow down, the route itself evidently being a matter of agreement beforehand. The men spoke little to one another, but the older one engaged Charley in conversation. He took off his hat and said it was about worn out. When he asked Charley his name, the firm precise reply was "Charles Brewster Ross."

Walter had been dismayed at their direction being away from Main Street, but he became interested in the road and asked frequent questions as to the names of streets and bridges, to which the man gave him ready answers. A black bottle lay on the seat. Twice the wagon rolled to a halt and Walter was sent to get water from a pump by the road. When he handed up the tin cup found hanging by the pump, the men added liquid from the black bottle and drank. The second stop appeared to be at a hotel, where both men also got out. Walter noticed a number of people around, but no one seemed to pay much attention to the wagon stopping for refreshments.

After they had traveled a considerable distance, Charley said he wanted to go home and began to cry. He was told they would soon be at Aunt Susie's. When he continued to verge on tears he was pacified by a helping of candy, and the wagon continued its long circuitous route through the heavily populated city streets.

At Palmer and Richmond it finally came to a halt in front of a cigar store which had an array of fireworks displayed in the window. Walter was given twenty-five cents and told to go in and buy firecrackers. At this, Charley recovered his composure sufficiently to say he wanted a torpedo, which Walter was ordered to add to his list. He went into the tobacco shop and ordered two packages of crackers and a torpedo. With these in hand and four cents change, he hurried back to the street. The wagon was gone. He looked up and down Palmer but it was nowhere in sight. Panic-stricken, he began to cry, and a crowd started gathering. A little girl tried to pacify him. Her place was taken by two sympathetic women, who were at his side when Mr. Peacock arrived. Walter was still clutching his purchases when the latter delivered him to his father some time later.

After hearing Walter's story, the Lewises and Ross debated whether to telegraph Atlantic City and inform Mrs. Ross of Charley's disappearance. They decided they would make a further search before alarming her. A letter was dispatched to Henry Lewis, another of Mrs. Ross's brothers, in Europe on a business trip. Christian Ross also sent word to two of his own brothers, Joseph and James Ross, both residents of Philadelphia.

Ross and his nephew then went downtown to the Central Police Station. For the first time they met William Heins, a painstaking officer of Teutonic origin, not given to rash action. Heins had no further word, but his men again expressed the view that the boy had been taken away during a drinking spree and would shortly be set loose, probably in the Kensington area.

Lewis and Ross next stopped off to meet Peacock, who had been given the rest of the day off, at the office where he worked. Accompanied by Officer Joyce the three returned to Kensington and began combing the neighborhood. They could find no one who had seen the men except the little girl who had comforted Walter. She recalled seeing the wagon drive up Palmer to the first small street, turn and disappear in an easterly direction. Her impressions were vague. John Hay, the young proprietor of the tobacco shop, recalled Walter, whom he had taken for a boy from the neighborhood, but he had made no note of the wagon outside. James Logan, the master of the nearby Shackamaxon Street Ferry, was interviewed but had seen neither the men nor the wagon.

While Peacock and Joyce remained at the district station house, Ross and his nephew hired a horse and buggy and drove over the usual route from Kensington to Washington Lane, inquiring at liveries, feed stores, and watering places if anyone had seen or rented a horse of the description given by Walter. No one had.

At the end of their fruitless journey they returned home. With Walter they set out again in the middle of the afternoon, taking the route to Kensington as he remembered traveling it. It was a far different journey from the one they had followed in the morning, twisting, turning, zigzagging to no apparent purpose other than that of throwing pursuers off the trail. As Walter recalled pumps, bridges, and other landmarks whose names he had elicited from his abductors, he remembered that one of them said he was a farmer and owned a lot of ground. Even now they were approaching the house the man had pointed out to Walter. On reaching the area Ross stopped to inquire. He was told the occupant had been for a ride on July 1, had returned on the second, and could probably be found at the tavern next door. Seizing on this clue, Ross went to the tavern, where he learned that the man could be found in a rather debauched condition in a cowshed nearby. On seeing the man, Walter did not recognize him, nor was there any apparent connection between him and the abductors. The journey ended with no further clues.

In the late afternoon Ross went again to the Central Police Station. When nothing new was reported, he prepared the following advertisement for the Lost and Found column of the newspapers:

LOST — A SMALL BOY, ABOUT FOUR YEARS of age, light complexion, and light curly hair. A suitable reward will be given by returning him to E. L. JOYCE, Central Police Station.

The advertisement was prepared in time to appear in the July 3 editions of the *Public Ledger,* the *Press,* the *Inquirer,* and one or two other dailies. It arrived too late at several other newspaper offices. Officer Joyce's name was used so that Mrs. Ross, should she read the Philadelphia papers in Atlantic City, would not be alarmed.

In the same columns appeared pleas for the return of a silk umbrella, a pair of gold spectacles, a striped gray cat answering to the name Dick, a gilt-mounted carriage lamp, a light yellow Scotch terrier dog, a large bloodhound, a brown steer, and a red bullock, weight about fifteen hundred pounds. The human loss, however, headed the list.

Having confirmed the insertions at the police station, Ross took a seven o'clock commuter train for home. His neighbors were convinced that little Charley was being held with the hope of getting a reward, perhaps by people other than the two men who had carried him away. When Ross told them of the steps he had taken, they felt sure that the lure of a few dollars would bring the boy safely home. With this thought to console him, the tired father ate a quiet dinner and went to bed.

6

SLEEP DID NOT come easily. Several times during the night Ross went to the window and then outside, pausing on the steps to tie his robe before walking down to the lane. The servants, their sleep likewise troubled, caught glimpses of his trim, wiry figure, his sandy-red beard in silhouette as he peered first one way, then the other down Washington Lane. His shoulders were stooped as he returned slowly to the house. He thought of his ailing wife in Atlantic City. Would he be able to hold off much longer telling her the news? What, indeed, could he say? Boys had, of course, been stolen before, but usually by individuals of the lower classes who trained them to beg and lived off their proceeds. Such boys were almost always taken from poor parents who were unable to raise much of an outcry on their behalf. Often they were recovered after a time. Why had Charley been taken? Too much time had elapsed for the drunken frolic theory to hold true. The morning of the next day would tell if the announcement of a reward would bring the desired result. There was nothing to do but wait.

Ross's neighbors had mentioned that Samuel Johnson, who lived a short distance down the lane, had told of seeing the men give candy to the boys. As his first activity of Friday morning, Ross, accompanied by his nephew, went to visit Johnson. True, he had seen the men one afternoon. To him they had seemed like farmers, but he had not been close enough to be sure. In fact, he could supply little in the way of a description. Peter Callahan, the Boutilliers' gardener, had already given a description of the younger of the two men which tallied with Walter's. He had also seen the older man walking down the lane, but since he had held a handkerchief over his face the gardener could say little about his appearance.

Returning to the house, Ross found a visitor waiting for him. He was Dr. M. M. Walker, a Germantown physician who said that he had heard of the boy's disappearance and that several times he had encountered the men who had taken him away. On Thursday, June 25, while paying a house call he had met one of them on Washington Lane not far from Main Street. Seated in a yacht-bodied buggy with a falling or collapsible top, a variety Walker knew to be peculiar to Bucks County, the man was driving a nice-looking bay about fifteen and one-half hands high. The horse, a good traveler, was going at a rate of eight miles an hour or more, but was not at all jaded.

Walker recalled the man as medium-sized, about forty, with brown hair, not very thick, a mustache with a few gray hairs in it, a side beard of healthy growth, and a long chin beard. He wore goggles, a light, soiled straw hat with a broad band, and a gray alpaca duster. As he drove past, the man scowled. Walker was struck by the flat shape of the nose, which carried an indentation that caused it to turn up at the end in an unsightly deformity.

On June 27 Dr. Walker saw the same man driving rapidly near the Ross house. On the morning of June 30 he saw him with the same horse for the third time. His wagon was standing at the top of the hill near the Ross house. This time a second man clambered off a wall at Mr. Homer's residence nearby and got into the wagon. The second man had a round full face, short brown hair, not very thick, and a light, short mustache. He wore a light linen duster and a straw hat. He and his partner sat in the hot sun, although there was shade on the other side of the street. When Walker passed the wagon he remembered that the men lowered the curtain but remained in the same spot. At first he had thought they were gas men, but now he began to feel they might be burglars. He was looking about for a policeman, with a view to having them watched, when he was called in to attend a child who had fallen from a tree on East Walnut Street. Detained by the youngster's injuries, he thought no more of the men until the news of the abduction reached him.

With these accounts, which on the whole reinforced one another despite variations of detail, Ross and Frank Lewis went to the Central Police Station, listed in the advertisement appearing that day. Their eyes swept the premises as they entered, but little Charley was nowhere to be seen. Instead a formidable array of city officials was on hand to meet them, headed by Mayor Stokley himself. Also present were District Attorney William B. Mann, Chief of Police Jones, Captain

Heins, and a complete lineup of district police lieutenants. Ross was requested to tell the full story of the abduction. After he had concluded he was asked if he had any suggestions. Reflecting a moment, he indicated that while the two men might for a time elude a police dragnet, a well-described horse and buggy, the latter an uncommon type, could surely not disappear from view quite so readily. Chief Jones then ordered his district lieutenants to detail men in civilian dress to inspect every livery stable, blacksmith shop, and all other places where a horse and wagon might be kept. He also gave orders to his entire force to be on the lookout for a suspicious person or persons accompanying a child.

This business accomplished, the mood of the conference suddenly switched in a manner that startled Ross and his nephew. From the assembled authorities came a barrage of personal questions. Was there any dissension in the Ross family? What were Ross's relations with his servants? Had there been any trouble? Had any retainers been discharged? What about his creditors? Had he had any arguments recently with anyone? What about jury duty? Had he served on any jury which had convicted a man of a crime?

Ross was assured that the interrogation was necessary to get at the root of the mystery. The boy had obviously not been picked up as a drunken prank or he would by now have been released. The announcement of a reward, which had appeared in the morning papers, had as yet brought no results. There must be a motive behind the abduction.

The harassed father, shaken by the questioning and experiencing a strange, nebulous feeling of guilt for which he could not account, said he could think of no reason why the child had been stolen. In his family there were only the most harmonious relations. He and Mrs. Ross were devoted to one another and loved their children. A servant or two had been discharged some time earlier, but without rancor. Names were supplied and Chief Jones gave orders that they be traced. Ross admitted that his business was unable at the moment to answer its creditors, but he said he had made arrangements, satisfactory to all concerned, to defer payments. He could think of no one who bore him ill will or to whom he bore resentment. He had, indeed, served on a jury that had convicted a man, whom Chief Jones now gave his staff orders to trace — the man proved to have no connection with the case. At the conclusion of the conference Officer Joyce gave his opinion that the motive for the abduction might well become apparent through receipt of an anonymous letter.

While the city officials dispersed to their various duties, Ross and Lewis remained in the station house, hoping to see the lost boy returned. Hour after hour went by. During the late afternoon, word was received of a band of gypsies who had broken camp after spending the night not far from Washington Lane and were now passing down Main Street. Residents who had seen Ross's advertisement in the papers reported to police that they had heard a child crying in one of the wagons. When the band encamped for the evening near 55th and Walnut streets, three police officers accompanied by Ross's brother Joseph hurried to the spot. They found a small group with two wagons drawn by handsome horses. As they attempted to search the grounds one of the band became belligerent and threatened to use his gun. He was subdued by the officers, who uncovered a sufficient amount of laces, jewelry, and pistols to warrant taking the gypsies back to the station house for questioning. No child was found.

While waiting at the station, Ross helped police officers prepare posters containing an account of the abduction and a description of the lost boy. The posters gave Ross's full name and business address, since unlike the newspapers, it was not probable that Mrs. Ross would see or hear of them. They were hurriedly put up in post offices, railroad depots, and other public places.

With his nephew, Ross also prepared a second advertisement for the newspapers. In the *Public Ledger* it was given special prominence on page one under the heading TOO LATE FOR CLASSIFICATION :

> $300 REWARD WILL BE PAID TO THE person returning to No. 5 North Sixth Street, a small boy, having long, curly, flaxen hair, hazel eyes, clear, light skin and round face, dressed in a brown linen suit with short skirt, broad-brimmed straw hat and laced shoes. This child was lost from Germantown on Wednesday afternoon, 1st instant, between 4 and 5 o'clock.

No. 5 North Sixth Street was the address of the Germantown district police station.

Midnight came, and the moderate weather began to turn blustering and wet. Ross and his nephew, keeping their lonely vigil, watched the officers bring in the band of gypsies and learned with dismay that they were charged only with theft. At four in the morning Frank Lewis went home and Ross was left alone. As the dark hours passed, he searched his mind for the motive behind the mysterious abduction. What could it conceivably be?

7

THE MORNING of the Fourth of July was gray in Philadelphia. At an early hour city officials decided to postpone the fireworks, but they were determined to go ahead with the opening of the Girard Avenue Bridge and the laying of the cornerstone of the new City Hall. Mayor Stokley made plans to give an accelerated reading of his prepared speech, probably between bursts of showers. Parents who had promised their children a trip to the new Zoological Gardens went ahead with these arrangements. Their hearts were not with the holiday, however. Posters and Ross's advertisements, newspaper accounts and word of mouth had told them of the little lost boy of Germantown. It seemed incredible that a child could be taken off the street in broad daylight in their proud city. What, they wondered, had happened to little Charley Ross?

In the forenoon Christian Ross visited the district station house at 5 North Sixth Street. The posting of the reward, which had listed that address, had brought no result several hours later, and Ross wearily returned to the Central Station, headquarters for all police activities in the city. He had barely arrived when Joseph Ross rushed in wild-eyed, shouting, "I have it! I have it!" With a trembling hand he produced a letter delivered only minutes before to the family place of business on nearby Market Street. Christian Ross gazed intently at the envelope with its weird handwriting that leaned first to right and then to left as it sprawled across the page. Opening it, he read in silence the words which would dispel the awesome mystery of his boy's disappearance.

July 3 — Mr. Ros — *be not uneasy you son charly bruster be al writ we is got him and no powers on earth can deliver out of our hand* — *You will hav two pay us befor you git him from us* — *an pay us a big cent. to if you put the cops hunting for him you is only defeating yu own end* — *we is got him fix so no living power can gits him from us a live* — *if any aproch is maid to his hidin place that is the signil for his instant anihilation* — *if yu regard his lif puts no one to search for him you money can fech him out alive an no other existin powers dont deceve yuself an think the detectives can git him from us for that is one imposebel*

  you here from us in few day

As the full realization of the unsigned letter's sinister import closed in, Ross began to shake. Unable to speak, he handed the document to Captain Heins, whose oval, florid countenance blanched as he read. Somberly, Heins put his arm around Ross's shoulder and guided him to a private room. Here the letter was read aloud to the assembled detectives and officials. There was a stunned silence, followed by expressions of incredulity and indignation. The mystery was solved. A monster walked the earth who had committed the unspeakable crime of child-stealing for ransom. In the supposedly civilized city of Philadelphia had been perpetrated a barbaric act hitherto associated only with the bandits of Sicily.

For a brief moment Ross had a sense of relief. The known fact, even when it is ghastly, can be welcome after long suspense. And the feeling of guilt which had been aroused by the official questioning was now abated by the revelations of the letter which lay on the table before the detectives.

But relief was followed by horror. There was no question but that the anonymous correspondents were in possession of Charley. Their use of the middle name Brewster, which was known to few but which Walter remembered as having been elicited from his brother by the abductors, was a conclusive point. The absence of a signature on the letter, the apparently deliberate misspellings and efforts to disguise the handwriting by varying its slant seemed to fit an overall design. The warning to steer away from the police and the torment of suspense inflicted by the final words, "you here from us in few day," added to the impression of a meticulously arranged abduction.

Captain Heins and his lieutenants reread the letter and expressed their conviction that the crime was not only against the Ross family, but one which posed a potential threat to every home in Philadelphia and the land. If the bandits got away with this first instance, would it not encourage other lawbreakers to emulate them? Where then would it stop? What child was safe? Everything must be done to apprehend these cruel and ruthless criminals.

During the morning Mayor Stokley was informed of the letter and he reiterated this conviction, appealing to Police Chief Jones and Captain Heins to do everything within their power to catch the abductors and restore little Charley to his home. The best men on the police force were assigned to special duty in civilian dress. They were ordered to search every vessel on the city's two rivers, the Schuylkill and the Delaware, and to inspect all ferries leading to New Jersey. They were ordered to stop all covered wagons passing over the city's various bridges and to question the keepers of tollgates in the surrounding counties and in nearby New Jersey. They were ordered to watch railroad depots and other public meeting places, and to search all barns, liveries, and unoccupied or suspicious dwellings, as well as known haunts of the criminal class. Because child-stealing was associated with Sicilians, houses of immigrant Italians were to be searched, as well as houses inhabited by professional beggars and women of ill repute. Men with criminal records were put under surveillance.

Officer Charles Wood and Frank Lewis prepared another advertisement, giving a more complete description of the lost boy with his full name and the circumstances of the abduction. This advertisement, which again offered a reward of $300 for little Charley's return, appeared in the Sunday papers and all the following week. Bills giving the same information were printed and detectives posted them in public places throughout the city, the surrounding countryside, and adjacent areas of New Jersey.

After conferring with members of his family, Ross determined to make the trip to Atlantic City to inform his wife. In a savage rainstorm he reached her cottage at eight in the evening, accompanied by Walter. Mrs. Ross, a handsome woman of patrician bearing, came to the door. Her face showed the effect of recent cares but lit up when she saw her visitors.

"Why did you not bring Charley along with you?" she asked immediately. "Is he well?"

To the woman who had borne his children, Christian Ross now had to tell the story of the abduction of their youngest boy and of the events that had followed. He tried to shield her as much as possible, but her eagerness to glean every bit of information concerning her lost child made his task doubly difficult. He described the anonymous letter but said nothing of its cruel threats and sinister tone. Instead he stressed that while his news was bad, the hope was that Charley would be with them again within a few days. Together the sorrowing parents and little Walter and his sister Sophia knelt in prayer for the return of the lost one.

8

ON MONDAY, JULY 6, having made arrangements to maintain a close liaison with key city officials on developments in the Ross case, Mayor Stokley left for his summer vacation retreat at Long Branch. Many of the well-to-do inhabitants of the city followed his course, settling in the various resorts along the Atlantic Coast. Newspapers carried the reward notice for the lost boy but, unaware of the arrival of a letter, had little to add in their news columns. Under the heading A MYSTERY, the *Inquirer* gave an account of the abduction, using proper names for the first time and concluding on a hollow note: "No motive can be assigned for the carrying away of the little one, and at the present time the whole affair is wrapped in mystery."

With his wife and two children, Ross had spent Sunday in Atlantic City attending church and helping his wife pack for the return trip to Philadelphia. On Monday morning, sending his family directly home after the journey, he stopped off at his store, where his brother was waiting for him. Joseph Ross handed him a letter received through the post office that morning. Ross looked at the familiar handwriting scrawled across the page, which his brother had already read, and his heart sank as he read.

PHILA. *July 6.* — Mr. Ros. — *we supos yu got the other leter that teld yu we had yu child all saf and sound.*

yu mite ofer one $1000000 it woud avale yu nothing. to be plaen with yu yu mite invok al the powers of the universe and that cold not get yu child from us. we set god, man and devel at defiance to rest him ot of our hands. this is the lever that moved the rock that hides him from yu $20000. not one doler lest — imposible — imposible — you cannot get him without it. if yu love money more than child yu be its murderer not us for the money we will have if we dont get from yu we be sure to get it from some one els for we will mak example of yure child that others may be wiser. we give yu al the time yu want to consider wel wat yu be duing. yu money or his lif we wil hav — dont flater yuself yu wil trap us under pretens of paying the ransom that be imposible, imposible — don let the detectives mislede yu thay tel yu thay can get him and arest us to — if yu set the detectives in search for him as we teld yu befor they only serch for his lif. for if any aproch be made to his hidin place by detective his lif wil be instant sacrificed you wil see yu child dead or alive if we get yu money yu get him live if no money yu get him ded. wen you get ready to bisnes with us advertise the folering in Ledger *personals (Ros we be redy to negociate) we look for yu answer in* Ledger.

The boldness, the ruthless calculation of the abductors was now apparent. Calmly they were outlining their conditions for the return of the boy. Ross read again the passage warning him not to traffic with the police. He reread the chilling phrases which defied God, man, or devil to wrest the boy from his abductors' hands and which promised his death if Ross crossed them and did not pay the ransom.

The demand for the enormous sum of $20,000 left him with a heavy heart. The panic of 1873 had hit the entire country, but it had begun in Philadelphia with the collapse of the firm of Jay Cooke and Company. Ross had felt its impact, and only the indulgence of his creditors had allowed him to keep open the doors of his business. Where would the required sum come from? He had good friends who would surely give him what help they could, but many of them had also been hurt by the panic. Should he turn to his family? Or to his wife's family? When would he ever be able to repay them?

One thing was certain. He would tell his wife of the arrival of the second letter but he would shield her from its savage threats. After a brief visit with her, Ross took the letter to the Central Police Station, where it was read to District Attorney Mann, City Solicitor Charles H. T. Collis, and the assembled detectives. All agreed that under no circumstances should the ransom be paid. It was clear that the sole motive for the abduction was money. Once the abductors realized that no money would be forthcoming they would turn the boy loose. The police were certain the threats in the letters would never be carried out. Their goal was to find the writer of the letters and thereby rescue the child.

Ross listened to the detectives' plans. They were already canvassing within a ten- to twelve-mile radius from the scene of the abduction. They were keeping a watch on all known criminals and in particular confidence men of the type apparently involved in the case. All hotel registers would be

checked to see if any signature corresponded with the handwriting in the letters, and to turn up strange or suspicious
characters recently come to town. The handwriting of the letters was put under close scrutiny. While it was generally con-
ceded that the writer had the child, there was still a slight
possibility that he had nothing to do with the case and was
merely a blackmailer seeking to profit by the occasion. To
lead on the author of the correspondence Ross was instructed
to insert the stipulated personal, "Ros, we be ready to negociate," in the *Public Ledger*'s edition of the following morning.

Once he had left the Central Station, Ross began to have
the strongest misgivings. Little Charley was in the hands of
the calculating criminals whose letters were now tormenting
him. "Yu money or his lif we wil hav" was the phrase which
echoed in his head. Conspiring with detectives to apprehend
them would be useless, the abductors' letters had warned.
Only the ransom could bring little Charley home. And now
the police and the city authorities had determined that he
should pay no ransom. They felt certain the boy would be
freed once the hope of gaining money for him was clearly
withdrawn. But what made everyone so sure? It was *his*
child who served as the pawn in this cruel chess game. And
how could the matter be explained to his wife? Even if here
he succeeded, could he really convince himself? Was the
course being followed, so fraught with peril, truly the wisest
one?

9

PERSONAL COLUMNS in the newspapers were a much used form
of communication in the 1870's. It was not until late in the
decade that Alexander Graham Bell patented a device known

as the telephone, and while the telegraph had come into use some years earlier, it was a medium employed chiefly in business and government. In the personals lawyers searched for missing heirs, lovers arranged assignations, and salesmen advertised their wares. In the summer of 1874 Schenck's Mandrake pills and Seaweed tonic were praised for their effectiveness against the injurious effects of a change of water and diet, especially on summer vacations, while Prussian salve was hawked as "the only positive cure for corns and bunions." Interspersed with such items on the morning of Tuesday, July 7, was the little notice, "Ros, we be ready to negociate."

Its author, Christian Ross, read the personals in the *Ledger* before bidding goodbye to his nephew. Frank Lewis was on his way to New York to deliver a supply of posters to the police of that city. It was their first official notification of the facts of the case, although the New York *Times* and most other papers had carried accounts of the abduction.

The Brooklyn *Daily Eagle,* whose masthead boasted a circulation "larger than that of any other evening paper of its class in the United States," was preoccupied with the Henry Ward Beecher scandal on its own doorstep. While it barely mentioned the Philadelphia abduction, it found space to tell of troubles in the New York police department. Two commissioners had recently been tried and removed from their positions for malfeasance in office. When Frank Lewis arrived in New York on July 7 with posters detailing the abduction of his nephew, the department was in a state of turmoil. Later in the month, the Charley Ross case developed a New York aspect and it was a newly appointed superintendent of police who had taken charge.

In Philadelphia, meanwhile, the morning of July 7 brought a telegram to the police from a New Jersey town postmaster: THE ROSS CHILD HERE, SEND IMMEDIATELY. With all dispatch, a

boy in supposedly suspicious company was traced to a county
almshouse, where he was discovered to be nine years old, of a
dark — probably Mediterranean, judging by his accent —
complexion and bearing no resemblance to the missing boy.
It was the first of a multitude of mistaken identities.

Ross was not spared the disappointment of the futile police
chase, nor the contents of the third letter from the kidnappers. It arrived at his store office at two o'clock in reply to
the *Ledger* personal which had appeared only hours before.

*Phila., July 7. — Mr. Ros: we se yu answer in Leger the
question with yu is be yu wilin to pay for thosand ponds for
the ransom of yu child. without it yu can never get him alive
if yu be ready to come to terms say so. if not say so, and we
wil act acordinly. we take yu anser either way as granted
and wil act on it. we care nothin bout yu schemin and plotin
to detect us. that is only childrens play with us. this thing is
wel understod with us and is taken out of the power every
humin bein to detect us. yu wil find it so at the end of this
bisines. the only answer we want form yu now is, be yu wilin
to pay $20,000 to save Charley. if yu love yu mony more than
him his blood be upon yu and not us fo wil show him up to yu
either dead or a live (it is left with yu) anser the folering in
evnin herald or star. Ros. — wil come to terms. Ros. — wil
not come to terms. omit either line yu pleas try the experi-
ment. offer $100,000 reward se if it avales any thing. use the
detectives as yu pleas but dont let them mislede yu to the sacrifice of Charley. dont concent to any thing only in good
faith. we wil act upon yu word, if yu prove faithles we will
prove to yu heart's sorow that wil keep our word to the
very letter.*

Ross's glance went back to the final words. What manner of
men were these, he wondered, who could alternate the most

coldhearted threats with talk of faith? He remembered that
the opening words of the first letter appeared to be an expression of human concern directed toward himself, the
parent. Perhaps it would be wise to deal with the abductors.
Were they not in the saddle? Was not the longed-for prize in
their possession? Would it not be best to somehow raise the
extravagant sum and count on the good faith of the criminals?

Myriad thoughts and conflicting emotions vied for his attention as he walked from his office to the Central Station.
Glancing about him, he saw that among the police authorities,
in whose hands he had placed the case from the very beginning, there was no indecision. Grim-faced, they told him that
to pay the ransom would be to compound the felony and encourage the spread of kidnapping. No child would be safe.
The crime that had been committed was not only against him
but against the entire community. He must stand firm.

The last letter had asked for an answer in the evening *Herald* or *Star*. It had stated very clearly that the message should
read either ''Ros. — wil come to terms'' or ''Ros. — wil not
come to terms.'' At the direction of the police, Ross inserted
into both papers' personal columns of July 8 a text which did
not follow these instructions, but which instead read: ''Ros
wil come to terms to the extent of his ability.'' With troubled
heart, he went home to the silent house on Washington Lane.
Perhaps by some miracle, through God's providence, when he
arrived little Charley would be there.

10

POLICE TOOK NOTE of the mention of four thousand pounds in
the last letter and, hoping that the abductors had unwittingly
given them a clue as to identity, checked their files for criminals with an English background. They turned up nothing.

Because it was feared that giving further information to the newspapers could easily work to the benefit of the abductors, a lid was clamped on press relations, and reporters who besieged the Central Station were turned away with the repeated assertion that there were no new developments. They listened to these negative statements with cynical doubt as they observed the heavy activity among detectives who filed in and out of the station doors.

Many reporters were friends of members of the detective squad, and only a short time elapsed before news of the anonymous letters and their demand for ransom on pain of killing the stolen boy leaked to the press. The outcry in print was loud and strident, typified by an editorial in the *Inquirer*:

. . . . Here at our very door, and in our crowded streets, a child is stolen and hid away so successfully that neither its parents nor the authorities can find trace of either the stealer or the stolen. The business is so serious that it should engage the attention and enlist the profoundest interest of every citizen, for if the child of Mr. Ross can be stolen and hid away for many days together, the children of any other citizen may be stolen and hid away forever. They must find those who stole him, in order that the law may deal with them so rigorously as to make the punishment of the guilty a restraining terror to any who may think to make profit by stealing away children. There must be no compounding of the felony committed.

In New York the *World* was similarly outraged, and went on to attack Ross for presumably contemplating negotiations with the kidnappers, mistakenly deduced from the first personal which had appeared in the *Ledger*, "Ros, we be ready to negociate":

The startling story which comes to us today from Philadelphia shows that brigandage as audacious flourishes in the most populous and cultivated regions of the United States as any that have survived the light of modern civilization or withstood the attacks of modern police in Greece, Italy, or in Spain. . . . This Philadelphia father might have remembered that no harm was likely to come to the child held for ransom, since to do it harm would be both to increase the risk and diminish the possible profit to the kidnappers, and if he took no notice of the demands, except to put the police in possession of the facts, his child would in all probability be restored to him sooner than if he acceded to them.

Ross, while in effect cooperating fully with the authorities, was quietly feeling out friends and business acquaintances in an attempt to raise the necessary $20,000. Meanwhile the campaign in the press, added to the visible police activity, had led to a feverish word of mouth among the sympathizing and alarmed populace. Almost instinctively the citizenry was organizing itself into a massive public posse. Again and again word was brought to the police department by individuals who had seen a horse or a horse and buggy resembling the descriptions. Private citizens reported countless instances of suspicious-appearing persons. Often they followed them on their own, not just for hours but sometimes for days on end, dropping all other activities. Amateur detectives offered their services, and offers of help came from criminals in penal institutions.

Wherever a band of gypsies was observed, reports drifted into the Central Station that a small boy fitting little Charley's description had been seen in their company. While officers were pursuing such a band near Havre de Grace, Maryland, they heard of another party consisting of two men with a small boy who were traveling over little-used roads winding along the streams of the countryside. After ascertaining that the gypsy band was not connected with the case, the officers trailed these men and caught up with them at a mill along a back route. The men were selling patent rights. This necessitated their using little-traveled roads to reach mills and factories located on streams. The officers returned to Philadelphia empty-handed.

In the northeastern section of the city a livery stable owner named Foulke recalled that two men whose looks he didn't like, and of whom the descriptions of the abductors reminded him, had come to his stable on June 19 to hire a wagon. They came again on June 20 and June 22, taking a wagon out in early morning and returning in midafternoon. On June 23 they had tried to rent the wagon for five days, but when they were unable to offer security Foulke refused and never saw them again. Witnesses were located who said they had seen the men in Germantown, where they had asked questions about the incomes of local houseowners. Police traced the men and arrested them, along with two women companions. An investigation proved that they were taking orders for trees and shrubbery for a reputable New Jersey firm. The inquiries they had made were germane to their business. All were eventually released.

11

THE DECISION to continue the bizarre semipublic correspondence with the authors of the anonymous letters was made with the hope that somewhere they would commit a blunder which would permit police to trace them. Answers to the letters were deliberately framed to necessitate further correspondence. To the evasive reply in the personals to their third letter, the kidnappers dispatched a fourth communication. The tone was brisk and businesslike.

Phila., July 9. — Ros. we is set your price. we ask no more. we takes no les we no the extent yu bility. how mucht time yu want to obtain this money. yu is only in part answered our

*question. the only question for yu to answer is is u got it
and be wilin to pay it then we wil proceed to bisiness at once.
is it necessary to repeat the fatle consequences of delayin to
give time to detectives to find his hidin place. we teld yu it
be posible to find his place, but imposible to find him. no
aproch can be made to it without a known signal and any
stranger forcibly comin to it wold be the signal for his instant
anihilation were he wold never be herd of. this makes our
party safe and shows yu that if it come to extremes we wil
spare not the child. thus yu se al the detectives in the country
could avale yu nothin only Jeopodosin his life. Ros this under-
taken cost us $1000 to prepare the machenery to perform the
work therefor consider wel befor yu consent to pay it. for pay
it you have to or sacrifice yu child. we want no other anser
but this and on the fath of yu word his lif hang. Ros i is got it
and be wilin to pay it. this anser or omition it satifies us.*

As he continued the correspondence, Ross experienced a
mounting sense of hopelessness. The renewed threats took
their toll on his nerves, but it was the abductors' insistence on
their invulnerability, on the impossibility of discovery, that
was undermining his spirit. The inability of the police to turn
up a single clue, despite their unceasing activity, reinforced
this feeling of emptiness. And the anguish of Mrs. Ross, her
saddened eyes looking into his, appealing for relief, brought
him to a state of torment. He thought again and again of the
criminals' apparent awareness of the tactics being employed
against them, their warning that delaying to give detectives
time to discover their hiding place would have fatal consequences.

Only the most resolute exertion of will enabled him to accede to the authorities in the wording of a personal in reply to
the fourth letter. "Ros i is got it and be wilin to pay it,"
the letter had asked him to reply, or, if he wished to sacrifice

the life of his child, to omit. "Ros is willing; have not got it; am doing my best to raise it," read the personal prepared by the police and inserted into the *Public Ledger* of Thursday, July 9, the same day the letter was received.

Although the criminals had demonstrated that it was within their power to use the public mails for replies within a matter of hours, this personal, which deviated from their instructions, drew no reply on Friday, July 10. On Saturday a puzzling document arrived, an envelope enclosing a postal card, blank except for the faint words in pencil, "bully boy." There was some question whether this communication came from the same writers.

During the day Ross helped police prepare cards which were later delivered to the pastors of the various churches in the city with a request that they be read from the pulpit on Sunday. The cards gave an account of the abduction and a thorough description of the lost boy, and appealed for help in locating him. Larger posters were also prepared and put in heavily traveled spots throughout the metropolitan area.

When no further word from the anonymous letter writers reached Ross on Sunday, July 12, the authorities prepared a new personal to appear the following day. "Ros. — I is got it and be wilin to pay it," read the text as demanded.

On Monday, July 13, a group of prominent men of Philadelphia formed an ad hoc committee and met with Ross. Included in the committee were the mayor's friend William V. McKean, manager and editor of the *Public Ledger*; John C. Bullitt, a member of one of Philadelphia's oldest families, and George L. Harrison, president of the Board of Public Charities. These men announced their intention of helping Ross in every way they could to bring the criminals to justice and restore the lost boy to his home. In order to enter into their task with unequivocal zeal, they stated it would be necessary once more to examine the private affairs of the Ross family in order to be sure that no motive other than money existed for the crime.

So Christian Ross submitted to another examination of his home life, his social relationships, and his business affairs. It was easier for him to talk of private matters with these men, some of whom he had known for years, than with the police. At the meeting's end he promised to inform the committee of all significant events in the case and agreed to obtain their approval for any important plan. All agreed that every effort must be made to find the criminals and restore the child, and even more firmly that this must be done without paying the ransom and thereby compounding the felony.

After this fateful conference Ross went on to another. From a perfect stranger had come a request for an interview.

"If you will tell me your real condition," began this man, clearly a person of means, "I may be able to assist you."

Ross gave him an account of the abduction, the activities that had involved him since, and of his financial circumstances.

"Do you wish to pay the ransom?" asked the man at the end of this recital. "If you do, I will *give* you twenty thousand dollars and never ask you to return one cent."

This extraordinary generosity touched Ross deeply. It also renewed the conflict which had been raging in his heart, whether to use money to ransom his boy or follow the path dictated by the authorities. Only minutes before he had given his promise that he would act in the best interests of society. He was reminded of the press's view of the matter. "Mr. Ross owes a duty to society as well as to himself, and to allow the success of such an outrageous attempt at extortion would be to encourage a repetition of the crime in some other neighborhood," the Germantown *News* had written of the case, adding, "Once put a premium on criminality and it will rapidly increase. We think the strong arm of the law is the proper one to accomplish the rescue."

Steeling himself, he now turned down the proffered financial aid. "I thank you, sir, but I cannot accept your generous offer," he began, "for having taken the position that I would not compound the felony, I prefer continuing to make efforts to find the criminals, hoping, if successful in getting them, that I will recover my child, and probably prevent a repetition of child-stealing for a ransom."

When the visitor asked whether Mrs. Ross shared these sentiments, Ross replied that she was willing to make almost any sacrifice to bring back her boy, but that she was also willing to endure whatever hardships her family and friends thought necessary. Clasping Ross's hand, the stranger bade him goodbye.

The trials of the day were not yet over for the weary father. Despite the fact that plainclothes detectives had been assigned to scrutinize those posting mail at the main post office, a letter from the abductors, number five, was somehow dropped unobserved into one of its boxes and delivered to Ross. He had just reaffirmed his decision not to negotiate in good faith with the criminals and now their first words were a warning that if he had the intention of double-dealing in order to try to trap them, the only consequence would be death for his child.

Phila., July 31. — Ros: *yu say yu be redy to comply. we presume yu have wel considered be for yu maid this promis we take yu at yu word and we hold the lif of yu son to the strictest performanc of yu word. we want yu mony. yu want yu child. the question between us is do yu mean to give the mony or do yu think by holdin out a fals promis to ensnare us into the hands of the authority. i want to explane this mater to yu so yu wil not deceve yu self for it is imposible for the wole detective force combind to put even one of us in the power of the law. in transfering yu mony to us be for yu get yu child yu have got to rely entirely on our word. we ask* *no more money. we wil take no les. if we wanted more we wold ask it now. in 5 ours after we receive the mony and find it corect, yu wil se yu child home saf. Aft we gets the mony we has no further use for the child, an it is our interest then to restor him home unharmed, so that others will rely on our word. if we don't get the mony from yu the child's life wil an shall be sacrificed. consider wel, then, wat yu be doin, for any promis yu mak us we hold the life yu child to bind you to it. Ros, it would be more satisfact to yu to give this mony to the detectives than us, but if we git it yu git yu child — if not yu child must die, that we can sho others that we mak no threths wich we don't kepe. Ros, it is our place to dictate, yues to comply. be you redy to pay it as we dictate. if so, have the $20,000 in United States notes. in denomination not excedin "tens." have yu money were yu can git it any moment wen cal for, the detectives, wen they read this, wil tel yu they have now got the key that opens the secret, but don't be misled by them (we alone hold the lock wich is yu child, if they open the dor for yu it wil only revele his (ded body) if yu regard his life let a fatherly love be yu gide. Ros, yu have inevitably got to part with yu mony or yu child, wich is certain as death itself. any fals act on yu part seals the fate of yu child an closes any further bisiness with us. consider wel, and if these terms agre with yu anser the folerin. Ros, it is redy, yu have my word for it. we look for the answer in the* Evenin Star.

The aspect of this letter which most impressed the police and committee of prominent men was the kidnappers' avowed intention to continue in the business of child-stealing for ransom. This confirmed their worst fears, that the Ross case was only the beginning of a new crime wave. Police efforts to apprehend the abductors were redoubled. Ross agreed that two plainclothes detectives should be detailed to keep him constantly in their sight. When he went out into the street they were to saunter along in the immediate vicinity. When he went to work at 304 Market Street they were to install themselves in a section of the store where they could observe without themselves being seen. While Ross was at home they were to be stationed, out of view, in the house.

Together the police and the committee prepared for insertion next day in the *Public Ledger* a personal which basically followed the form required: "Ros — came too late for *Evening Star*. It is redy. You have my word for it."

As the second week of his son's disappearance wore toward its close, Ross could not keep his mind from the subject which was almost too painful to contemplate. Where was little Charley? Was he being treated kindly? Was he crying out even now for his mother and his home? Was he well? The questions would not stop and the answers would not come.

12

ON TUESDAY, JULY 14, the editors of all newspapers in Philadelphia received the following note:

> *Office of Chief of Police*
> *Philadelphia, July 13, 1874*
>
> Dear Sir:
>
> In the interest of public justice, I ask that you will give orders that nothing be published in your papers touching the case of Mr. Ross' child for a few days.
>
> Yours respectfully,
> KENNARD H. JONES, Chief of Police

The Philadelphia police had now turned to active muzzling of the press. The attempt, like so many others before and after, led to widespread criticism of the department and eventually produced an effect opposite from the one intended.

There had never in the history of the country been a manhunt such as the one for Charley Ross. A private sorrow had become public property, and in the morning the first question asked at the breakfast table was about the stolen boy. Obviously the mysterious abduction was good copy. Every edition which reported new developments quickly sold out and was followed up by extras.

The press had already been frustrated when it found the police uncommunicative in the early days of the case. On hearing of the anonymous letters, newspapers had begged for copies. These were not forthcoming, as the police feared that once they were shown, further letters could be counterfeited, complicating their efforts. Ross was also anxious to withhold publication of the letters because he did not want his wife to see them. Similarly, when illustrated papers demanded a photo of the stolen child they were refused. The only photo in the hands of the family showed little Charley at the age of two. Ross and his wife felt that reproducing it would be misleading since his appearance had changed so much in the interim. Chief Jones's note was the last straw. To a public clamoring for information, the press was able to give little more than speculation and a scant few facts dug up by its reporters.

Some justification for the police curtain derived from the fact that one newspaper, the *Inquirer,* had just said in its columns that the post office was being watched by detectives day and night. Whereas up to now all letters had been dropped in boxes at the main postal station, where there was a hope of trapping the criminals, it was feared — and correctly — that after this revelation letters would be dropped into street boxes, which were much harder to patrol. Volunteers were engaged to fulfill this function, but the instance confirmed the police in their view that the press could be harmful in the case.

Chief Jones's plea for a news blackout was observed, although with great reluctance, by many of the Philadelphia papers, most notably by the *Public Ledger* and the *Evening Star,* both of whose personal columns had been used to communicate with the abductors. From the one important Democratic organ in the city came a swift rebuff to the detectives. The largest newspaper published in Philadelphia, the *Illustrated New Age* proclaimed itself "a journal for the people, a complete news, business, and family paper." The Ross case was of profound interest to the people, and the *New Age* began to see in it disturbing elements of bungling by the police and other municipal authorities of the incumbent Republican party. Its editorial columns began unleashing an attack.

"The police may as well attempt to muzzle the public as the press in this matter," it began, "for the press is the public in council, and it must and will talk with itself about this abduction which concerns it so dearly." To put things bluntly, said the writer, the paper had more confidence in public indignation aroused by the press than by police "spotting" of certain localities like the post office. "Spotting" was less likely to lead to recovery of the boy than a press and public outcry.

From out-of-town newspapers came bitter criticism of Philadelphia authorities, exemplified by a blast from the Baltimore *News*: "We think the Quaker City had better improve its police organization before it undertakes its centennial display."

Such outbursts paled in comparison with the barbs tossed by the New York journals. The *World,* the *Tribune,* and others had sent special correspondents to Philadelphia to provide daily accounts of the case, but the paper which soon took the lead in capturing every fact and nuance and innuendo of the case and in blasting the local authorities was the New York *Herald,* under the stewardship of the volatile, aggressive

James Gordon Bennett, son of its founder. Jones's appeal
only whetted Bennett's appetite. One of his top men was put
on the train to Philadelphia and was soon sending back criti-
cal dispatches like the following:

The absolute unsoundness of our police system is well exemplified
by the failure of the Philadelphia detectives to find any trace of the
kidnapped child. Many days have now elapsed since Charley Ross
was spirited away, and though the perpetrators of the outrage have
received and answered communications, no clew has been obtained as
to their identity. This is the more discreditable to the police because
the men who took the child are known to have appeared several
times in the neighborhood where the abduction took place, and a
more or less reliable description of their appearance has been furnished as a clew to work upon. Notwithstanding the advantages, the
detectives seem unable even to get upon their tracks.

The problem was said to lie with the system in which men
were appointed to all classes of public employment, including
the police force, without reference to their fitness, as a reward
for political service. Through an oversight, certainly, rather
than through consideration, the *Herald* neglected to mention
that Captain Heins, in charge of Philadelphia's fourteen-man
detective squad, had been in office only since January 1873,
when the newly elected Mayor Stokley had appointed him.
Heins's previous occupations had been housesmith, telephone
operator, and alderman.

The *Herald* had pointed out disturbing facts which could
not be wished away. Despite the efforts of a police force of
eight hundred men, criminals were defying the law with impunity. They were using the public mails to set their terms.
Not one clue had they dropped. Not one blunder had they
committed. More than two weeks after the crime, the police
were no better off than on the day of the abduction. Horse
and buggy had disappeared as completely as rain that sinks

into the earth. Of the abductors and their young prey there
was not a trace of a trace. The leader of the criminals, it was
clear, was a man of cunning and skill, a mastermind at work.

13

THE MASTERMIND left his victims hanging through the four-
teenth, when the personal he had asked for appeared in the
Public Ledger. When no reply arrived, the authorities repeated the same personal in the *Ledger* columns of July 15.
Once again the day passed without word. Not until Thursday,
July 16, was there an answer. Letter number six, the first not
deposited in the main post office, had been dropped into a
letter box on Delaware Avenue near Spruce Street.

Phila., July 16 — Ros: *the reason we did not respond to yu
answer was we had to go a bit out in the country an the
blasted old orse give out so we could not get back in time.
We went as much as anything to se how Charley was. Yu
have our word that he is yet safe — in health an no harm
done him thoug he is uneasy to get home with Walter. he is
afraid he won't get home in time to go to Atlantic City with
his mother when Sofy comes back. Ros, yu understand the
condition the money was to be given us. We wold glady give
yu Charley befor we got the mony but that wold be imposible
under the existing circumstances. Yu must satisfy yuself that
yu wil get him after we git the mony an find it corect and no
sly marks put on the notes. We told yu we wold place him in
yu hands in 5 ours after we fond the mony corect but that we
can not do but our word for it that yu shall have him insid of
10 ours an may our blasted sols be eternaly damed if we do
not keep our word with yu — as we said befor after we gits*

the mony we have no further use for the child but we have a big object in restoring him to yu safe and sound. We shall be redy we think by Saturday to efect a change with yu (the child for the mony). Ros — we want to impres upon yu mind the grate danger in efecting this change — the danger lies intirely with yuself if yu wish to make a change an absolute certainty yu must comply in every particular as we instruct yu then a failure is imposible. the first place, yu must not let the detectives no how yu are to setle this bisiness (not that we fear them at all) in aresting one of us for as we told yu that is imposible — but they wil secretly interfear in this bisiness in some underhanded way to prevent the mony from findin its way to us — we are going to deal with yu alone an yu only, an if yu call in any others to give you a counter advice from ours then yu mistake wil be yu own misfortune. let yu friends advise yu and not the detectives they study their own interest an the interest of society. yu have a duty to perform to yuself that stands paramount to all else in the world an if yu ever expect to regain yu child a live, yu alone with the advice of yu friends must perform it. we wil give you this much incite into our bisiness — that if any arest is made it wil be an inocent person who wil be ignorant of the part he is actin. but it is imaterial with us wether it be an inocent person or one of our own party the moment any arest is made or any clandestine movements in transmiting this mony to us it will be conclusive evidence with us that yu have broken yu faith with us an that our we pledge our selves befor all the gods in the universe if there be an god exist that yu child shal die an we wil give yu an oculd prof of it an then all further business with us ceases. (yu have answered al that is necesary at present. we have yu word for it.) we want yu to nail this mony up in a smal strong ruf box an have it were yu can git it at a minutes notice. mark on it (Drugs for H H H.)

The letter displayed again the writer's uncanny ability to put himself in Ross's shoes. He should let his friends advise him and not the detectives, who followed their own interest and that of society, said the text, summing up with remarkable accuracy the father's dilemma. As matters appeared to be drawing to a perilous close, he dismissed any doubts he might have had about the writers' possession of the boy. They spoke of little Charley's anxiety about being home in time to go to join his mother in Atlantic City, a family matter which only he could have brought to their attention. Apparently the abductors had separated themselves from the boy, putting him in the care of others, and at some distance. Apparently, too, they were able to travel about the countryside without danger of detection. The hopelessness of the situation was stifling. And now Ross was left to wait.

When the terms of the delivery leaked to the public — the public offered advice, which was duly reported in the papers. A farsighted Connecticut pedagogue said the ransom notes should be marked, and after delivery every grocery store and banker's counter in the land should be carefully watched. Another amateur sleuth suggested turning over counterfeit notes in the ransom box.

The authorities prepared a box with the designated markings, DRUGS FOR H. H. H., but apart from this decoy, police and the public committee devised ways to trap the criminals. Their intention was to allow the box, filled with counterfeit bills, to be taken and then to follow the caller and arrest those with whom he established contact, this despite the fact that the letter clearly said such deception would lead to the arrest of innocent third parties and to the certain death of the child — on the other hand, the criminals had sworn that compliance with their plan of exchange would deliver the boy within ten hours into the hands of his family.

The scene now was a page torn from classical tragedy. On a

man and his wife a terrifying choice had been thrust. Would they risk the life of their child for the common weal? With aching hearts Christian and Sarah Ross answered yes. On Friday evening, July 17, after the children had been put to bed, officers secreted themselves in the Ross house and took their positions. A terrifying silence pervaded the atmosphere. Having made their painful decision, the courageous father and mother waited. At midnight a pounding at the door roused them from their restless vigil. Signaling to the officers, Ross went slowly forth while Mrs. Ross, trembling, stood at the head of the stairs. Ross flung open the door. Two strangers appeared, come to give him information they thought might lead to the recovery of the boy. The information was useless.

14

So THE HARROWING WATCH continued. Saturday, the day designated for the exchange, passed with agonizing slowness for the Ross household on Washington Lane. A few days earlier a New Jersey paper had printed startling news that the lost boy had been found on a Jersey ferryboat. Now, as Philadelphia journals repeated the story, friends of Mrs. Ross rushed to her house to embrace and congratulate her, but that weary, worn woman had already learned that the rumor was false. Another rumor, that the abductors were captured and locked in the Town Hall in Germantown, likewise turned out to be unfounded.

The previous afternoon, while Ross paid a brief visit to his neglected store, a group of spiritualists came to Washington Lane and persuaded Mrs. Ross that they had inside knowledge of the boy's whereabouts. With her permission they saddled a pair of horses from the Ross stable and rode off, saying they would bring back little Charley. At the store Ross received his wife's wire: COME HOME QUICKLY; GOOD NEWS, and rushed back to the house. The spiritualists had already returned empty-handed, the tired horses panting. The episode, along with the rumor, provided additional Saturday morning reading for Philadelphians.

Mayor Stokley, who had suffered a slight attack of vertigo during the week, nonetheless returned to the city from his Long Branch retreat to follow the case more closely. One of the first things brought to his attention was the arrest on scant grounds of a suspect named Christian Wooster. Another was the mounting reaction to the abduction. Seldom had the mayor seen Philadelphia so aroused.

In an editorial entitled "The Unpardonable Crime," the *Public Ledger,* while refraining from publishing new developments, declared the base and inhuman act of abduction was of such a nature as to excite the most intense anxiety in the mind of every parent: "We have never known sympathy with the individual grief of a person in private life to be so universal. Nor so intense a desire that the perpetrators of a crime shall be hunted down and punished at any cost." The abductors had made a fatal blunder in choosing liberty-loving Philadelphia in which to commit their atrocious crime. "This is not the city in which such business can be carried on," the paper proclaimed. "We have had traffic made of a great many extraordinary subjects, but an attempt to trade upon the heart-agonies of a whole community will not do. There is but one way open to the brigands, and that is to restore the child with the least possible delay, and then get away from Philadelphia as far and as fast as possible."

"It would be impossible to overestimate the intensity of the feeling of indignation pervading this community against the brigands who stole the child of Mr. Ross," editorialized the

Inquirer. "There is nothing that is more certainly resolved than that there shall be no compromise with the guilty parties; that they shall be hunted down and punished for the crime they have committed, not only against the parents of the abducted child but against the security, peace and happiness of all other parents." Every man was concerned, said the paper, and every man must now become a detective.

Every railway station and train should be under rigid inspection by all who travel, and also every steamboat, canalboat, stagecoach and vehicles of every description, enjoined another paper. Every foot passenger should be watched, every highway and byway should have its vigilant guards, and every person with a human heart should keep a lookout on every house in every neighborhood, whether in town or country. Places believed to be resorts of disreputable characters should have the concentrated public gaze fixed upon them. By these means the whole population of the country could be turned into a universal detective police.

The *New Age* spoke of "the awful reverberations of the hue-and-cry of a whole people which is now gathering its echoes to roll them through the length and breadth of all the land."

"The kidnappers of Charley Ross knew not what they did or they would rather have their hands cut off than have ever touched him," said the editorial's ringing conclusion. "They thought they were only stealing Mr. Ross's child. They will learn yet in the appalling indignation of the nation that they have stolen the child of a whole people."

A great popular concern was that, whereas in many nations of Europe abducting a child was a capital offense, in the United States kidnapping was a misdemeanor, punishable only by fine and imprisonment not exceeding seven years. Interviewed on the subject, District Attorney Mann said the nation never anticipated such a "peculiarly shocking and cold-blooded case.'' He evinced the belief that the ''elasticity of law'' could come into play, so that the criminals could be convicted of engaging in a conspiracy to extort money. This would add several years to their sentence. They could also be given three years for taking the boy's jacket, three for stealing his hat, three for his shoes, and so on with each article of clothing worn by the boy at the time he was kidnapped. The sentence could thus become tantamount to life.

The first object, however, was to use every possible means to put down street brigandage in Philadelphia. One of the most obvious would be the posting of a reward for the apprehension of the abductors, said the *New Age*. Yet no public official of the confused administration had the authority to do so, not the mayor, not the chief of police, nor the district attorney, nor the comptroller. A public committee formed to raise money had not acted. This left things up to the father, who did not have the means to offer a reward, and who was now divided between willingness to sacrifice everything to recover his child and a repugnance to set the ruinous example of condoning so heartless a crime. ''While we cannot blame him — for the voice of nature is stronger than reason — we emphatically condemn the precedent he is setting, and which cannot fail to afford the worst possible stimulus to a crime hitherto almost unknown in America,'' the paper said of Ross's reported efforts at raising what it termed ''blood money.''

Announcing that a vigilance committee had been formed to mete out punishment to the abductors, the *New Age* admitted that vigilantes engage in unlawful proceedings, but asserted the present case offered a tremendous provocation. ''If found, as we doubt not will soon be the case, their fate will be made a warning to others,'' the paper said of the criminals. ''Neither will the law be permitted to save them, nor will mercy be shown them.''

While one journal questioned whether the anonymous letter writers were not impostors, and suggested that to prove their authenticity they forward a piece of little Charley's clothing or a lock of his hair, most of the nation's press was concerned with the means of administering justice to the criminals.

"The Philadelphia papers are complaining that there is no law to punish child stealing," said the Washington *Star*. "If the kidnappers of Charley Ross are once caught, let them be turned over to a jury of eight or ten anxious parents in the neighborhood of his home about the dusk of the evening, and we think they will be able to find a law that will suit the case."

"If captured, nothing would save them from the gallows," said the semiweekly New York *Evening Post*. "They can be punished both for kidnapping and for threatening life, and judge and jury will be ingenious in figuring up a round term of years."

"This single act of blackmailing brigandage in Philadelphia makes every mother who has heard the story feel insecure in the possession of her children," intoned an editorial in the New York *Herald*. "Even air and exercise will be denied the little ones in every city if this heartless abduction is not speedily punished, and every parent has and cannot fail to feel a personal interest in the discovery of the criminals."

15

LIKE MANY OTHERS, the *Herald* editorial said hardly a word about restoring the lost boy to his parents. In many instances newspapers solemnly warned Ross against any compromise with the criminals, declaring that a grave question of public morals was involved which automatically removed freedom of action from his hands. It is not surprising that the abductors, whose letters showed them to be avid readers of the daily papers, became alarmed.

Saturday, July 18, came and went without the appearance of the kidnappers' messenger. In his stead came a lengthy letter.

Phila., July 18. — Ros: *we be at a los to understand yu a week ago yu sed yu had the amont an was wilin to pay it the editorials seme to speak as if the mony wus yet to be contributed befor yu could pay it. this wold be a terable mistake for yu to have it caled for an yu had it not to hand out for it wold never be solicited the second time. if yu mean square bsiness with us we wil do al we promis yu. if yu mean stratigem it is imaterial whether yu hav the mony or not yu can try the game as wel without the mony as with it. if yu trap any one it wil be some one we care nothin abot only we lose the mony (yu lose the child) we be redy to test it soon as you say mony is redy. we se the pealers has coped a lad an grate prase is given them for their efficiency but we care nothin for him but if it was one of our chums they had, yu child wold have dide within an our after it, an al further negotiations wold cease at once. yu wil find in the end that the cops can do nothn for yu in this case, thay are as far of the track now as the day they started in persuit of the game. we cautioned yu against seting the pealers or cops as som here cal them lookin for the child. don't yu believe us when we tel yu that they only search for the child's life. The blasted editorials have got the city in such a feve bout the child that we can hardly do anything. i tel you they endanger the child's life at every stroke of the pen. one editor wants to kno why we dont give yu some prof that we ever had the child by sendin some of his close or a lock of hair we have our reason for not sending them. to satisfy yu we have him yu remember his striped*

*stockins are darned in two or three places were they had holes
in. ask Walter if we did not put the blanket up in front of
him an Charley in behind to hide them. ask Walter if we did
not say we wold go down to aunt Susans befor we went out on
the mane street to buy torpedoes. Ros — if yu ever want yu
child restored to yu a live yu have got to act with us alone yu
and yu friends only. we tel yu positivly if yu love yu child
the detectives are yu worst enemies. if yu have them in yu
service they will be the means of yu losin yu child forever. if
they interfea in our bisines we can never efect the change an
death inevitably will be the result. we can not keep the child
forever. we don't want to keep him any longer than to give
yu time to procur the mony we thought yu were better fixt
for money or we would never took yu child but since we have
him we shal cary out our plan with him. this corosponence
with us must stop short we wil not keep it up longer. befor yu
git this we shal join our friends at a distance but we wil notice
al yu have to say either in ledger star or herald or sunday
dispatch anything you wish to communicate to us head it
C R R instead of Ros. dont let yu wife be foolishly led by
the Spiritualist to think they can tel her anything bout Charley, there is but one thing on earth outside of us that has the
power to tel yu an that is the money. yu wil find in the end
that we speak truth for once, This man Woster is innocent he
has nothin to do with us, do as yu please with him an make
the most out of him yu can. our advice to yu is an we hope yu
will take it for once that is dont yu state in personals that yu
have the mony until yu have it naled up in the box we described to you an redy to give wen caled for. the brokers we
se have had a metin an think they can restor yu child an bring
us to justice — they mean wel to yu but they be actin under a
great delusion — if they be friends to yu let them make the
mony up which is the only thing can restor the child — if they
will not do that yu drop them unless yu want to cut yu child's*

*throat — if they want revenge let them git it after yu get yu
child. this is a friendly advice do as yu think best — yu hear
no more from us til we no yu mind — we have told yu that yu
will see yu child again but it depends with yu an yu only in
what condition you se him. We thought we would be ready to
setle this bisines to-day but it must be delayed.*

This latest word from the criminals showed that they had
read of attempts to raise reward money for their apprehension, of Ross's alleged efforts to raise ransom money, of
suspect Wooster's arrest, and of the spiritualists' encounter
with Mrs. Ross. They raised various points of identification
which Walter confirmed. The violence of the clamor about the
case admittedly upset them, forcing them to redouble their
caution. In fear they left Philadelphia and removed themselves from the center of the dragnet enveloping them.

16

THE SUSPECT the police had arrested to satisfy the public demand for action was a colorful confidence man, blackmailer,
and thief. Christian Wooster had been arrested so often over
the years that he called many men of the force by their first
names. In one instance he had blithely given the name of a
United States marshal as a reference in order to make off with
a horse and buggy, and he had not hesitated to rob the pastor
of a prosperous Presbyterian church. Recently he had been
released from prison in Philadelphia, where he was held on a
charge of attempted blackmail, under the two-term rule which
specifies that if a prisoner's case does not come up in court
within two terms he is automatically released.

"It is with genuine pleasure that we this morning announce

the arrest, made yesterday, of a man of whom there is every reason to believe is closely connected with the abduction of Charles Brewster Ross," trumpeted the *Inquirer* in Philadelphia the day after the arrest. In New York, the *Herald* would have none of it. "It is true that one man has been arrested, but except that he has been observed to meet three other men at the same hour for several days, and his previous bad character, there is no ground for suspecting his complicity in the case," the paper reported. "The truth seems to be that the police have simply arrested a noted criminal at hazard in order to make believe that they have found a clew," it concluded. "This kind of humbug is too frequently adopted by our inefficient police to cover their own want of energy and skill."

While the city police had known about Wooster for some time, they had not actually arrested him. It was a former municipal detective named Joshua Taggart who took in the acquiescent suspect. With two associates Taggart ran a private agency, the Pennsylvania Detective Bureau. Before booking Wooster, he went to see District Attorney Mann and City Solicitor Collis. He showed them letters which Wooster had written and which he felt closely resembled the handwriting on the anonymous correspondence received by Ross. He further indicated that while the arrested man was born in Massachusetts, his ancestry was English. It was still generally believed that the abductors must be foreigners, and because of the reference to four thousand pounds in the third letter, probably English.

To newspapermen Mann said he had little doubt Wooster "and his gang" were involved in the abduction. Forty-eight hours would very likely produce sufficient evidence to prove his complicity in the case.

A reporter who called on Collis found the city solicitor at his office on South Seventh Street. Asked if he thought Taggart had the right man, Collis replied, "I have not the slightest doubt of it and future developments will prove what I say."

On being booked by Taggart, who was described by the press as "careful and cool, not at all enthusiastic or very sanguine or apt to jump at conclusions," Wooster made a voluble statement:

"I returned to this healthy city and was fastened on again for a little blackmailing job and sent below. I got out on the twenty-fourth of April and went to New York. Well, I didn't do much there, but what I did worked all right. I returned to Philadelphia on the eighteenth of June, and about the twenty-third I quarreled with somebody in a saloon and received an elegant black eye, which laid me up for almost two weeks. I had a finely colored eye when the boy Ross was stolen, and was at home."

In their last letter the abductors had taken note of an arrest by the "pealers or cops" and declared that the man in custody was innocent and had nothing to do with them. Had he been a member of their band, they warned, his arrest would have meant the death of the boy. Since this letter arrived while Wooster, the suspected author, was in police hands, it appeared to rule him out as a suspect. The authorities were not so easily convinced.

When Wooster was taken to the Ross store to be confronted by little Walter, the boy shook his head. Nevertheless, Wooster was kept in custody, where for a few days he became a favorite of the press and the public, as well as the police. At his request, Taggart came to see him at Moyamemsing County Prison. After a friendly chat, Wooster declared his innocence.

To Moyamemsing also trooped the alert *New Age* reporter. The latticework cell door was thrown open by the guard and out stepped a wiry pleasant-featured man of medium height, close to forty years of age. Wooster's hair and side whiskers were ringed with gray. He looked at the reporter with bright intelligent eyes and greeted him in a cheerful tone: "You must excuse the looks of this cell. I haven't fixed it up yet."

After settling back on his cot, Wooster described his youth, his English parents, his graduation from Greenleaf Academy in Massachusetts. "There is no doubt great pains were taken to make something of me," he related. "The stuff was in me, but never mind that." He had fallen in with bad characters in New York and Boston and that was that. In fact, he added with a twinkle, had the reporter ever heard of the swindling pawn ticket game currently being played in New York? "I invented that," he said with some pride. In New York as in Philadelphia he knew most of the boys on the police squad by name. As for the Ross case, he was simply the victim of Taggart's zeal to best his old pals.

"Down I went with Josh, and by the way he is a pretty good sort of fellow, but he wanted badly to do something, he and the Central men being at loggerheads," he said of the arrest. "God knows I am bad enough, but the police have got me for something now that I don't know anything about. I am still able to work, but there is plenty of other and more certain ways of making a big stake then by child-stealing."

The police had clearly bungled, he went on. The letter business was all "bosh." "I am of a very nervous temperament, and you might pick out four of my letters and they might all appear to be written by different persons," Wooster confided, throwing himself back on his cot and laughing heartily. He concluded his interview on a buoyant note by saying that when he got out he might very well deliver one or two lectures on the inefficiency of the Philadelphia police. A word about their New York compatriots might also be in order.

While Wooster remained in prison, the New York *Herald* reported that a diary found on his person documented his movements since the kidnapping, as if preparing an alibi.

This led the *Herald* to reverse its earlier judgment of his innocence:

Chris Wooster's character and conduct, in a word, clearly indicate those of a criminal, who, anticipating arrest, ranged all his plans beforehand, wrote his letters, devised his assistants, and now remains uncomplainingly in durance, confident that his companions can attain their desired ends, after the successful accomplishment of which he must needs be released because nothing has been proved against him.

Shortly, the *Herald* came full circle by veering once again to the view that Wooster was an innocent victim of the incompetent Philadelphia detectives.

On Thursday, July 23, after a week of rather congenial imprisonment, Wooster was released. He promised to lead a different life if only the police would let him. Ever communicative, he explained that at one time, intending to reform, he had gone to Kansas and prospered. A desire for public office led him to aspire to a seat in the legislature of that state, but at a crucial point in the campaign a paragraph in a Leavenworth newspaper mentioned that he had been the proprietor of a panel house in the East. The revelation ruined his aspirations and forced him back into his old life. If given another chance, he hoped to do better.

At this point the New York *Herald* saw that it was missing out on some first-rate copy, and sent its troubleshooter to interview Wooster at a downtown rendezvous. The tone of the questioning, which the *Herald* published on July 25, made it clear that the released man was now considered not only to be innocent, but virtually an elder statesman in the police field.

"What do you think of the case, Wooster?"

"I'll tell you just what I think of it," replied the genial con man, rising easily to the occasion. "I say to you, just as I said to Mr. Ross last evening when I called on him, that

this boy will never be forthcoming until the money is paid —
that is, unless the abductors make some egregious blunder.
The best 'cross men' in the world are liable to get into trouble
in that way."

"Why do you think so?"

"Simply because, speaking professionally, they would be
fools to do so. Their danger is by no means a common one. I
am sure that the case could have been compromised for five
thousand dollars within a week of the abduction of the child.
As soon as the men could have been convinced that they had
made a mistake in their man, they would have closed up the
job on the best possible terms and avoided further publicity.
The case was badly managed at first, and now it has become
so notorious that the men will never give up the boy until they
can get rid of him to advantage. To a thief or a burglar
twenty thousand dollars seems little enough money for the
compromise of the case as it stands today."

"What has raised the price?"

"The bungling of the police and the conviction of the kidnappers that the police can never catch them. The newspaper
publicity has also had the effect of making them more careful.
I ask you then, as Charles Reade advises every man to do, to
'put yourselves in their place,' and see what you would reckon
as a fair compensation for giving up home and being an exile
for the rest of your life? Is twenty thousand dollars too much
when you are debarred from such rich, gullible cities as Philadelphia and Boston, with such police forces as they have, to
work in? I guess not. Don't think from what I say that I
sympathize with these scoundrels. Not a bit of it. I would
travel the breadth of this country to give such men away. If I
have no sympathy for a man's pocket, I have for his heart.
I tell you if any man were to come and steal one of my bright-
eyed little pets, I would have his blood if I hanged for it.
Yes, sir, before God I would."

"Your family are in Philadelphia, then?"

"They have not been away from the city. I'll give you my address. Come out and see my boys."

"Thanks. How about your lectures?"

"They are a thing of the future yet. I am afraid I can't get under way before Saturday evening."

With a hearty handshake, the *Herald* journalist bade his host adieu and hurried off to other tasks.

Wooster's attack of the platform mania was in earnest. Reports circulated that he had engaged the Opera House in Germantown for an evening during which he promised to tell all he knew about the police of Philadelphia. Other reports, emanating from Wooster himself, stated a manager had offered him three hundred dollars a week for six weeks of lectures but that he preferred to manage himself. The Germantown lecture was canceled when adequate financing was not forthcoming in time.

A week later, August 1, large posters were stuck up on all the street corners of Frankford, a wide-awake town to the north. The posters announced Wooster's lecture scheduled for that evening at the Odd Fellows Hall. The Christopher Columbus Band, four lively pieces, had been engaged for the occasion. In order to make a suitable appearance Wooster had his hair shampooed at Dollard's, a smart local emporium. He had his white vest neatly cleaned and pressed at one of the town's Chinese laundries. He purchased a handsome new plum-colored coat and a pair of narrow tight-fitting pumps. Strutting about town he cut a dapper figure as he waited for the gala Saturday evening to begin.

When the Christopher Columbus Band struck up its introductory chords, however, the dismayed lecturer gazed about to see the Odd Fellows Hall virtually empty. The citizens of Frankford were in the streets and stores doing their marketing and exchanging pleasantries of the day. To his audience

— which consisted of three newspapermen, a friend who had advanced him some money on expectation of cleaning up a tidy profit, a slouched figure come up from the city to see if any chance might develop to pick a pocket, and an agent for the sale of unadulterated liquors — Wooster began to relate his tale of woe and to vent his indignation on the Quaker City's "smart detectives." It was difficult to muster up enthusiasm for so sparse an audience. Wooster made the attempt, then regretfully announced the lecture would be postponed until a more fitting time. The agent for unadulterated liquors, already somewhat groggy from frequent tasting of his samples, lurched to his feet and slapped the disappointed lecturer on the back.

"My good feller," he said with a thoroughly blurred diction, "let's take a drink."

"No, sir, excuse me. I'm not on that," Wooster replied firmly.

"No yer don't. Drink you must," said the agent with surprising determination. Under his perseverance, Wooster's resolution gave way. Together the two hurried off.

The reform effort had failed. The local papers, in announcing Wooster's lecture, had also published his police record. He had tried to follow an honest path but once again his past had tripped him up. He was seen no more on the lecture platform, and he was thereafter out of the case, whose point of emphasis, in any event, had long since shifted elsewhere.

17

To FILL THE GAP caused by police ineffectiveness, the *New Age* undertook its own detective work. It obtained the route which Walter traveled with the abductors and sent its man over the same roads at the same hour. The reporter found them teeming with people, many seated on porches cooling themselves in the shade. To his astonishment there was hardly a policeman in sight, although more than two hundred were technically assigned to the areas covered. When he finally saw a member of the force, "the man was holding on to a lamp post, gazing at the sky. There was evidently nothing on earth worthy of his attention." Over the entire route only three officers appeared, the other two in deep conversation about the heat.

In his travels above the Limekiln Pike, the reporter found a farmer who said that on the evening of July 1 he saw two men and a boy in a buggy as it pulled up before a tavern. One man got out and took a drink. When he was finished, the other descended. On his return, the little boy began to cry, but the man pacified him by playing a harmonica. A second farmer testified that he saw what appeared to be the same party stop at a tavern on July 2 at eight o'clock.

Earlier it was rumored that a woman living above the Limekiln Pike had also seen the party on July 2, the small boy's head partly hidden by a linen wrapper. The boy was said to be crying as the wagon went by the house going *into* Germantown. This appeared to be significant, but when the reporter caught up with the woman she said the story was false. It developed from a chance remark she had made many weeks earlier about a wagon that passed her house with a child inside crying.

Mrs. Ross, seated on the porch of her home and surrounded by women friends, spoke briefly to the *New Age* sleuth. She told him the police had no reliable knowledge of anyone having seen little Charley in the neighborhood after the abduction.

The paper was undismayed by this washing out of its research. It turned immediately to the reward which it had long insisted should be posted for information leading to the boy's return. In an interview Mayor Stokley declared that while he could not act without direction of the Common Council, scheduled to meet in September, he would offer no reward even if it were in his power to do so:

"When I became mayor of Philadelphia I said to myself, 'There is to be no more compounding of felonies.' When goods are stolen I don't wish them returned so much as I wish those who stole them brought to justice. I must have the thieves. If anyone on the force turns up stolen goods without bringing the thief to prison, the officer will be discharged from the force. I tell you I am doing my best to keep Philadelphia clear of rogues, and my men are determined to hunt down the fellows who stole the little boy."

Despite the mayor's recalcitrance the *New Age* reported a proposed meeting of Germantown residents to raise money for a reward, as well as a public meeting in Independence Square to express the sympathy of the people. "Not an hour in the day but the imaginary little face I have pictured rises before me and a pang of renewed grief is felt as I hear of its continued captivity," wrote the editor.

The New York *Herald* reiterated its criticisms of the police. "Of how much the country towards the northward of the Limekiln Pike has been looked over by the police, the people will of course be kept in utter ignorance until a *Herald* correspondent penetrates the region." Furthermore, it had not been ascertained whether the buggy was driven over the identical road to and from every visit to the Ross mansion or whether it came from different avenues of approach. "This is an important point which the police may afford to overlook, but a newspaper correspondent cannot," the dispatch concluded.

On Tuesday, July 21, the *Herald* used its front page to say it had unearthed the kidnappers' plan for effecting an exchange of the ransom money for the stolen boy. The place they had selected was a lonely bridge in the extreme northern portion of the county, and the hour at which the business was to be transacted, if transacted at all, was set down at about midnight. The bridge was surrounded on all sides by a flat and open country so that one standing on its abutment could witness an approach from any direction. The plan stated that Ross must come to this bridge with the money. While en route to the designated point, and before he arrived at it, he would be met by a man who would stop him and say: "Good evening, sir." To this Ross was to render an immediate reply and then pass on. Before reaching the bridge he would be approached in the same manner by a second man. To his salutation Ross was also to render an appropriate reply. On reaching the bridge he would meet a third man, who would ask the following question, "Mr. Ross, have you got that?" This would be the signal for turning over the ransom. After Ross had paid the money there would be a slight delay, but in a few minutes little Charley would be delivered.

"The robbers evade all possibility of detection by the following conditions," the *Herald* reported. "The three will be armed and in disguise. If Mr. Ross does not come alone or if a single soul is seen lurking anywhere in the neighborhood, the robbers will fail to keep their appointment. The bridge stands all by itself, three different roads intersecting near its site, and the country being open and level as the floor, the confederates stationed out along the different roads can see Mr. Ross for a long distance off and know whether he came alone or with someone else. Moreover, Mr. Ross will be watched from the time he leaves the city until the time he is accosted by the first man, and any attempt to assemble a posse of citizens or police near the bridge would be sure to be seen by the kidnappers, who, of course, the policemen do not know."

While the "bridge plot" was never broached by the anonymous letter writers, and was apparently the fabrication of a feverish journalistic mind, Ross was besieged by people who offered plans on how to cope with it. A Southerner wrote to say bloodhounds could be put on the trail of the criminals even as much as six hours after they had left the area. A man from California suggested that large logs be hollowed out and put under the bridge with men secreted in them. When the child had been turned over and was safe, the men could come out and apprehend the criminals. The man offered himself as a volunteer.

Asked his opinion, Christian Wooster was convulsed with laughter. "Well, that is the most absurd story I ever heard. How could any such job be carried out? It's too bad that any newspaper should have been fooled on such a matter."

His own suggestion for the carrying out of the exchange was ingenious: "The friends of Mr. Ross or an officer can go to a house on the Canadian side of the border, say across the bridge at Niagara Falls, and the very moment the money is paid the child can be brought from the adjoining room and delivered over. The kidnappers can laugh at the men who propose to take them. No warrant could be obtained to take anybody out of Canada on such a charge. This is my opinion regarding the easiest method of settling this matter up. You have asked me and this is what I tell you."

Later it was learned that the kidnappers read this interview in the papers and decided to check into the matter. They were to discover that Wooster was correct in his belief that there was no clause in the extradition treaty with Canada on the subject of kidnapping. Other crimes, robbery and extortion, were covered, they learned to their dismay, for on these charges they were vulnerable.

While the New York *Herald* was cooking up its "bridge plot," the *Evening Star* in Philadelphia obtained a revealing interview with Christian Ross in which he discussed the letters which the papers were so eager to print but which he would not furnish. Because of the tremendous interest in these letters, many other papers reprinted the interview:

"Of course you have heard of these letters and I don't see any use in keeping their contents secret any longer," Ross began. "The parties who have been negotiating with me by letter ask that I shall agree to pay them the ransom they demand and they promise to return the child within ten hours after the receipt of the money. Such an exchange could be done very easily. They ask that I shall first agree to their terms. It will then be understood that I will have the money at hand whenever called upon, whether that be at the mid hour of the night, at my store, or on the street. It is proposed that I shall be approached by someone who will ask for and receive the money. The delivery of the child will follow. In the letters I am asked to place confidence in these men. They say they intend to be faithful to their promises and they expect me to be faithful to mine. They add that they will deal fairly so that others may know it. From this I infer that they intend to continue the business. Of course I place no confidence in these men and shall not do as they request. Thus far I have no fears for the child's safety. All the letters assure me that the child is safe and in good health. By the way, they confess that they have got the wrong child. If they had known my circumstances, they would not have taken my child. I think they are anxious to get rid of him — indeed, they substantially say so. My greatest apprehension is that, finding they do not get the money, the child may suffer for it."

Ross found it difficult to voice the sentiments in this interview; in fact, it was largely dictated by the police and the public committee advising him. Its intent was to convince the kidnappers that no money was forthcoming, so that they would abandon their plans and release the captive boy. Ross was not confident of this reasoning, and to another source he acknowledged that while his family had not offered him the ransom sum, he had been enabled to raise it. His tortured mind kept wavering on this point.

On the morning of Tuesday, July 21, he was told that George Philler, president of the First National Bank of Philadelphia, had called a meeting to raise $20,000 in sums of $250 and $500, on condition that the money be paid only when the child was recovered and his kidnappers convicted. The meeting was held in the mayor's office, and at it, in addition to Philler and Mayor Stokley, were William McKean of the *Ledger,* George L. Harrison, John C. Bullitt, and other prominent men of the city. Pledges for the desired amount were given. The next day the following ad was prepared for the newspapers and also for use on large handbills in conspicuous locations throughout the metropolitan area.

$20,000 REWARD FOR THE KIDNAPPERS
Mayor's Office
City of Philadelphia, July 22, 1874
At the instance of the citizens of Philadelphia, I hereby offer a reward of twenty thousand dollars for the arrest and conviction of the abductors of CHARLES BREWSTER ROSS, son of Christian K. Ross, of Philadelphia, and the restoration of that child to his parents.

William S. Stokley
Mayor of Philadelphia

The proclamation was followed by an account of the abduction and a detailed description of the lost boy, who was said to have no blemish, mark, or scar on any part of his person, except from vaccination on one arm, but on which arm it was uncertain. Caution in identification was urged since little

Charley's appearance might well have been altered by cutting his hair, dressing him as a girl, or by other means.

The notice described the horse and buggy, and the two abductors:

No. 1 — was a man of rather large size, probably 5 feet 8 or 9 inches high; he was only seen sitting; age believed to be from 35 to 45 years, moustache and full beard or whiskers, rather long on the chin, of brown or sandy-brown color, and brown hair; he wore a ring on the little finger of right hand.

No. 2 — was a man 5 feet 8 or 10 inches high, about 25 or 30 years of age, of light, or with a tendency to sandy, complexion, sandy moustache, and rather red nose and face, having the appearance of a drinking man.

One of the men wore a broad-brimmed straw hat, looking as if it had been worn a season or two, and much sun-browned. The other wore a high-crowned, dark-colored straw hat. One wore a linen duster, the other a gray alpaca duster. One of the men wore large glasses or goggles of dark color, probably as a disguise.

Obvious difficulties had presented themselves in the preparation of this proclamation. Gardener Peter Callahan and Dr. Walker had seen the abductors only at a distance. Walter had been very close to them, but he was a child unaccustomed to describing people in terms of height, age, and other identifying characteristics. As a consequence, the proclamation compromised on variations in detail and produced a composite picture of the two men. Despite the fact that Walter had seen both on foot, it stated that the older "was only seen sitting." While Walter had said the older man wore two gold rings on a middle finger, the proclamation spoke only of a ring on the little finger of the right hand. In these and other instances, the versions of Callahan or Dr. Walker prevailed. Elsewhere, Walter's account was credited.

Overall, the descriptions of the two abductors provided few

telling marks of identification — the younger man's face and the older's use of goggles were perhaps the most valuable. By an incredible oversight, the older man's most conspicuous characteristics, the deformed nose, was not mentioned at all! Still, the proclamation did indicate general features of two abductors, and it gave a clear picture of the stolen child, the horse, and the unusual type of buggy.

A postscript asked every newspaper in the United States and Canada to publicize the proclamation, an appeal which drew wide response. To give added emphasis, Chief Jones shortly let it be known that all officers of his department would forego any part of the reward in favor of the person or persons who would communicate with him, secretly or otherwise, and provide information leading to the arrest and conviction of the abductors of the child.

When Ross saw the text's emphasis on the apprehension of the abductors, he remembered the criminals' admonition which referred to just such a situation: "if they want revenge let them git it after yu get yu child." The mayor's proclamation was designed to lure an informant, since every other measure had already been taken. Would it succeed? At what cost? Physicians were freely administering opiates to the distraught mother, but for Ross, who held himself responsible for the actions being taken, there was no drug to dull his pain.

To add to the suspense, the wildest stories continued to circulate. A dispatch from Belair, Maryland, said Charley Ross had passed through with detectives twenty-four hours behind. The child supposed to be Charley was later traced to Baltimore, where he turned out to be a nine-year-old boy. Little Charley had been found in the woods near Gloucester, New Jersey, and the abductors were safely locked in jail, went another report, which also said one of the men had been seen handcuffed to an officer, the child at his side, walking down toward the courthouse on Market Street in Camden. The individuals described were found to have no bearing on the Ross case. In another instance, a man and woman were detained in the 24th Police District on information that they had been seen with a child answering to the description. The couple were arrested and taken into custody, but later released when the child was found to be a girl. Still another rumor, that the boy had been found in the cellar of a house near Philadelphia's Girard College, proved false. To a reporter who asked Joseph Ross if anything meaningful had developed, a somber answer was given: "All is dark, dark. We know nothing."

18

ON THE SAME Tuesday morning that the meeting was held to raise money for the mayor's proclamation, a reply was finally framed to the criminals' seventh letter, received the previous Saturday. "Yu hear no more from us til we no yu mind," that letter had stated. In the *Ledger, Star,* and other papers of the twenty-first, the following personal was inserted by the authorities: "C.R.R. — Money is ready. How shall I know your agent?"

A reply arrived the next day. It was dated Burlington, July 21, and postmarked Camden, New Jersey.

Burlington, July 21. — Ros. *yu statement in Monday Star is so conflictin with yu statement in this mornin personals that we are yet unable to comprehend yu nevertheless we wil act upon yu promise as if it was made by an angle. in monday Star yu say yu can have no faith in us neither do we have any faith in yu from the nature of this bisines it is to be presumed neither can have implicit confidence. the way this bisiness*

stands is this yu pay us the money yu are left without anything to bind us to our promis but our own word which yu say
yu do not believe. then on what ground can we efect the
change. we have seen yu own statement that yu would not
comply with our terms an yet yu say (the money is redy how
shal I no yu agent) the fact of us having yu child and you
having paid us every dollar we demanded what further use
could we have for him? He has answered the end for which
we took him; this is one reason why we should give him up.
The next reason is, if we should ever play the same game in
any other part of the country, who would have any confidence
in getin their child after they had paid the ransom if you
should lose yu child we don't say we shal ever play this trick
in this country again, for the popular outcry is a most to
great. It has been stated that since the great outcry of the
people that we would gladly surrender the child without a
ransom. Do not deceive yuself on that, for we could set the
child at liberty at any moment, but we never wil alive without
the money, no never, never, never! Ros, in order to ever get
yu child alive there is but one way left yu an that is the way
we point out to yu. Yu must comply with our terms in every
particular, and met our agent step by step as we instruct yu.
If yu mean to act in faith to us yu can have no objection to
this course. The fair an the faulce part is left with yu to
chose, for it is with yu alone we shal presume to act an the
life of Charley shal bind yu to yu word. do not deceive yuself
an think this is only to frighten yu. we appeal to the highest
power exist on high to bear us witnes. (we solomly swear befor the twelve houses of heaven so sure as the sun rises in the
east an sets in the west, so sure shall Charly die if yu brake
yu promis with us an may the same curse fal upon us if we do
not keep our promis with yu. Ros we want to caution yu stil
more for this is a question involves the life or death of yu
child. do yu desire to make a change of yu money for the

*child if yu are sincere take advice from us who yu think are yu
worst enemies but in the end yu will find we were yu best advisers the advice is that if yu want to regain yu child drop
the police entirely have nothing to do with them while yu are
transacting this bisines with us or the whole thing wil prove
a failure an yu child must die if yu mean to ensare us then
our advice is enlist al the power yu can invoke but be sure yu
prove succesful for one false step seals the fate of yu child.
We have told yu it is impossible to ensnare one of our friends.
Do yu not believe us, or are yu wilin to put the life of yu child
at issue an test it with us. In all of our letters we have told yu
the life of yu child shal be the bond that bind yu tu yu promise; any stratagem or false promise on yu part must an shall
seal the fate of your child and you have none to blame for yu
be his murderer an not us — for one false promise from yu we
shal stop at nothing until we haveing given yu a prof that we
can keep our word even unto blood. i repeat if yu want yu
child yu comply with our terms in every particular. One false
step on yu part will make yu and yu family weep tears of
blood but if yu act in faith with us al wil go wel with yu.
What have the authorities done towards findin yu child. They
have done nothin yet and they are as far from his hidin place
to-day as they were on the 6th day of July (yu money alone
can find him) if these terms suit yu answer the following in
the* Ledger *personals.*

C R R. i will agree to the terms in every particular.

*P.S. — have the money ready as we described we wil send
prof with him so yu can no him when he comes.*

Authorities inserted the prescribed personal in the papers
of Wednesday, July 22: "C.R.R. I will agree to the terms in
every particular." On Friday, July 24, a reply posted in
Philadelphia was delivered to Ross. Apparently the abductors
had returned to the city, or as the authorities suspected, a

member of their band was stationed in Philadelphia and able
to post letters sent there.

Phila., July 24 — Ros. *we have seen yu reply in personal
(yu agree to the terms in every particular) we accept yu
offer for we consider yu fuly understand the great an momen-
tus obligation yu place youself under when you assented tu
this agreement. we be sory that we cannot effect the chang
to-day. our creed is such that it forbids us to any bisines of
this kind only at a certain quarter of the moon an the phace
of the moon has just passed over so we have got tu wate one
week befor we can transact any bisines between us. this delay
may be a great sorce of torture tu yu but it cannot be avoided.
we pledge ourselves in the mean time yu child shal not suffer
for any thing only the close confinement which is necesary
for his safe keepin. we have him so that we feel at ease against
all the detective force in the country ever feritin him out. the
authorities have offered $20,000 for the recovery of the child
an detection of us if they had yu interest at hart this would
be the worst thing they could do. this is only oferin a reward
for the sacrifice of yu child, We told yu at the beginin that yu
child could never be takin from us a live that he was so situated that we could destroy him in one instant. an forever out
of al prof against us but yu seam to have no faith in our word.
nevertheless yu have nothin to fear on that point for he can
never be found by any detective force. neither can any reward no matter how large be any temptation to us to peach
one on the other for we are sworn an blood bound unto death
tu never give each other away. Ros. one week must intervene
befor we can negotiate for the restoration of Charley by that
time there will be an $100,000 reward yu will se by that time
the detectives can avail yu nothin or yu wil se that we spak
trought from the beginin. that there was no earthly hope left
yu only in payin the ransom in good faith an then yu get*

yu child what we mean in good faith is tu set no trap. We no it is not posible for yu to trap us. but by any stratigem on yu part or connivance it wil thwart our perposes an the money wil never come to us. if this result takes place through any act or connivance of yuse then yu lose yu (child forever.) If yu do as we instruct yu an this money gits lost (it shal be our los and not yuse) an yu shall git yu child just as if we got the mony. no matter what our instruction is for yu to do with the mony yu do it an yu child shal be restored to yu. if we tel yu to burn it up do so, if we tel yu to throw it off the dock do so, if we tel yu to give it to any one do so, an yu child wil be restored yu wether the mony gits lost or not through any act of ours. Ros. the whole contract is sumed up in these words. yu pay us the mony in good faith in denominations from 1s to 10s in U. S. notes an no private marks fixed on them, then we consider yu have fulfilled yu part and yu shal have yu child restored safe to yu. if we do not fulfil our part in good faith to yu, we invoke the vengeance of hell, if there be an hell, to be our eternal portion. we have told yu that we wil transact this bisines with yu and yu friends only. we know a true friend wil not advise yu rong if he has the interest of yu child at heart we shall no nothing about detectives in the bisines if yu cal them in for advice or asistance it wil be at the peral of yu child's life for in their eigerness to arrest us, which they never can do, they will surely be the means of sac-rificing yu child. we shal never cal on yu but once for the mony so it is yu part to have it at a minute's notice. but yu have plenty of time yet. due notice wil be given yu when to have it at hand (we request no answer tu this) till yu hear from us again which perhaps wil be one week. in the mean-time yu and yu family console youself that yu child is wel an safe tu yu. an to us against al detective power. nothing sur-prised us more after we had told yu the imposibility of findin the child an the risk it wold be tu the child's life tu find his *hidin place yet yu in disregard of this advise persisted in havin the detectives search for him. time wil tel yu that we do not lie in every word we write. the reward signifies nothin, with us wether it be $20,000 or $20,000,000 it wil accomplish nothin with us an the authorities wil fail on that point tu bribe one of us as yu wil se in the end of this bisines. Ros our word for it no harm shal befal yu child intentionaly til yu hear from us again 7 days by that time yu must be prepared for his ransom if yu ever expect him alive. Ros mark the selfishness of Mr. Stokley an his committe of brokers what do they say. not one cent for ransom but millions for conviction. do they have yu interest at heart. no it is a selfish motive. they are wilin to sacrifice yu child that theirs be safe. why do they not pay their mony to have yours restored first, an then offer a reward for our conviction.*

As the extraordinary correspondence continued, Ross noted again the apparent touches of humanity in the criminals. They apologized for their delay in exchanging the boy for the ransom money and promised that in the interim little Charley would not suffer except from his necessarily close confinement. Ross's agony could only increase with this news of his boy and the abductors' insistence that they had sworn a blood oath which no reward money could force them to betray. They told him to mark the selfishness of the mayor and his committee of brokers, who were willing to sacrifice his child that theirs might be safe. Once more Ross was left with his doubts while, powerless, he was forced to endure the suspense of waiting.

19

THE POSTING OF a reward by the mayor fanned public excitement to fever pitch. Extra editions of the papers hawked every new rumor. Letters and suggestions poured in on Ross, many from well-meaning sympathizers, others from spiritualists, astrologers, soothsayers, crackpots and confidence men. To the house on Washington Lane and to the family business on Market Street they flocked each day of the week, with Sunday a particular favorite. One man stationed himself in the family stable and read prayers of incantation to the rhythm of a turning wheel, saying that each revolution of the wheel brought Charley one mile nearer home. Another called to say Ross was being punished for cutting his hair and beard, forbidden by the Bible, and that the boy would return when Ross allowed his hair to grow. A youth from North Carolina wrote that with a peach tree sprout he could trace little Charley from his place of disappearance to his present abiding place. Still another expounded an elaborate ritual — take the fresh egg of a hen, a hen untouched by woman's hands; place it in a wicker basket containing no metal reinforcement; cross the road in front of the house three times, et cetera, et cetera.

Many declared that if given a piece of the boy's clothing or a lock of his hair, they could locate him. A prisoner from Sing Sing offered his professional services. At times Ross felt as though every person, from near and far, whose mind was unbalanced or whose mania verged on a particular subject, was bound to come to him with a plan for finding the lost child.

For the harassed man the visits and correspondence were time-consuming and often disheartening, yet he answered every letter that seemed reasonable and saw many people, looking for any thread that might lead to a meaningful clue.

The inability of the police to turn up one piece of useful information led to a feeling of desperation on their part, on the part of Ross, and on the part of the press. The newspapers were at a total loss to understand the case, and their speculations began to take on forms which increased the ordeal of Christian Ross.

In Philadelphia, the *New Age* gave voice to a theory that the boy had been kidnapped in order to put him into training for some acrobatic purpose, following a practice common in England in past eras. The process was described in these terms:

These poor little victims were bathed in or with hot oil, incessantly, so as to cause unusual fluidity of muscular parts; and the various joints, after each immersion and bathing for lubrication, were tortured into "doubleness," as it is technically called. The result of this process is an abnormal elasticity and doublejointedness, until at middle age nature asserts her rights and the twisted form of the erstwhile human eel mocks the past triumphs of circus trainers.

In New York, the *Times* recalled cases in which the motive for abduction was "the desire of depraved wretches to witness the writhings and convulsions of human beings under various forms of torture."

Not surprisingly, the New York *Herald* correspondent came up with a special supplement on child-stealing, in which he recalled that from the earliest ages the practice had existed among barbarous races as a means of increasing the tribe, and also as revenge upon the parents. Later on there was profiteering as children were sold into slavery, a case in point being the Biblical Joseph, who was sold into captivity in Egypt by his jealous brothers. Gypsies were well known, of course, for stealing children to replace offspring of their own who had died prematurely, and in modern times the system of large estates in European countries, with strict laws of inheritance, had often led to child-stealing or even murder by envious relatives.

Recounted in detail were the stories of Kaspar Hauser, the mysterious boy who was found wandering destitute and unsure of his origins on the streets of Nuremberg in 1828, and of the boy who appeared early in the eighteenth century among a tribe of Indians in New York State and exhibited many remarkable traits which led to the belief that he was the lost Dauphin, the son of Marie Antoinette.

The most bloodcurdling section was reserved for the description of a particularly savage type of child-stealing dramatized by Victor Hugo in his book *The Man Who Laughs*. Hugo told of a group called *comprachicos*, who for money trained the human form into hideous shapes. The *comprachicos* would singe an intelligent-looking face and turn it into a leering mask, form a straight-backed boy into a hunchback. So thorough was their process of torture and disfigurement that even a mother could no longer recognize her child.

A day after printing this historical summary of kidnapping, the paper ran the following in its personal columns:

A New York Gentleman, of Ample Means, in the hope of saving the life of his invalid wife, who is growing insane over the Ross abduction, will pay an amount equal to the reward — viz. $20,000, for the return to him of Charles Brewster Ross, in order that he may restore the child to its parents. While opposed to compromising a felony, he will act squarely in this case for the above reasons. On receipt of an answer from the right parties proposing any reasonable plan for the exchange of child and money, money and man will be ready. Business now. Address ARTHUR PURCELL, General Post Office. Philadelphia.

It was generally assumed that *Herald* editor James Gordon

Bennett was responsible for this personal; that he had hired a private detective who was using the name Purcell while trying to unshroud the mystery of the disappearance and thereby bring credit to the paper.

Another figure who tried to divert the kidnappers' correspondence toward himself was Joshua Taggart, who inserted the following notice in the papers:

$5,000 reward will be paid by us to any persons who will give us a clue which will lead to the detection of the kidnappers of Charles Brewster Ross, and the name of the person giving us the information shall be kept secret, if desired.

The notice was signed by Taggart and Edward G. Carlin and R. A. Luken, two of his associates at the Pennsylvania Detective Bureau. After its appearance Taggart became a frequent visitor at the office of the attorney for the reward committee, often popping his head in the door to learn if anything had developed. "Nothing for you yet," the attorney would say and Taggart would disappear.

From time to time personals appeared in the paper addressed to Ross, Taggart, and others, the efforts of sundry characters who claimed knowledge which money could buy. All were false leads.

20

WHILE the *Herald* had turned up little more than rumors and fabrications, it decided to give itself an editorial pat on the back:

"It should be here stated out of simple justice to journalistic spirit and enterprise that the New York *Herald* has communicated more to the police and the public concerning the mysterious abduction of Charlie Ross than all the other New York and Philadelphia journals combined.''

When Philadelphia police announced they were debating a plan to search every house in the city, many New York papers ridiculed the idea as an act of desperation. The search would be ineffectual, they said. It would also be illegal. Ross noted the attacks. But he could not have guessed, nor would he have believed, that an onslaught of unheard-of virulence was about to be launched against himself and his family.

In its columns of Saturday, July 25, the New York *Herald* used bold-leaded heads and subheads to talk of STRANGE QUESTIONS ARISING OUT OF THE CASE; REMARKABLE DISCREPANCIES AND CONTRADICTIONS; and STARTLING SUSPICIONS. ''Dark, grave suspicions begin to influence the community, but they are of such a foul and unnatural character that nothing but the most conclusive proof that they were true could force your correspondent to transfer them to paper,'' began the text.

The ''conclusive proof'' came in the form of a letter to the editor from a suspicious citizen, who signed himself Vindex. The most important aspect of the abduction had never been reported, the letter began: ''It has been mooted in the family circle; it has been spoken of upon the street; it has been discussed, pro and con, by the representatives of every newspaper in the city, and yet no newspaper or its representative has as yet walked up to 'the ghost' stalking in the midst of the city of homes and taken it by the throat.''

A few well-put questions would pinpoint ''the ghost.'' Since the boy was abducted on July 1, why was the first official notice of his loss delayed two days until July 3? Why was the piddling sum of $300 offered as a reward, a sum much too small to tempt the cupidity of the rascals who allegedly ''stole'' the boy? Why was Christian Ross's name not given to the reporters at an early date? Why did Ross refuse a generous offer of pecuniary assistance? Why was Mrs. Ross described as being ill when she was actually bathing on the beach at Atlantic City? Why, if there were anonymous letters from the abductors — and rumor had it that Mrs. Ross had burned the letters because of incriminating facts they contained — were they not shown to the press and the public? Why had the father refused to allow the picture of the stolen boy to be issued in the illustrated journals? Why had Mrs. Ross told a reporter that she felt the child would not be harmed and that such things had to be borne, if she did not have some inside information? Had Ross allowed a fund-raising campaign and arranged privately with a detective to give him pertinent information allowing him to recover the boy, thus enabling the detective to walk off with the $20,000 reward and then split with him?

"In this day of widespread financial ruin, in this day of Jay Cooke embarrassment and Franklin Savings Fund frauds, it would be a possible thing for a person who had been in financial difficulty, and compromised with his creditors at three, six, nine, and twelve months, to go into a conspiracy of this very character to raise the wind and start anew," the writer opined.

Detective Joshua Taggart was quoted as saying: "I know more about this case than you do, if I could only tell you now, but I can't. Can it be possible there is an American citizen of African descent in the woodpile?"

The letter writer said he was asking his questions in the cause of truth and humanity, hoping that their appearance in the paper's columns would spur those working for these ends. "To recover the child at all hazards," he concluded, "without any compromise whatever, is the sincere desire of yours, VINDEX."

Christian Ross was aware of an undercurrent of rumor and innuendo which had evidenced itself in letters he had received, as well as in correspondence and calls directed to the mayor and the police. Many times the suggestion had been made that the family had secrets. Some said that Charley was not the child of Mrs. Ross and that a designing second woman was involved in his abduction. Others declared the father was an accomplice of the villains, or that the boy was concealed in the Ross house. A correspondent suggested digging to a depth of one or two feet all around the house in a search for the boy's body.

Ross had been disturbed by the whisperings about his private life, but he had considered them products of aberrant minds. When the ugliest of the rumors were printed in the columns of a prominent New York journal, he was shocked.

"Here in Philadelphia, where Mr. Ross is known, such a story needs no contradiction," said the *Inquirer,* which interviewed him and described Vindex as a "villainous piece of business." The defense in the *Ledger* was more passionate: "It is a wanton cruelty, adding a crushing humiliation to a terrible affliction, to be suggesting that the parents of little Charley Ross have any other knowledge of the disappearance of their child than that he was stolen in order that the bandits might make money out of his abduction." The principal ground for the innuendos, stated the *Ledger,* was the refusal of Ross to permit publication of the anonymous letters, in which instance he was conforming to the counsel of his legal advisers.

The *New Age* interviewed Ross the day after the letter appeared and found that the father had satisfactory answers to each of the questions posed. Attributing the attacks on him to the cruel collusion of wicked men, it said the father appealed to "no one for anything save that sympathy which must well up in the heart of every parent in the land. He wants the kidnappers caught, but above and over all in his heart is his paternal love for his little one." In this regard the paper said Ross had not received any money from his rela-

tives, but had by other means raised the required sum. He
was willing to pay it for the recovery of his boy, who had not
been ransomed as yet because negotiations with the kidnappers had been temporarily suspended, possibly through fear of
detection.

Having paid its homage to Ross's integrity, the *New Age*
proceeded gradually to impugn it. Most pertinently at issue
were the anonymous letters, which every paper had demanded
to see but which were shown only to George W. Childs, publisher of the *Public Ledger*. Chosen as a competent authority,
Childs expressed satisfaction that they did not implicate Ross
in the abduction. The favor extended to a rival publisher
further angered the *New Age*:

From the moment we were refused access to the letters we began
to surmise that the story of the abduction might not be altogether
straight. This surmise has gained strength every day since, and much
of the attention our reportorial corps has given to the case has been
on the assumption that it was not dealing with a genuine case of
kidnapping for ransom. . . . This celebrated abduction case begins
to look very much like no abduction at all.

Again and again the *New Age* declared that the anonymous
letters should be published, that they contained vicious slanders and unspeakable language against Mrs. Ross, that a
knowledge of their contents might lead to a solution of the
mystery. After all, the whole case appeared to rest almost
entirely on the testimony of little Walter, recounted not by
himself but through his father. And Walter's account of the
abduction was full of holes. To Peacock, Walter had said
nothing of a second man and nothing of Charley. On the other
hand he had mentioned that the man who took him in the
wagon knew his mother. And if Walter's description of the
route was accurate, why had no one over the heavily crowded
area seen the horse and buggy? If Walter had told the truth,

summed up the *New Age,* a strong ground existed for believing his brother had been kidnapped. If he had not told the truth, there was no ground for believing in the abduction at all.

In a particularly bitter mood, the paper quoted its New York rivals, starting with the *World:*

Walter is a boy some seven or eight years old; he may even be nine. He has an oddish look. His eyes are small. He has a quick, nervous, twitching countenance. He has a sharp, cunning, secretive look. He is a very knowing boy, a prematurely old boy, and is capable of using sarcasm and irony in his conversation. . . . Why may not this prematurely sharp and prevaricating youngster . . . be lying?

The quote ended with the *World* declaring it was painful to cast a suspicion upon "this possibly entirely innocent child," but "justice begins with suspicion." If the paper had been in charge of the case, its very first step "in this mysterious affair would have been to arrest and thoroughly examine every member of the family; above all, the single one who professes to have any direct knowledge of the alleged abduction."

In addition to the *World* extract, the *New Age* reprinted a long column from the hated New York *Herald* which declared the ransom did not seriously figure in the case. The long, vituperative letters abusing the mother clearly indicated that personal enmity toward her, the gratification of a personal revenge, was the diabolical motive that lay behind the case. It was certainly obvious that professional thieves were not involved, for they would not have been so stupid as to choose an unfortunate bankrupt.

In this view of the case the *Herald* was supported and perhaps inspired by Joshua Taggart, who was interviewed at the Pennsylvania Detective Agency at Fifth and Spruce:

"If professionals had been engaged in the affair, we would have got down to them before this. Whoever has possession of that child is perfectly aware of the fact that there is not one cent in the case, and no persons would know this sooner than professionals. That is what makes the case all the more mysterious and causes it to be so strange that the child is not returned."

While he said there might be some family feud or difficulty behind the abduction, Taggart admitted there was no evidence to support this view. "I should not be surprised to hear that the child was picked up, either in the street or in the country somewhere near Mr. Ross's residence, by some stranger and carried home," he concluded.

Shortly after the Vindex letter appeared, the *Herald* correspondent visited the Central Police Station in Philaldelphia and immediately ran into Captain Heins, who, he reported, looked at him in a severe manner and demanded, "Do you know, you're charged with the authorship of the Vindex letter?" Laughing at the accusation, the correspondent left the headquarters office and went to see the object of Vindex's venom, Christian Ross. He came away with a remarkable impression:

I had a long talk with Mr. Christian K. Ross today. The more I see him the more thoroughly am I impressed with the injustice of Vindex's allegations. The man is worried to death by all manner of rumors and by great numbers of calls. All sorts of people visit his office daily with all sorts of theories. . . . The sorrows and cares of the past month weigh heavily enough on his head without the addition of any more such letters as that from Vindex. The poor mother, too, whose sadness seemed to me something so noble, so hopeful, and so womanly, never deserved this blow.

Under the heading "The Mother's Story," the *Herald* also carried an interview with Mrs. Ross:

The lady was seated on the veranda, and as she rose to welcome your correspondent, while his card was handed her, there was to be seen all the grace and carriage of a courageous, resolute woman, suffering under a terrible affliction. There was a mother's grief in every feature of that calm, pale face.

Mrs. Ross explained to the correspondent that her husband had withheld some information from her to shield her health. She had been overcome by the boy's disappearance: "It was a dreadful shock. The knowledge of Charley's death would not have equaled it. But I am trying to be hopeful. I believe in the Almighty and justice."

The conversation resolved other supposedly suspicious points. In particular, Mrs. Ross emphatically denied that Walter had said one of the abductors knew his mother.

Within days of this soft line, the *Herald* reverted to form, demanding to know why the letters of abuse were not published, declaring that yesterday Walter told one story to relate the events of the abduction, the number of stops made, and so on, while today he told another, and summing up by blaming the entire messy case on the Republican party of Philadelphia. This ruling group would not allow the letters to be published because they knew the correspondence might contain clues which, while apparently of no value to the Philadelphia police, could help others. Thus the case might be solved out of New York and the local Republicans suffer a rousing defeat in the coming elections. Ross was the dupe of the politicians, the entire case a subject for political jobbery.

As a result of the calumny heaped upon him by the *Herald*, Ross withdrew from all communication with it. One day to his dismay he found himself on a New York–Philadelphia train with the offending correspondent, who thrust his card into his hand.

"I have nothing whatever to say," Ross said stiffly. "When

a man's character has been assaulted as mine has been . . . it behooves him to say nothing until the proper moment. My first object is to find my son. My next will be to vindicate my character.''

When the correspondent said he was forced to go to the streets for news because Ross withheld information, the weary father quietly admonished him: ''A newspaperman should report nothing unless he knows what he is reporting is true.''

''All that has been said that you imagine hostile to yourself was uttered after you had denied the newspapers the only means they had to secure the truth,'' the reporter pleaded.

''Be that as it may, I do not care to talk now. . . . I believe that God will see me safely through yet.''

Ross tried to conclude the interview by explaining that the letters were not devoted to wholesale abuse of his wife, as alleged; he had withheld publication because they used such strong language in threatening the child that he feared knowledge of the contents would kill the mother. Had this been made known, the correspondent said, the insinuations against the Ross family would never have arisen, for people could not fathom why thieves who stole a child for ransom could waste their time in abusing that child's mother. Not understanding, they made up their minds that the child had been taken not for money but for revenge.

In an attempt to hold Ross's attention, the *Herald* reporter asked, ''Do you believe there is any other way in the world for you to get your boy, without bargaining with the kidnappers and fully complying with their demands?''

''I see no other way at all,'' replied Ross and refused further comment.

It was later disclosed that the *Herald* had offered him five hundred dollars for facsimiles of the letters, which he refused, saying that at the proper time he would make the correspondence available to all the Philadelphia papers at no cost.

Ross considered bringing libel charges against the *Herald* for what he termed "base fabrication," but because of the many drains on his energy he abandoned the idea. Two months later, he did take to the courts against the proprietors, editors, and publishers of the Reading *Daily Eagle*. In an article entitled "The Ross Case All Humbug," the editors of that Pennsylvania journal said they were neighbors of Ross and offered a theory. They recounted that ten years earlier, when Ross's business was prospering, he had married a wealthy Western lady of good family who had borne him two children, Walter Lewis and Charles Brewster. The family had been happy until Ross began to lead the life of a *débauché*. He sought out other company than his wife's. His business began to fail and he became a bankrupt. The woman fled without the formality of a divorce, and the present Mrs. Ross took her place. Some months before the abduction Ross had received letters from his first wife. The paper theorized that the first wife had Charley in her custody, and that the anonymous letters were forgeries written by Ross or his friends to divert public attention from the real facts. "We think Mr. Ross knows now and always did know where his child is, but refrains from making it public for family reasons," concluded the malicious attack, which the proprietors rushed into print and sent to Philadelphia, where it caused a great stir.

To support his libel suit, Ross appeared in court and stated that all the charges were completely untrue. His only marriage had been to Sarah Ann Lewis, his present wife, who had borne all his children. While he admitted that in April last his firm was compelled to suspend payment of debts, this was wholly due to business reasons. A pale, brokenhearted Mrs. Ross appeared on the witness stand to testify to the exceptional purity and fidelity of Ross's life as a husband and father.

At the conclusion of the trial, the proprietors of the Reading

Daily Eagle were fined a thousand dollars and reprimanded for gross abuse of the press. For Ross it was a shallow victory.

21

BEFORE PUBLICATION of the Vindex letter, the abduction had been carried in the papers under such headings as "The Stolen Boy" and "The Ross Abduction." These leads changed to "The Ross Case" as the slanders were blazoned over the front pages. When this vein of reportage was at least partially exhausted, the old headings reappeared.

The campaigns of innuendo caught Ross at a time when his physical and psychological strength was being worn to the breaking point. Again and again police called on him to investigate what appeared to be tangible clues.

In Richmond, Virginia, authorities arrested a man named Myron Leasure when it was discovered that he was traveling with a child. His story was that he had left his New York home with his son three weeks earlier for a trip west. When he arrived in White Sulphur Springs, West Virginia, the child died. Leasure, his equilibrium upset by the event, continued to travel with the dead child and brought him to Richmond. Investigating his strange story, detectives obtained a certificate from a White Sulphur Springs doctor indicating that the child had died of natural causes — and was, moreover, only ten months old.

Several days later a little boy with light golden ringlets was seen at the West Philadelphia depot in the company of a well-dressed woman. Passengers about the station noted that many aspects of his appearance corresponded to the published description of little Charley Ross and detained the woman while police were sent for. The officers were likewise startled by the resemblance and immediately sent for Christian Ross. When the father entered the station, a large, noisy crowd was swirling about the child and his guardian. One look told Ross that it was not his boy.

The woman explained that she had purposely avoided putting a brown linen suit on her son, although he owned one, because the mayor's award proclamation had described Charley as having worn such a suit. To prevent further detentions of the party, Ross signed a certificate, endorsed by the police with the seal of the city, and gave it to the woman. It was the first of hundreds of such certificates presented to individuals detained by overzealous citizens.

Near the end of the month, while Ross was enduring the week before the "certain quarter of the moon an the phace of the moon" the abductors' "creed" required to transact business, he was informed of reports that little Charley had been seen shortly after the abduction in the Allentown area. An employee of the Reading Express Company had first seen him at the railroad depot in the company of a suspicious-looking man. While the boy was light-haired, the man, obviously a stranger to his charge, was dark. When the boy, acting as if under some mild opiate, cried "Mama," the man had addressed him as "Deacon Harry." This led to the belief that the boy was Charley, whose slow, old-fashioned gait and deliberate speech had earned him, as noted, the nickname of "little William Penn."

When the suspicious man took the child to a millinery shop, the female proprietor, seeing that the boy was dirty and unkempt, scrubbed his face and hands but found she could do nothing with his hair, so matted and kinky as to be unmanageable. She suggested that while she fitted out a suit for the boy, the man should take him to the barber. This he did, leading the youngster to an emporium run by one William Able, better known as Fancy Bill. Later in the afternoon, the man and the boy, his hair neatly cut, his face and hands clean, and wearing the new suit from the millinery shop, boarded a train for Mauch Chunk.

Many people in Allentown noticed the incongruous couple and some remarked on the boy's sorrowful expression. In particular, Fancy Bill continued to mull the matter over, and some ten days after he had seen the mysterious couple he wrote the Philadelphia police to tell them of the little boy who had come in to have his "hare kut," avowing that he was the man "as had kut it." By now newspaper reports were telling of the horse and buggy employed by the abductors, and as a result the imaginative Allentown barber suddenly remembered the child's being driven up in a wagon. For added spice he declared that a strange woman had accompanied the man and the little boy.

Unaware of Fancy Bill's propensity for embroidery, Captain Heins sent one of his detectives, Lieutenant Kraft, to Allentown. Kraft made his first call at the barbershop, located in a basement under the offices of the First National Bank, and found Fancy Bill awaiting him in a lush-looking velvet coat, a jeweled cross over his shirt front, bogus jewels on every finger. After leaving the barbershop, Lieutenant Kraft spoke to others who had seen the man and boy. He was soon able to discredit Fancy Bill's version.

The Allentown story led to a long series of reports from Harrisburg, Reading, Mauch Chunk, and other Pennsylvania cities, all saying the boy and his guardian had been seen passing through. One man said he had spoken to the mysterious traveler, who told him he had come two thousand miles with the child. Another said the man asked the boy not to speak to strangers. Each successive clue was checked. After a long pursuit the suspicious party was arrested. The little boy turned out to be blue-eyed and barely two years old.

Privately, Ross was reported to have expressed dismay with

the way detectives had handled the case, and to feel that if he had had his way the boy would long ago have been recovered. He was seen less frequently at the Central Police Station, to which he had earlier paid daily visits. In his public statements, however, he continued to express confidence in the detectives.

In addition to tracing the unending series of clues which were being brought to their attention, the police force, in late July, was given the order to undertake a house-by-house search of the entire city. Every dwelling place, public and private, a total of well over a hundred thousand houses, was searched over a period of weeks. Philadelphians of every social level, from Supreme Court justices to garbage collectors, answered their doorbells to find uniformed men of the law sternly asking, "Is Charles Brewster Ross concealed in this house?" Hearing a negative answer, the officers announced that they must then explore the premises. In a city famed as a defender of human and civil rights this illegal procedure — no search warrants were produced — met with not a murmur of protest. To Philadelphians there was no matter so urgent as the recovery of their lost boy.

So all-pervasive was the police activity that for many weeks the city was free of crime. The mammoth hunt led to numerous arrests as officers found vast quantities of stolen goods. During their investigations, they also uncovered scenes of poverty and deprivation. Spinsters and hermits were frightened and ladies of little virtue were sometimes surprised at their work. The search turned the city upside down, but it did not lead to a single clue as to the whereabouts of little Charley Ross or his abductors.

The press continued to insist that a breakthrough might be achieved by the publication of a photo of the lost boy. The one extant photo of Charley at the age of two was bound to show a family resemblance and this would be valuable. The

Evening Star finally managed to gain access to this baby picture and reproduced a drawing derived from it on its front page on July 27. At the same time several papers ran pictures of Walter, identifying him as the elder brother; others, less scrupulous, as Charley himself.

Ross and the authorities had earlier agreed upon a plan to meet the need for an up-to-date likeness of little Charley. At the *New Age*'s behest they allowed Austin Street, a well-known Philadelphia portrait painter, to take the early photo and, aided by suggestions and criticisms from members of the Ross family, to produce an updated life-size portrait. A woodcut of this oil painting by Street was reproduced near the end of July in the *New Age*, which stated that Mr. and Mrs. Ross, little Walter, and other members of the family pronounced it a perfect likeness.

Electrotypes were made available to illustrated papers in Philadelphia and other cities; police posters incorporated it into their descriptions of the abduction. In response to public demand, a copy of the portrait was placed in a conspicuous window in downtown Philadelphia, on Chestnut Street just west of Ninth. Here great crowds of people stopped to fix in their minds the image of the lost boy. As a result of the portrait's widespread circulation, the citizenry redoubled its efforts. People were more than ever on the alert for a boy resembling it. A strange man driving through the country accompanied by a child was almost certain to be overtaken and questioned.

Theories continued to abound and each one had its opposite: The child was being kept in a low haunt in the city — he had been taken out of Philadelphia on the day of the abduction and placed in the hands of a third party in the country; the child had long since been killed — he was alive and would probably be left anonymously at a charitable institution; the abductors had rented their horse and wagon — they owned them; there were at least four criminals involved, probably two men and an elderly couple put in charge of the child — two men and a lone woman were involved; the abductors were English — they were of Italian origin. Speculation was unending. Suspense, melodrama, even humor made their appearance in the case. Only facts remained conspicuous by their absence.

22

AMIDST THIS ACTIVITY, Ross remained under the surveillance of detectives. He appeared to be increasingly bewildered, and was described by his brother Joseph as "not the same man." Mrs. Ross, under the care of a physician, sat at home unable to keep her mind from morbid thoughts. At the sound of every carriage wheel she would rush to the door, thinking that her Charley had returned. With each disappointment she returned more wearily to the chair and silence. "If only she could cry, I think it would relieve her," said Joseph Ross. "She has to take an opiate every night to produce sleep."

The trials the afflicted couple were about to endure seemed to exceed even those they had already experienced. On Tuesday, July 28, the day began with the arrival of a new letter from the criminals.

Philada., July 28. — Ros are yu not convinced by this time that the detectives can render yu no service whatever. are yu agoing let them keep yu under the delusion that they can yet recover yu child an bring us to justice. we tel yu the thing is imposible we fear them not — neither do we fear they wil ever find Charley until we find him for yu. We se in the personals that Mr. Percll a milionaire of New York offers to pay the required amount to redeem yu child an ask no questions,

*but we have no confidence in him neither would we treat with
him if he offered one milion in hand an no questions asked.
in the transaction of this bisines we are determined to no no
one but yu, an if yu suffer these letters to go out of yu hands so
that they can personate yu in effectin this change we shal hold
the child subject to the fulfillment of yu promise an one fals
step by yu or by any one acting for yu, yu may consider the
bisenes is at an end, an the trap has sprung that render further negotiation useles to yu. At the end of this week must
end this biseness; it must place him in yu hands safe an sound
or must place him in the grave; it is left entirely with yu. if
yu have not the mony to redeem him an ask for an extension
of time we wil keep him for yu but under no other circumstances we wil not. We are not afraid to keep him for we set
the whole force at defiance to find his hidin place. No matter
how grate the reward is, it signifies nothin with us — they are
goin to search every house in the city. we wil give yu the
satisfaction to tel you he is not in the city nor ever has been
since the day he left home, nor he never wil be again unles we
return him to yu for the ransom, we wil give you the satisfaction of knowin that he is within 100 miles of this city an yet
we defy al the devels out of hell to find him. we tel yu sin-
cerely we have prepared this place for every emergency an it
is death for yu to find him while he is in our custody. we told
yu in our last letter we could not transact any business for one
week. we are now prepared to effect the change as soon as yu
be redy, but under no circumstances say yu be redy when yu
be not able to put yu hand on it, an hand it out. rest assured
if our agent cals for it an he does not get it without waiting,
he will never come again an the our of redemption is forever
gone by with you. from you former promises we take it as
granted that yu be agoin to redeem yu child in good faith, it is
unnecessary therefore to repeat the consequences of any per-
fidey or fals step on yu part. we teld yu to put the mony in a*

*box, but we now tel yu to put the mony in a strong, white,
leather valise, locked an double straped an be prepared to
give it or take it wherever we direct yu. if yu are directed to
cary it yuself yu may take al the friends yu please with yu —
but dont let the cops know yu bisines nor go with yu unles
yu want the bisines to turnout a failure. if yu want to trap
take the whole force with yu an then be sure yu know what yu
be doin — for we know what we be doin. this is al the caution
necesary for yu to save yu child alive. if you can have all
things ready as we have directed yu by thursday the 30th
insert the folowin in the ledger personal (John — it shall be
as you desire on the 30th.) Ros you may fix any other date
that is convenient for you. Ros yu have sed yu had no confidence in these men an would not do as they requested yu. now
we say yu must do as we request yu, or there is no earthly
hope left yu to save yu child alive. this is the only alternitive
given yu an yu will find we are prepared for every emergency.
detection is impossible if yu do not ransom him, he must die.
if yu attempt to arrest any of our agents, he must die. If yu
fail to comply with the terms after promising — he must die.*

In reply to the letter's command, authorities placed the
specified personal in the *Ledger:* "John. — It shall be as you
desire on the 30th."

On the morning of the thirtieth, however, another development in the case occupied Ross and the public, and occasioned
perhaps the wildest popular excitement experienced by the
Quaker City since the days of the Revolution. A front-page
announcement in the Philadelphia *Times* blazoned, "It affords
us inexpressible satisfaction to announce at last to the sympathetic people of Philadelphia the joyful tidings that little
Charley Brewster Ross has been restored to his family! The
lost is found, and there is sunshine once more in the darkened
cottage home!"

The rumor that little Charley had been found — and despite the headline, as yet it was only a rumor — had begun at eight in the morning when a telegram was received at the Central Police Station saying two detectives of Pottsville, some seventy-five miles distant, had found a gypsy camp near Hamburg which was harboring a four-year-old boy who conformed exactly to the description of little Charley Ross. When the citizens of Hamburg first noted the boy's presence among the band, they had turned out en masse to form a posse that locked arms and completely surrounded the camp until police officers arrived.

By ten o'clock in the morning, contents of the dispatch had spread over Philadelphia. Men, women, and children began a race to the Central Police Station and the Ross place of business. Thoroughfares in front of newspaper offices were blocked as throngs gathered before bulletin boards to await further news. To the right and left of the mayor's office on Chestnut Street a mass of anxious citizens barricaded the street, while at the railroad station an angry crowd gathered to lynch the gypsies. In hotels, overwrought guests swarmed through the lobbies. Members of fashionable clubs, the exclusive Union League, the Reform, and the Philadelphia, dropped all business at hand and assembled to await news. The intense excitement had brought the city's life to a single focal point.

On receiving the telegram, Chief of Police Jones swiftly decided he himself, along with several officers, would make the two-hour journey to Hamburg to bring back the boy and his abductors. Because Christian Ross was anxiously awaiting another letter from his anonymous correspondents, he remained at home. To make the identification, his brother-in-law Joseph Lewis prepared to accompany the police chief. A special train of the Reading line was proffered and hurriedly made up. The entire line between Philadelphia and Hamburg was cleared and coal trains put on sidings. At each station large crowds gathered.

By eleven o'clock newspaper extras appeared on the street with these developments and newsboys found it impossible to carry enough papers to meet the demand. A new telegram told of how the entire gypsy band had been arrested. The boy had been taken from the hands of a woman and man who claimed him. At noon the agent from the mail train arrived at the Central Police Station and brought excitement to a new peak with his news. The mail train did not have a stop at Hamburg, but because of the activity there the engineer had slowed down to observe the scene at the station. An immense crowd was gathered around a tall slim man carrying in his arms a little child with flaxen curls. "Great heavens, that is the very child," the agent had cried out. "Thank God!"

In the early afternoon definite news arrived. A telegram destroyed built-up hopes with the words "It is not the child." A chill disappointment swept the anxious crowd. Silently the men returned to their offices to stare at their work, while the women took their children by the hand and sadly led them home. The stolen boy had not been found. The city's sorrow was not yet at an end.

In the middle of the afternoon Joseph Lewis stopped by the Ross house to tell what had happened in Hamburg. On their arrival he and Chief Jones had made their way through the crowd to the beleaguered gypsies. It was immediately clear that the boy, little more than a baby and nearly as brown as a mulatto, bore a strong resemblance to his mother, who was present. Obviously no proper attention had been paid to the descriptions of the missing Charley, spread far and wide in the newspapers, nor to the photos circulated several days past in thousands of post offices and railroad stations. Seeing the error, Chief Jones and Lewis immediately turned and left. They were followed by the boy's mother, who made loud complaints about her arrest and demanded satisfaction for her detention. She was promptly released, along with others of the gypsy band.

The disappointment of the Hamburg episode had barely affected Ross and his wife before they received another letter from the kidnappers, which arrived at four in the afternoon, having been posted in the city during the day.

PHIL., *July 30.* — Ros: *from yu answer this day yu signify every thing is redy, every thing is redy with us. we now give yu a wide margin for preparation to make an arrest if yu be pleased to do so — your actions this day desides Charley's fate — it is left with yu alone wether he shall live or die. we caution once an the last time do not think we are trifling. Ros. you are to take the 12 p. m. train to night from West Phila for New York it arrives at New York 5.05* A.M. *take a cab at cortland or disbrosser sts New York, an ride directly to the grand central station at 4 ave and 42d streets. take the 8* A.M. *northern express by way of hudson river (take notice) you are to stand on the rear car and the rear plat form, from the time yu leave west phila depot until yu arrive at jersey city — yu are then to stand on the rear platform of hudson river car from the time yu leave the grand centeral at New York until yu arrive at albany. if our agent do not meet yu befor yu arrive in albany yu wil find a letter in post office at albany addressed to C. K. Walter directing yu where yu are then to go. Ros — the probibility is yu may not go one mile before our agent meets yu and yet yu may go 250 miles before he intercepts yu but be it where it may yu must be prepared to throw the valise to him regardless of all risks. the risk of being lost we assume an yu get your child without fail. these are the signals: if it be dark the moment the rear car passes him he wil exhibit a bright torch in one hand an a white flag in the other hand but if it be light he wil ring a bell with one hand and a white flag in the other hand. the instant yu see either of these signals yu are to drop it on the track an yu may get out at the next station, if the cars continue on their course we consider yu have kept your word an yu child shal be returned yu safe but if they stop to arrest our agent then your childs fate is sealed. this letter ends all things in regard to the restoration of yu child.*

The moment of truth was at hand. A badly shaken Ross noted that the very tone of the letter reflected an air of impending climax. The spelling was now generally correct except for a few words like "yu" and "redy." The circumstances of the exchange of little Charley for the ransom had been worked out to a fine detail, demonstrating a remarkable ingenuity on the part of the abductors. The time was short.

Accompanied by Frank Lewis, Ross hurried to the Central Police Station, where he was met by Captain Heins and Detective Wood, as well as several members of the public committee, among them William McKean and John Bullitt. A hasty conference was held in an atmosphere of growing tension. It was agreed that Ross should go on the journey as directed. His nephew and a plainclothes detective were to accompany him. The valise was prepared according to instructions, with only one exception — instead of $20,000 in denominations of from one to ten, as demanded by the criminals, it was empty save for a letter prepared by the authorities. This letter was another patent attempt to trap the kidnappers by leading them on. While emphasizing a desire to act in good faith, it was actually a fine specimen of duplicity, reversing the position previously taken. Rather than following through with the abductors' plans for an exchange, it demanded that the exchange be simultaneous. Though there was no doubt in anyone's mind that the letter writers had the boy, it asked for new proof. It also asked for a new mode of communication on the pretext that the old was too public. The text read as follows:

Philadelphia, July 30, 1874

Sir: — *Your letter of this date is received. I am anxious to end the suffering and suspense of the terrible four weeks that I have just passed through, but I am compelled to tell you that I cannot throw away twenty thousand dollars on the wild plan you suggest. It is a plan where all the chances are on your side, and I have not the smallest assurance that I will ever get my dear child into my possession again. It is impossible for me to give you twenty thousand dollars ($20,000), and trust to you to bring me my child at some subsequent time. I desire to act with you in good faith, but as your whole correspondence leads me strongly to suspect deception, I must insist upon having some positive, tangible proof that you have the child, and that after receiving this I must in some way and at some place suggested by you, meet either you or yours and see that you have my child in my presence, so that I may take him simultaneously with your receiving the money. I shall look for a letter from you in Philadelphia in answer to this.*

I have come here in response to your call with a friend (not an officer) as suggested by you in your letter of 28th instant, and in so doing have complied so far as a reasonable man can with your plan. I cannot give you one cent until I see my child before me. It is my purpose, as I have said, to act in good faith; but I must, before going further, receive every assurance which can possibly be given me, first, that you have the child, and second, that his delivery to me will be simultaneous with the delivery of the money to you.

I will add that the public mode I have used in compliance with your suggestions of answering your letters is not satisfactory to me, as it informs the police and everybody else of what we are doing. We must have some better mode of communication.

C. K. Ross

Final plans for the fateful journey were drawn up in John Bullitt's downtown office. A copy of the prepared letter was fastened to the outside of the valise. It was 11:30 P.M. when Ross and his nephew left Bullitt's office for the railroad depot. The officer in civilian clothes inconspicuously boarded the train and took a seat in the same car. At midnight the train for New York pulled out of the station. It was now clear why the criminals had said their creed forbade effecting the exchange except at a certain quarter of the moon. Their plan called for a bright clear night. As midnight passed and the early hours of July 31 began, a full moon shone brightly. There was not a cloud in the sky.

The abductors had said Ross might be asked to drop the valise within minutes of leaving the station or perhaps he would have to travel two hundred and fifty miles before receiving a signal. As he stood on the rear platform he grasped the rail with one hand and clung to the valise with the other. His eyes searched the night, sweeping over every bush and building, looking for a man with a torch and a white flag. Each time the train stopped, the plainclothes detective wandered out to the platform and waited until it had departed, to prevent the valise from being suddenly snatched from Ross's hand.

The fatiguing trip wore on. In the haste of departure Ross had not thought to bring an overcoat. In the early morning hours the dense mist from the New Jersey swamps drenched his light flannel suit, leaving him wet and chilled. After five hours of anxious, uncomfortable travel, the train pulled into the Pennsylvania Railroad's station in New York. There had been no signal. Ironically, Ross heard a sleeping car porter remark, "That man must have a pile of money in his valise. He's been standing there ever since we left the depot in Philadelphia, and he has two men with him to guard him."

Following instructions, Ross and his nephew took a carriage

at Desbrosses Street and drove to Grand Central Station, where they caught the 8:00 A.M. train that followed the Hudson River toward Albany. Although a brief rest at the station helped revive his spirits, Ross found the daytime journey more oppressive than the night trip from Philadelphia. The morning heat became stifling on the rear platform, where he stood exposed, his arms stiff from clasping the empty valise, which felt heavy as lead, and the rail. The speeding train churned up a billowy cloud of dust which trailed behind and enveloped him. As the road curved, engine smoke whirled in gusts into his face, forcing him to strain his eyes in search of the elusive signal. Each time he saw a railroad flagman he became apprehensive, knowing that he must act on the instant. Several times he was on the verge of dropping the valise. His senses numbed, his body begrimed with sweat, dust, and smoke, the exhausted Ross was on the point of collapse when the train pulled into the Albany station at one in the afternoon. There had been no signal, no white torch, no flag, no ringing of a bell.

With his nephew he took rooms at a hotel and tried to rest. Later in the afternoon, he went to the post office. The kidnappers had said that if their agent did not meet him before his arrival in Albany, a letter would be waiting addressed to C. K. Walter. No such letter had arrived. Ross and his nephew ate dinner in Albany. When the expected word had still not come the next day, they left for home and arrived in Philadelphia at seven in the morning. A letter from the abductors, the twelfth of the series, had been delivered to Ross, Schott, and Company during Ross's absence. It was dated July 31 and posted from Philadelphia.

Phila 31 July. — Ros : *yu seem to have no faith in us whatever. we told yu to be at yu store on thursday and this bisines would be all settled up but yu seem to pay no attention to it.*

at the time we supposed yu wer gitin redy to effect the change yu were as the Evening Star *stated on you way to potsvill to see some child there. if yu ever except to git yu child yu must look to us and no one else for there is no other existin powers that can restore him we have told yu to let the detectives take their own way an do as they pleas for they wil do yu no good and we don't think they can do much harm if yu had done as the last letter instructed you and let the potsvill affair alone yu would now have the plasure of seeing yu child safe at home after we had seen that yu had gone to potsvill we did not instruct our agent to meet yu from the fact we thought it was no use. if yu are trifling with us yu will find we are not the right party to be trifled with but if yu mean squar bisines with us although we are perhaps the worst men in the world we wil act honorably with yu in this affair. we told yu the last letter was the only one yu should ever reseive from us an we would keep our word but we are inclined to think yu did not get it befor yu started for potsvill. to save yu al further trouble an vexation in runing around to false reports that yu child is found here, and found there, we tel yu candidly that yu child is not in the possession of any woman or family or that his hair is cut off short. to save yu further troble pay no attention to any telegrams of that description for it is only trouble in vain for yu. your childs hair is the same length that it ever was an there is no disfigurement whatever in him but he is kept where no human eye can behold him yu have expressed the opinion that we would git tired of keeping him an turn him over to some charitable institution. dont flatter yurself with such an idea we have told yu what his end is, if yu do not redeem him we shal never digress from that. he wil never be taken from the place he is now concealed unless he is brought out to be restored to yu. Ros. if yu want to redeem yu child yu must come to us. you can reach us through the personals of the* Ledger *or* Evening Star. *our address is John. a*

*change can be easily accomplished if yu desire it. remember
you have our word in 10 ours the whole thing shall be consum-
mated yu git yu child an we git the money.*

23

THE NEWSPAPERS had earlier tipped off the abductors that the
main post office was being watched. The later stories of the
Pottsville expedition, they said, led them to believe that Ross
had accompanied the detectives to Hamburg. At any rate,
the father's painful journey to Albany was made in vain.
The next step was up to him.

On Sunday, August 2, the authorities met with Ross at
John Bullitt's house and prepared a personal which was inserted in Monday's *Ledger:* "John. — Your directions were
followed. You did not keep faith. Point out some sure and
less public way of communicating, either by letter or person."

The next morning, the thirteenth letter from the kidnappers arrived.

*Phila. Aug, 3. — Ros — in not keepin our apointment with
yu was entirely a mistake from the fact of havin seen a statement in evening star that yu had gone to potsvill on the day
you was to setle this bisines with us. we saw the mistake but
not in time to communicate with our agent or to notify yu not
to go as we directed yu. Yu say yu want us to point out some
sure way by which this money can be transmited to us — of
course we can not call on yu personaly neither can we receive
it by letter. Ros — We will make the followin proposition to
yu and if yu comply with the terms propounded we wil settle
this bisines in very quick time satisfactory to both parties
concerned so far as the restoration of your child is concerned.*

We assure yu that yu child is now well and in as good health as when he left yu home — do yu consent to the followin proposition and stake the life of Charley on the faith of yu promise.

Proposition 1st. Yu wil hand the box with the amount in to our agent when he calls to yu store.

Proposition 2d. Yu will hand him the box, ask him no questions — not folow him — not put any one to folow him — not tel him what the box contains — not notify the detectives so they can folow him — not do anything that wil interupt its transit to us.

Do yu agree to the first and second proposition while we hold the life of Charley to bind yu to yur promise. Remember when yu promise your word is life or death to yu child. If yu consent to these terms answer the folowing in Ledger *or Evening Star to save time. (John i agree to the 1st and 2d propositions.) The reason we have warned yu in al our letters about the detectives to keep them ignorant of this compromise bisines is not that we fear detection but we now they wil interfear and baffle us from receiving the money and yu from giting yu child. we told yu in our last this corrospondonce must end but it was a mistak on our part therefor we be wilin to give yu a fair opportunity to redeem yu son if you wil. when our agent call on yu he will give yu a symbol of which yu wil previously receive a facsimilar so there wil be no posibly mistake in him, if there be it shal be our loss and not yours providing yu do as instructed. if we lose the money through our agent yu get yu child just as if we got every dollar.*

At this point police and municipal authorities decided on a radical step. Frustrated by the continuing correspondence which was yielding no workable clues, they decided to ignore the restrictions of the criminals' proposals. They would henceforth frame their answers not in the language asked for, but in terms demanded by the circumstances. In accordance with this new hard line, a personal was inserted into the *Ledger* of August 4: "John. Propositions are impossible. Action must be simultaneous."

The next day, the kidnappers' reply arrived.

Phila., August 4. — Ros: *we saw yu ansur. yu say it is imposible to agree to the terms, then we say emphaticaly yu can never redeem yu child from us. yu requested a more sure way of paying yu money for yu child we agreed to give yu a satisfactory way which would have made the change sure and safe for yu and safe for us, the way we propounded was the sure test of your sincerity and yu answer implies distinctly that yu son is not worth that amount to save him, yu may be entertaining the idea that if the money is not paid we will turn him loose. yu will find when it is to late that this was a grate mistake. we tel yu plainly and positively that the chances of yu ever geting yu child again is ninety-nine out of an hundred against yu. if yu do not redeem him he is just as good as the money to us for we have him for reference though we may never work this thing in this country again. be where it may we have the Ros child to show that we do about what we say when we told yu your child should stand responsible for our word to us we ment just what we said and any perfidy on yu part would have brought instant death on his head. now we are convinced that you would not keep faith with us, if yu could violate it with impunity to yu child and yet we do not blame yu for that, and yet do yu supose that we would pro- duce the child and hand him over to you the instant yu paid the money to us. the thing is absurd to think of such a change, we are not redy yet to have chains put on us for life. we did think once that we might effect the change in canidy in that way, but we find that cannot be, for yu could hold us there on robbery and extortion until yu could get us here and then yu would have us on the whole. Mr. Ros the way the case* *stands now, it looks as if yu dont want to redeem yu child, or at least yu must redeem him on yu own terms. That is impossible: we repeat it, that is absolutely impossible. If yu ever get him from us, and we are sure yu never will get him from any other than us, yu have got to come to us on our own terms and our terms wil be more stringent than ever. One has suggested to redeem yu child with counterfeit money; another to mark all the money, and then we could be traped after with the money. We say if yu had redeemed yu child with counterfeit money, or with money privately marked, we would not restored yu child till yu had replace the marked money double-fold. A woman has proposed to Tagget to produce Charley and his abductors for $5,000. This will be by far the cheapest way for yu to git yu child, for we will never restor him for one dollar less than the amount we first named. when we found out yu circumstances was not good, we were goin to throw off one-half the amount an accept $10,000 but the public have raised hell so, and smpathised for yu in offring such large rewards that we shall have the whole or none. but they took good care in offering it in such away that they would never have to pay one dollar of it. if they ment bisines why did they not offer so much for the child and so much for the abductors. the reason is they thought one or the other rewards might have to be paid. but we dont think they would ever have to pay a dollar for either child or us. yu wil find the truth of this in the end (if i no myself). Mr. Ross we leave the city to-night. we shal not communicate with yu any more unless yu can satisfy us yu want to redeem yu child on our terms which will be $20,000 and not one dollar less and it must be paid to us as we prescribe. when yu receive this we shall be at least 200 miles from here we leave the detectives of phila and Mr tagget to work out their clues. we think we have left no clues behind us. Charley wil remain where he was taken the second night after he left home. if Mr tagget can find a clue*

to that place he wil no doubt get the reward we have no femi-
nines into that place. charley will never come out of there. it
shal be his everlasting tomb — unless the ransom brings him
out. we are not destitute of a few dollars yet, charley shal
never starve to death if death it must be, it shal come upon
him as instant as the lightning strock itself. Mr. Ros, if you
have anything to say to us it must be through the personals of
New York Herald. *we can see that, where ever we are and no*
doubt every day, we shal notice nothing only from you. no
matter what propositions others may make they wil receive no
attention. yu say the action must be symultanious from the
nature of this bisines that can never be, so that ends the bisines
we told yu in 10 ours after the receipt of mony if we found it
genuine, and not secretly marked al up, yu would then get yu
child in our way of passing him over to yu. this does not suit
yu so we wil leave yu to yu own way of giting and the detectives
to work out their clues.

The authorities, continuing their policy of toughness which
they hoped would bring the abductors to heel, decided that no
answer whatever should be made to this last letter. For three
tense, unbearable weeks they let the matter lie. Of this trying
time, Ross was later to say: "The public were clamorous for
the arrest and punishment of the kidnappers at any cost, yet
were ignorant of the risk to the life of my child and conse-
quent terror to which I was subjected. It is comparatively
easy to sacrifice another man's child for the public good, and
my anxious suspense is easier conceived than borne."

Book Two

24

As a consequence of the apparent dearth of developments in the Ross case, newspapers cast about in the rest of the country and abroad for other matter to fill their pages.

They reported regularly on Indian outbreaks, as the Comanches, Cheyennes, and other tribes took to the warpath. "The Red Barbarians" was a frequent heading for stories about cruelties and outrages allegedly perpetrated by the pampered Redman, but occasionally a voice such as the *Public Ledger* would criticize the Federal Government's treatment of its wards, pointing out that cries for action against them had by a remarkable coincidence grown loud only since gold and other precious metals had been found on Indian lands in the Black Hills.

In a lighter vein, the press assailed the origins and purposes of a new community which had just established itself. "Free Love on Valcour Island," began the dispatches, telling of the "detestable doctrines" of the group, which had dared to settle on an island "in the beautiful bosom of the bluest of American lakes, Champlain." Members called friends of the opposite sex their "affinities." Children did not bear the surnames of father or mother, but were known simply as "Brother" Bill, "Sister" Edna, and so on. Matrimony was a limited copartnership with easy rules for dissolution. In no uncertain terms the press described the "promiscuous philosophy" of the high priestess of the group, a woman whose motto was a question, "Is woman a dog to wear a collar?"

Marital relations came under more searching examination
when one of the wives — number nineteen, by count — of
Mormon leader Brigham Young charged him with adultery
and sued for divorce and alimony. Young did not deny having had relations with his other wives, but said he had done so
under the name of "celestial marriage," a kind of mutual
arrangement according to faith. As for the one in question,
she was never his legal spouse, since his first marriage — in
1834, in Kirtland, Ohio — had never been formally dissolved.
"Polygamy!" shouted the press, and indignantly described
this reasoning as "adultery sanctified."

"Passion's Perils," ran one lead for the most talked-about
scandal of the year, the trial of Henry Ward Beecher, pastor
of Brooklyn's Plymouth Church, on charges of adultery
brought by one of his parishioners. The conservative Quaker
City was inclined to judge the accused preacher harshly; the
majority of the dailies assumed his guilt in advance.

Then, as now, from passion to politics was the distance of a
column in the newspapers. During the summer of 1874,
President Grant had left the matter of a possible third term
up in the air, despite continued clamor for a statement of
intent. The press divided on party lines on the prospect of
his running again, and although national elections were two
years away, editorials bitterly debated the issue.

There was also a division of views on the reports that had
circulated for some time of the Pope's intention to send a
cardinal's hat to an American prelate. Those opposed maintained that a cardinal was a prince and therefore not suitable
for a democracy. Others, including the *Ledger,* looked favor-
ably on the prospect, seeing it as a recognition of the nation's
importance.

Elsewhere abroad, Bismarck's Machiavellian machinations
in Europe came in for considerable attention, as did the quarrel between China and Japan over Formosa. A natural

phenomenon was playing a role in that dispute. Coggia's comet, named for its discoverer, had for some weeks been visible in the Eastern sky. The wise men of Japan interpreted its appearance as a presage of victory in the war, while in China it produced the opposite effect, since astrologers of that land thought such phenomena to be harbingers of evil and feared that the comet's presence would make their statesmen accede to almost any terms demanded by the Japanese.

Although these events found their way to the front pages, the Ross case remained in the news. A variety of curious results were developing in its wake. Child nurses were suddenly in active demand. Photography received an unexpected impulse when it became apparent that having a good photo could be important. The buying of homes in suburban areas sharply slumped.

Overriding all such considerations was the extraordinary impasse to which things had come. Two men with a horse and wagon had appeared almost every day for a week at one place with the suddenness of apparitions, and then had vanished from sight as if dissolved by magic. Their appearance and movements had been such as to attract the close scrutiny of casual passersby, yet nobody had ever noticed them except in the close vicinity of the spot. Not one person had been found who had ever observed them on their way to the Ross house or after leaving it. Nor had they been seen after dropping off Walter on the day of the abduction.

Where had the horse and wagon been kept during the days of reconnoitering to and from Washington Lane? Had the search of liveries, blacksmith shops, and other likely places not been thorough enough? Had someone lied? A month's diligent activity provided no answers.

But certain factors were becoming clear. In cases of theft a usual practice was for a middleman to arrange a compromise whereby the victims accepted a loss but had the bulk of their

property restored for a sum of money. In the Ross case the
abductors dared not make use of the usual machinery, dared
not send an agent to negotiate. And if they had, there would
have been no intermediary willing to undertake the role. The
anger and purpose of the authorities, that there should be no
compounding of the crime to let the villains escape with their
"blood money" and without punishment, were barriers to
such a proceeding.

The villains knew as well as anyone that they faced other
perils besides the usual dangers of a negotiation and the risks
of a common trial. By fair means or foul, the populace was
calling for their death. The abductors were therefore obliged
to be wary in the highest degree, double-guarded against those
trivial exposures which frequently come to light by accident
and which put the police on the trail of malefactors. Again
and again they proposed a plan to obtain the ransom money,
but each time the fear of detection deterred them and left matters where they were — at a standstill. Excessive public concern was containing the criminals. It was also preventing
them from effecting the return of little Charley Ross.

25

AT THIS TIME Ross received startling information which gave
the case an entirely new aspect, moving its focus to New York.
Of this turn of events the press knew nothing and was to learn
nothing until much later.

In their August 4 letter the kidnappers had said they were
leaving Philadelphia that night. The authorities suspected
that they had decamped to New York. This view resulted
from events of early August, when the major activity in the
case shifted to that city and brought with it a new cast of
characters for a melodramatic second act.

On August 2, Philadelphia Police Chief Jones had received a telegram: SEND DETECTIVE HERE WITH ORIGINAL LETTERS OF KIDNAPPERS OF ROSS CHILD; THINK I HAVE INFORMATION. The dispatch bore the name of George Washington Walling, newly appointed superintendent of New York Police. The next day Captain Heins and Joseph Ross went to New York. They took with them all the anonymous letters received so far and delivered them to the superintendent, an imposing-looking man whose white beard circled a full, roundish face, compensating for a head which was bald save for a thin outer fringe of hair. In his brass-buttoned uniform replete with the insignia of office, he gave the appearance of a stiffly formal Civil War general, an impression quickly dispelled by his warm and genial manner.

"We hope that you at least have some trustworthy information," Captain Heins said as he turned over the letters.

"I think I have," Walling replied. "Through Captain Henry Hedden of the Thirteenth Police District I have heard of a man who professes to know who the abductors are. I will send for Captain Hedden."

After giving orders to bring in the officer, Walling brought Joseph Ross and Captain Heins up to date on the New York phase of the case. He had first heard of the abduction from newspaper accounts and from Frank Lewis, when that emissary came to the city with a supply of posters on July 7. Near the middle of the month Officer Doyle had told Captain Hedden that a man known as Old Gil Mosher suspected his brother Bill of having a hand in the abduction. Since the man had declined to give the reasons for his suspicions, Hedden placed little reliance on him. Old Gil had repeated his story to the then superintendent of police, George Matsell, who advised Hedden to follow up the lead and report back to him.

Meanwhile New York Mayor William T. Havemayer named

Matsell president of the police commissioners on July 23. On the same day he named Walling, for seventeen years a patrolman, detective, captain, and inspector, to the office of superintendent of police, in charge of the department's more than twenty-five hundred men. Thus Hedden now reported to Walling. What he had to say aroused the keen interest of the new executive head of the city's police force. Walling immediately sent for the informant.

Officer Doyle had found his man at home on Sheriff Street. He was a shipwright who worked on Long Island. For a time he had also been captain of a gentleman's yacht called the *Ida,* following the lead of his father, who had been both captain and owner of a coasting vessel. The elder Mosher had become prosperous and with his wife, a native of Westchester, had brought up a family of fifteen children, fourteen boys and one girl. Of these only three were still alive. Alfred, the youngest, was a tradesman who did not associate with the others. Clinton Gilbert, better known as Gil or Old Gil, was the senior member of the clan at fifty-seven. William Mosher was five years younger. It was at him that Gil pointed an accusing finger. Gil's wife Liz concurred in that accusation.

While Officer Doyle and Captain Hedden listened carefully to the story, they remembered that Gil's character was far from unblemished. In addition to the trade of shipwright, he had several times been involved in horse-stealing and served a term in state prison for that offense. He and Bill had also engaged in a series of burglaries. The Ross reward money appeared to be one of his motives in coming to the police. Revenge against his brother, with whom he had quarreled over a division of spoils, seemed to be the other.

"What are your reasons for suspecting that your brother William took part in the kidnapping of Charley Ross?" Walling began his questioning when Old Gil was brought into his office.

"Well, I was approached by Bill, who asked me if I would join him in carrying off some child who had rich parents. The plan was to steal one of Commodore Vanderbilt's grand-children," Gil replied.

"Which one of the children was to be taken?"

"The youngest one we could get."

"What would you do with it?"

"Hold it for a ransom."

"Where did he propose to conceal the child?"

"In a boat. And I was to negotiate the ransom."

"Well, what then?"

"I refused to have anything to do with the business."

"Why?"

"Because I thought there would be too much risk in trying to get money from the Vanderbilts. They were too rich, have too much power, and are not the kind of people to be fright-ened. There would be no trouble in stealing the child. The difficulty would be in negotiating for the ransom."

"So you gave up the plan?"

"Yes. I would not run the risk of being detected. I did not think it was a safe enterprise."

Further questions filled in the details of the plot which William Mosher had proposed to his brother only a few months before the Germantown abduction. The child was to be stolen while playing on the lawn at Throgs Neck on Long Island Sound, where the Vanderbilt family lived. A ransom of $50,000 was to be asked for returning the victim, who was to be secreted on a small vessel run out on the Sound. While one brother guarded the child, the other would negotiate the ransom, which they would later divide. Gil Mosher felt that the details of the Ross kidnapping were so similar that the same group was undoubtedly involved. He stated that his brother often went under the name of Johnson and for some years had been working with a man named Joseph Douglas, who also used the name Clark. He said he believed the two men lived in Baltimore.

Under Walling's orders, Hedden held a second meeting with Gil Mosher. Gil stated that he had last seen his brother Bill in the latter part of April on the landing at the foot of 93rd Street in New York. As youngsters they had gone to school together for a time, but then separated to follow different paths. Bill was handy at many trades but master of none. He was a voracious reader.

After a considerable length of time they had met again. Some ten years ago, his brother had begun scribbling away on a novel. Gil had taken up one of the pages. "It was a very dirty hand, much blurred, and very sprawling," he recalled. "I asked him why he turned the tail of his 'y' such a wide turn, wide enough to drive a horse and wagon through."

The elder brother also remembered the unusual way Bill folded his letters. He told Hedden that he could recognize both his brother's handwriting and his special way of folding letters. He was convinced Bill Mosher was the leader of the abductors, the man who had worked out the entire plan and written the letters.

When Hedden arrived on August 3 for the meeting with Joseph Ross, Captain Heins, and his superintendent, he repeated much of the story narrated by Gil and declared, "If my suspicions are correct, this William Mosher is the leader of the conspiracy. He arranged the plot and is the writer of the letters sent to Mr. Ross. From Gil's account I am familiar with Mosher's handwriting, and can tell if I see the letters whether he is the author of them."

At this, Captain Heins interjected, "Before we show you the letters, describe to us the peculiarities of Mosher's handwriting."

"He writes very rapidly, and is careless," said Hedden. "He seldom finishes a page without blotting it. He often

writes either above or below the lines. When he folds a letter
it is in a peculiar and awkward way."

At this point, Hedden was shown the anonymous letters.

"They are his without the shadow of a doubt," he said immediately. "Here is the handwriting, blots and all, just as I
told you. And you see for yourself, gentlemen, that the letters
are folded in a peculiar and awkward manner."

From Joseph Ross came an exclamation: "At last!"

26

IT WAS APPARENT that the thorny case had finally located its
first meaningful clue. The parties meeting in Walling's office
decided that Gil Mosher should try to locate his brother Bill,
alias Johnson, in Baltimore, along with his partner Joseph
Douglas, alias Clark. A letter to Bill at an old address was the
first step. In case there was no reply to this communication,
they would ask Gil to make the trip to Baltimore, reporting to
Officer Doyle, who would accompany him. They would also
ask him to secure specimens of his brother's handwriting.
While Hedden had described the eccentricities of Bill Mosher's pen in advance of seeing the anonymous letters, the
identification — which Gil shortly confirmed — was not considered conclusive so long as there was nothing with which to
compare the letters.

Walling and Hedden determined to try to find others who
knew Mosher and Douglas, both known criminals in New
York, in order to gather additional evidence. They also went
into the records to check the dossiers on the two men.

Joseph Ross and Captain Heins returned to Philadelphia
with the beginnings of a guarded hope in their hearts. Christian Ross was informed of the new developments and told he

would be contacted the moment there was further news. Captain Heins received a letter from New York two days later.

New York, August 5, 1874

Captain William R. Heins: — Dear Sir: We are doing everything possible to locate those parties, and with good prospect of success. I will write you again tomorrow, or will telegraph if anything important is developed.

Yours,

HENRY HEDDEN, Captain

Three days later, another letter arrived.

New York, August 8, 1874

Captain William R. Heins: — Dear Sir: We are busy, and hope to find something very soon. Please send me a few newspapers published in your city during two or three weeks past. I want those that contain small advertisements. Papers of the style of the New York *Sun* or *Evening News* are what I want.

Yours,

HENRY HEDDEN, Captain

From Gil Mosher and his wife and from their own files, New York detectives had derived valuable information. They learned that Douglas and Mosher manufactured an insecticide called Mothee, which, along with other articles, they peddled from door to door, traveling with a horse and wagon. Mothee provided a front for small-time stealing activities. The men had advertised it from time to time in the newspapers, and Hedden felt that a check of Philadelphia papers might turn up a clue. It did not.

It was further learned that William Mosher was born on Christmas Day of 1822 on New York's lower East Side. In 1848 he had married and opened an oyster saloon on Grant Street near Jackson. After two years his wife took to drink and he divorced her. Her sister, apparently also an alcoholic, committed suicide. Distressed by the failure of his marriage — the couple's child had died at sixteen months — Mosher gave up his oyster bar and turned to illegal pursuits, becoming a well-known river thief. His family largely disowned him, but when his mother died in 1860, Gil gave him the news. Subsequently the two worked together in crime. After their quarrel over the swag of one of their robberies they became estranged, and Bill Mosher took up with Joseph Douglas.

These two went from place to place in a small boat, traveling along the coasts of Long Island and out among the islands of the Sound, as well as along the shores of New Jersey and Connecticut, engaging in robberies of small boats. Gradually they turned to robbing commercial establishments and private dwellings along the shore. Both men knew every cove and inlet of the various rivers and coastlines. They would hide out with their loot in a secluded area, venturing forth to dispose of stolen goods only when their burglary had had time to cool off. On one occasion Bill Mosher was arrested and sent to Sing Sing for several years.

Although he and Douglas were later brought up before the police a good many times, authorities found it difficult to make their charges stick. In 1870 the thieves' luck ran out after they robbed a country store at Red Bank, New Jersey. As they were sailing back to a sheltered hut on Berrian Island with their plunder of silks, dry goods, and other articles, a fisherman sighted their boat and reported it to the police. Unaware that they had been observed, the river thieves moved in a leisurely manner. They hid their goods, and Douglas went to the mainland for supplies. Mosher was alone and sleeping in the isolated shanty when the police arrived. He was hauled off to the Monmouth County jail in Freehold to await trial. Among the arresting policemen were Officers Doyle, Silleck, and James Moran, of the New York

River Police. Silleck made a point of telling the New Jersey authorities they should be doubly careful, for Mosher, who gave them the name Thomas Henderson, would most likely try to break jail. Laughing heartily, local authorities said they were sure their jail was strong enough to hold him. In the morning their laughter had turned sour. The criminal had made his escape by cutting through the jail wall, knocking out one whole side of the structure. No charges were ever brought against Douglas. While Mosher was known to be in hiding because of the Red Bank affair, police felt that his partner's simultaneous disappearance pointed to his involvement in the Ross abduction.

Confirmation of Mosher's role was gained when Walling asked Detective Silleck to call on him at his office. Without explaining why he wanted him, Walling said he was after a man named Henderson, the Mosher alias in the Red Bank burglary. The name recalled no memory to the officer. The superintendent then relayed the descriptions of the abductor which had come from Philadelphia, including the fact that he wore goggles and had what Walter called a "monkey nose." At this Silleck at once exclaimed, "Why, I know him. That's Bill Mosher, the river thief."

Silleck explained that the middle cartilage of Mosher's nose was eaten away early in life by cancer and that the disease flattened out the nostrils, which turned up sharply at the end. Mosher was sensitive to the deformity and often raised a handkerchief to his face to hide it. He wore goggles because he wished to draw attention away from his unusually deep-set eyes. The criminal had one other distinguishing physical characteristic. A felon, or abscess, caused by a falling cask, had made the little finger of his left hand become atonic and wither away, leaving a pointed remnant shaped like a claw. To cover it Mosher sometimes wore a glove on the left hand, at other times a stall, or sheath, to hide the skeletal structure.

Silleck and Officers Doyle, Lawler, and Moran were among
those now assigned to the case by Walling. All were personally familiar with Mosher and Douglas, knew their haunts
and their mode of operation. Silleck went to Philadelphia to
give all possible aid to Captain Heins and the dozen Philadelphia detectives working full-time on the case. He called
on Christian Ross to say Superintendent Walling wanted him
to come to New York with Walter.

Ross and the boy checked into a New York hotel on August
10. Walling visited them and told Ross of the latest developments. Gil Mosher had not received an answer to the letter he
had written his brother in Baltimore, where he suspected him
of residing under an alias. With him, Gil assumed, were the
unmarried Douglas and Mosher's second wife Martha, whom
he had married some dozen years earlier when she was only
fifteen and he had just turned forty. The Moshers had had
six children, two of whom died. Surviving were Willie, nine;
Charles, a blue-eyed, round-faced child with straight light
hair whom they called Lovie, going on four; Georgie, eighteen
months old; and a baby born sometime in July of the current
year.

While the abductors and Mosher's wife were being hunted
down, Old Gil Mosher had spoken of another person he
thought might be implicated in the abduction. Martha Mosher
had a brother named William H. Westervelt, who lived in
New York. Westervelt had been a police officer in the city
from late 1872 until January 1874, when he had been dismissed from the force for failing to report a lottery office,
having listed it as 145 instead of 147 Hester Street. He insisted that the reason for his discharge was not the wrong
number, which he said was an error, but rather his refusal to
subscribe ten dollars to a political organization. Westervelt
was in the process of suing the commissioners of the New York
Police Department for dropping him.

On August 11, Captain Hedden asked Westervelt to come to his office, and arranged for Ross and Walter to observe him without his knowing it. Westervelt was a medium-sized man in his middle thirties, with a roughly trimmed mustache. As he entered the room, Walter immediately shook his head and said, "No, sir, never," when asked if he had seen the man before.

"I did not think he was one of the persons who took the child, but I wanted to be certain he was not," Hedden said. "Yet I believe he is connected with the matter, and is in communication with the abductors."

Hedden said he would remain in touch with Westervelt while placing his basic reliance on Gil Mosher, who had requested that his efforts be kept secret. Ross returned to Philadelphia, his spirits buoyed by the knowledge that the police were using varied means to trace the abductors. On the morning of August 12 Officer Doyle and Gil Mosher arrived in Philadelphia with a letter from Superintendent Walling.

Captain Heins — Dear Sir: — The bearer, Officer Doyle, and another man go to your city, and intend going on to Baltimore, where the family of Johnson lived a few weeks ago. Johnson, we think, is the prime mover in the Ross abduction. Mr. Doyle and the man who is with him both know Johnson and his family well. This Johnson has a wife and four children. Some time since he escaped from jail at Freehold, New Jersey, while awaiting trial for burglary. His correct name is Mosher. It may be that we are on the wrong scent, but I think not. If they can locate Johnson's family, we can certainly find his whereabouts.

Yours respectfully,
GEORGE W. WALLING, Superintendent

The next day, Walling again wrote Heins.

Captain Heins: — Dear Sir: — If we are right in our suspicions, and the parties that Detective Doyle and his companion are searching for in Baltimore are guilty of abducting the Ross child, in all probability the child is kept on board of a small boat, and may be in your vicinity.

Yours in haste,
GEORGE W. WALLING, Superintendent

As a result of Walling's letter a search was made in Philadelphia of all boats, vessels, and barges on the Delaware and Schuylkill rivers. It did not provide any clues. In Baltimore, Officer Doyle and Old Gil Mosher failed to locate Bill Mosher and Douglas, save for a vague clue that they had gone to Philadelphia. After several days of tracing this report, Doyle and Old Gil returned to New York. Despite the apparently powerful leads which had been provided, the authorities found themselves at a stalemate.

27

DISSATISFACTION with the results of police activity led a group of prominent Philadelphians, many of whom had earlier contributed the money for the mayor's reward proclamation, to raise new subscriptions totaling $20,000. With this money they retained the services of Allan Pinkerton and his National Detective Agency. The entire resources of the noted agency were thrown into the nationwide search for the lost boy of Germantown and his abductors.

Philadelphia's Pinkerton bureau was headed by Superintendent Benjamin Franklin. One of his first tasks was the preparation of a vast quantity of bills and posters offering various rewards for specific items of information. For facts concerning the owner of the horse and buggy used by the abductors, a thousand dollars was offered. Similarly, a thousand would go to anyone giving information about the house the kidnappers stayed in prior to the abduction. The agency also prepared a four-page circular which carried the photograph of Charley Ross at its head, followed by an account of the abduction, Mayor Stokley's reward proclamation, and a thorough description of both the stolen boy and his abductors. The older of the two abductors was said to have a "pug nose, or a nose in some way deformed." Also given prominence in the circular was a special section called "Questions for Identification," which showed how little Charley — the circular used the alternate spelling, Charlie — could be identified if found:

Tests may be made upon his memory. He can recite, "Jesus loves me, this I know, for the Bible tells me so." Knows "O" and "S" of the alphabet, but no other letters. Will state his name to be Charlie Ross, but when asked if he has any other name he will say, "Charlie Brewster Ross."

To the following questions he should answer, to-wit: —

Question — Who is your uncle on Washington Lane?
Answer — Uncle Joe.
Question — What is your cousin's name?
Answer — Cousin Joe or Cousin George or Cousin Frank.
Question — Who lives next door to papa?
Answer — Marcellus McDowell or Jennie McDowell.
Question — What horse does mama drive?
Answer — Polly.

In like manner, he can give the names of his brothers, Stoughton, Harry and Walter, and sisters, Sophia and Marry (for Marian) and of Doctor Dunton, the family physician; also the name of his Sunday-school teacher, Miss Mary Cope.

More than seven million copies of the circular were distributed, specimens going to the sheriff of every county in the United States, to every railroad office and steamship line, and to many foreign countries. It was thought necessary to provide these checks on the boy's identity because of the multiplicity of false clues which were increasingly occupying and misleading both police and members of the Ross family, who were constantly called upon to check boys brought forth by citizens of almost every state. Although the authorities were certain they were on the right track in pursuing Douglas and Mosher, they continued to explore each case.

In addition to the private Pinkerton agency, the head of the United States Secret Service volunteered assistance in the search. Bureau chiefs in every city were given photos and circulars and instructions to make private inquiries for little Charley Ross in every place where their usual business called them. Leads were turned over to appropriate police authorities.

At about the same time that the Secret Service and Pinkerton joined the search, another illustrious name, that of P. T. Barnum, the world's greatest showman, made its appearance in the Ross case. Barnum's Great Roman Hippodrome was scheduled to appear in Philadelphia for a two-week run. Giant-sized advertisements announced "the most magnificent pageant ever known, The Grand Congress of Nations, representing with historic truthfulness the Sovereigns of all Nations, and the manners and customs of nine centuries, its magnitude and grandeur without a parallel in the history of the world."

When Phineas Taylor Barnum arrived in Philadelphia to personally supervise advance promotion activities, he found the city had only one topic of conversation, the abduction from the streets of Germantown of little Charley Ross. He became deeply interested in the case and began forming in his mind a plan which was to bear fruit more than two years later. At the moment he was gifted with free publicity of an unexpected nature.

From Bennington, Vermont, a citizen sent a dispatch which said that a woman named Mrs. Fred Hamilton had come to town with a child of the same age as the stolen boy, the same color eyes and hair as Charley. The hair had only recently been cut. Questioned about the boy, the woman gave evasive answers, while the boy, speaking plainly, said he had once had a nice home.

Hours later, a second dispatch reached Christian Ross. Signed by the local police chief, it reported that the child had said, "My name is Charley Ross, but this mama says I must not tell anyone." The boy had also declared he now had two names, Charley Ross and Charles Augustus Hamilton. The police chief asked Philadelphia for an accurate description of the lost boy. This was sent. As a double check, Joseph Lewis boarded a train for Bennington.

When newspapers reported the story, the circumstances of a singular coincidence was unraveled. The boy's annoyed father sent a telegram from Boston, where he was head property man for Barnum's Hippodrome, currently in that city prior to appearing in Philadelphia. His wife, he declared, was visiting her grandmother in Bennington. They had adopted their little boy on March 1 and had proper adoption papers which would show that the child's original name was Charley Gross, the real father a tinsmith who worked on Fourth Avenue in New York. Arriving in Bennington, Joseph Lewis confirmed that the boy was not the sought-after Charley. Mrs. Hamilton was released from custody.

On the same day a flurry of excitement swept through Frankford, Pennsylvania, when a little curly-haired boy turned up in the streets and said his name was Charley Loss. Eager passersby were convinced the child was lisping and sent for the police. They learned that the boy had given his real name.

A special dispatch reached the Chicago *Tribune* from Odell,

Illinois, stating that a male child had been found dressed in girl's clothing. A man named Lewis Dungan had been arrested. A prominent Philadelphia citizen received a telegram from his old friend Dungan asking him to come to his aid. The Philadelphian promptly went to the police and explained that Dungan was traveling with his housekeeper and caring for several children of vacationing friends. The boy in question had been wearing a frock popular with boys of his age at the time. Dungan was released, but later instituted suit for false arrest.

A Denver citizen wrote Mayor Stokley that he thought he had found little Charley Ross in the company of two suspicious-looking men. "I fell in with the parties at Cheyenne, on their way from the East," the writer declared. "The peculiar actions of the two at once excited my suspicions. They put up at a German boarding house and I was so impressed by the evidence that I have been able to satisfy myself only by taking lodgings at the same place."

When Mayor Stokley sent a circular which listed the questions for identification, the man investigated and found that the boy failed the test completely. While he resembled the description of Charley, he was clearly much younger and spoke German as well as English.

From Barboursville, West Virginia, came the story of a little boy who had recently turned up under mysterious circumstances in the family of a man named Peyton. Police found that the boy had escaped from a neighboring poorhouse. Peyton had taken him in and was giving him a good home.

Canadian newspapers reported the discovery of Charley Ross in Canada. A woman recently arrived in the small town of St. Catherines, Ontario, had brought with her a boy she said she had found in the streets. When she refused to provide details, natives of the town informed police. Detectives went to make the arrest but learned the woman had decamped, leaving the child behind. A photograph was sent to the Pinkerton Detective Agency. While the photo resembled little Charley in many respects, it was another case of mistaken identity.

In New Haven, Connecticut, a man taking his evening meal in a public dining room looked up in alarm when a woman entered with a young boy who seemed to him an exact duplicate of the photos of little Charley Ross. Unable to finish his meal, the diner hired a restaurant employee to follow the suspected pair, but their trail was subsequently lost. The man nevertheless remained firm in his conviction, which he conveyed to the Philadelphia authorities, that Charley Ross had passed through New Haven. Detectives were sent to look for any clues that might be followed up.

Reports of little Charley's being found could often be discarded quickly as the facts came to light. In other cases excitement mounted as new details seemed to corroborate the story. In one such instance, the community of Goshen in Orange County, New York, was thrown into an uproar by the supposed presence of the abducted child.

Sheriff James W. Hoyt received the news, repeated from many sources, that a child answering the description of little Charley had been mysteriously secluded for several days past at the country mansion of David Henry Haight, a millionaire resident of the area. Because Haight was highly respected locally, the sheriff hesitated before making the trip to his estate, but eventually made up his mind there was no alternative. Haight, in keeping with his custom of spending six months of the year in New York, was absent. His wife received the sheriff and explained to him the presence of the boy.

Father Kenney, an Episcopal priest stationed in Cuba, had rescued the child from a woman who he suspected had stolen him. He had seen her cruelly whipping the boy with a strap that had a buckle on the end, causing severe cuts on the head and heavy bleeding. The priest had obtained the United States consul's permission to take the child out of the country. As a family friend, he knew of the Haights' generosity. This led him to place the boy in their home temporarily while he attended to other matters. After hearing this explanation, Sheriff Hoyt spoke briefly to the boy and went away satisfied that the case was closed.

Back at his office, villagers gathered to tell him they had earlier questioned the boy, who said he had been stolen from Philadelphia in a wagon and that his name was Charley. They added that the child's hair had recently been cut. A troubled Sheriff Hoyt took a Pinkerton circular with little Charley's photo and returned to the country estate, where Mrs. Haight, deeply offended that her word was not credited, ordered him away. Determinedly, she kept the child out of view. Only by using all his persuasive powers was he able to convince the excited woman that he had a duty to perform. Seeing the boy again, Hoyt found the resemblance to the photo striking, the familiar cowlick on the left side of the forehead, the very light eyebrows, the brown eyes, as well as other features.

In Philadelphia, a telegram arrived from the sheriff: THERE IS A CHILD HERE WHICH I BELIEVE IS THE LOST CHARLEY ROSS. Joseph Ross hurriedly made the trip to Goshen, where the anxious Mrs. Haight had retained counsel to help her keep the boy until Father Kenney's return. When Ross arrived, he saw that the boy was not little Charley. To the relieved Mrs. Haight he presented a certificate that would spare her further annoyance.

Several months later, when Father Kenney took back the boy and placed him in the School of the Holy Saviour in Cooperstown, New York, reports again started filtering into Philadelphia that Charley Ross had been found. Investigation

proved it to be the same child. And still later, when the same
boy made a trip to New Jersey, a third series of reports told
Christian Ross of the discovery of his lost boy.

The continuing search showed that a great many children
around the country were in the hands of people who did not
appear to be their lawful custodians. A remarkable propor-
tion of them seemed more or less closely to resemble the missing boy; others resembled him only in the most superficial
aspects, and yet anxious citizens brought them forth hopefully
as the lost child. Each day the case seemed to grow in com-
plexity.

From Reading, Pennsylvania, came the ever-recurring story
of little Charley's presence among a band of gypsies, in this
case some twenty people with four wagons and eight horses
passing up the town's Penn Street. In the rear wagon with
his supposed parents was a pretty young child with sunny
curls and a round face who greatly resembled the description
of the lost boy. While hundreds of people looked inquiringly
at the little fellow, who was merry and cheerful as he swung a
toy whip at his wagon's horses, police intercepted the band.
Officials soon determined the boy was much older than the reports had indicated.

Before the band moved on, their chief, who claimed to be a
real Spanish gypsy, gave the townspeople some insights into
his race. "Stealing of children by gypsies in this country is
not practiced," he said. "In the days of 1700 in Europe one
of the customs of our forefathers was the observed right of
child-stealing to replace one that had been taken away by
death. . . . Today you have telegraph and printing presses
here and it would be certain death for us to run away with a
child if we even desired to. The gypsy customs of the Old
World are not in vogue in this."

Commenting on the reappearance of little Charley among
the gypsies, the *Public Ledger* noted that it would puzzle

nine out of ten of those who reported these incidents to produce a well-authenticated example of the presence of veritable
gypsies. Groups of pea pickers and berry pickers did move
about the country, but were not true gypsies. Nor were the
little knots of vagrants who were ignorantly designated by
many as gypsies, or those groups who found it "a convenient
means of advertising their vocation as fortune-tellers to have
it believed that they were of the Bohemian order."

Savoring even more strongly of romance than the various
tales involving gypsies was a story which now came out of
Pittsburgh, chronicled in detail by that city's *Gazette*. Several days earlier, a tall spare man in his early thirties, his face
reddened by the sun, his scanty crop of yellowish hair covered
by a leghorn hat, had entered the counting room of the paper
and asked to look over its files. When business manager N. P.
Reed entered the room, he recognized the man as H. C. Carter, a journalist. Carter had once told him he left the New
York *Herald* because of a disagreement about the best way
to find little Charley Ross. Carter now took Reed aside and
asked him if he knew a shrewd detective, a man with nerves
of steel, to assist in a delicate and important undertaking.
Reed hesitated but was soon convinced that Carter, a good
talker with a ready knowledge of the ins and outs of journalistic life and jargon, had an actual lead on the famous case.

Reed sent for Peter Dressler, a detective employed in the
district attorney's office. Moments later Dressler was seen
arriving through one of the narrow doors of the newspaper
office. An air of secrecy prevailed as the trio retreated to a
small apartment in the rear of the counting room. Here Carter revealed that with the keen scent of a bloodhound he had
been on the trail of Charley Ross's abductors since the afternoon of July 3. He knew for a fact that the boy had been
kept in Germantown for five days after his abduction, after
which he was taken on a route that passed through Allentown

and Mauch Chunk before swerving west into the Monongahela valley, where the abductors had gone down the Monongahela River in a skiff and avoided all large cities. Carter had been right on their heels, he declared. He followed them overland as they moved through Ohio, then on to Chicago, and finally across the Mississippi at Burlington, Iowa. Five miles outside of Burlington, Carter tracked his prey to a secluded retreat. Seeing that they apparently planned to remain there for some time, he went to Philadelphia to alert Christian Ross to his boy's whereabouts, but Ross told him to go away and mind his own business.

Returning to Burlington, Carter visited the house and saw Charley in the hands of a man and two women. His face, neck, and arms had been stained an olive color from a bottle on the mantel which bore the label of Schenck's drugstore in Philadelphia. Carter spoke to the boy and to the man, who appeared sullen and said that he was tired of being buffed around and wanted his ransom money. This he would soon obtain when he went to New York to effect the exchange of the child for the ransom. On the same day he planned to sail for Europe.

Having related this stirring adventure story, Carter told his two gaping listeners in the *Gazette* office that the matter urgently called for action. He knew the house to which the child had already been taken on 36th Street in New York, and on the very next day the kidnappers intended to take a steamer to go abroad. Their plan was to give the boy to a third party, a decoy, to whom they would also give a receipt acknowledging that he had paid them $20,000. The exchange was to take place on the dock at a time known to Carter. This decoy would then take both the boy and the receipt to Philadelphia, where he would get the actual $20,000 from the reward committee. The money would be shared by several detectives, among them Heins, Wood, and Taggart, as well as by

Christian Ross and his brother, all of whom were in on the deal.

Dressler was completely overcome by the apparent cunning of the plot. Carter showed him a memorandum book swollen with documents, including a letter purportedly from Joseph Ross saying Carter should "keep his trap shut" and he'd do all right. He further stated that he needed a Pittsburgh detective to go in with him since he was certain that a New York or Philadelphia officer would sell out.

After two hours of this fascinating exposition Dressler paid his fare, along with Carter's, and the two men boarded an express train for New York. When they arrived they went directly to the residence on 36th Street where the child was presumably concealed. Hurrying up the steps they rapped loudly on the door of the quiet, lonely-looking house. After a moment they heard footsteps. The door was thrown open and a neatly dressed lady just past middle age asked what they wanted. On hearing they were looking for little Charley Ross, she was able to convince Dressler that the boy was not now and never had been in the house. Chagrined, Carter admitted that he must have been mistaken.

The next day Detective Dressler followed his companion to the landing where the exchange of little Charley for the ransom money was ostensibly to take place. Dressler's faith in Carter was now oozing out with each footfall. At the dock he saw neither the man who was to effect the exchange nor the little boy. Dressler angrily accused Carter of being a fraud and swore he would have him locked up if he ever reappeared in Pittsburgh.

No motive could be ascribed to Carter other than an apparent propensity for self-delusion and invention. As he returned to Pittsburgh on the train Dressler wondered if the *Gazette* had printed any of the material which had taken in business manager Reed and himself. To his dismay he found on arrival that his adventure had been thoroughly covered. Before outlining the exotic "facts" related by Carter, the paper made a sweeping statement:

This morning we present a partial statement of facts from one who is familiar with the kidnapping from the very hour of its occurrence until now, and it may be considered that the end is very near at hand, and that in all likelihood before the setting of today's sun the child will no longer be in the hands of those who stole it from its home.

Superintendent Walling heard the story in New York and called it "wholly unreliable." It was impossible, he said, for the boy to have been brought undetected to the city within the past week, since police officers had been stationed at all railroad depots and ferries.

28

THE SITUATION in New York, like that in Philadelphia, had regressed. Officers were secretly detailed in railroad depots, at ferries, wherever there was the hope of getting a clue to the abductors. Following reported leads, detectives searched suspicious houses within the city and traveled out to the countryside to make investigations. On numerous occasions men were sent to other states to track down stories. Inquiries were made in the Thirteenth Ward, where William Mosher used to live, and in the Eleventh, once the home of Joseph Douglas, but residents knew nothing of them.

The entrance onto the scene of Gil Mosher had been viewed as a very hopeful sign. His first interviews appeared to be fruitful. At a later meeting he recalled the theme of his brother's novel — the abduction of a little boy from his home! The authorities were already convinced that Bill Mosher was one of Charley Ross's kidnappers. When they learned that he had written a fictional account of an abduction, all doubts as to his guilt were removed from their minds.

The problem was to run down Mosher and his partner Douglas. Old Gil had been unable to find a trace of them in Baltimore. A follow-up investigation in Philadelphia led nowhere.

Superintendent Walling therefore decided to try another approach. Up to now William Westervelt had been seen only by Captain Hedden and Officer Doyle, both of whom felt that while he was not one of the actual kidnappers he was connected with the case. They had ascertained that in the past he had seen Bill Mosher and Douglas with some frequency. Although Westervelt was a discharged police officer, and to that extent of dubious reliability, Walling determined to deal with him.

On August 18 he asked Captain Hedden to bring Westervelt to his office at 300 Mulberry Street, New York City Police headquarters. His purpose in calling him in, he stated immediately, was to ask for his aid in locating William Mosher and Joseph Douglas, whom he suspected of being the abductors of Charley Ross.

Westervelt said he didn't believe them to be guilty. Mosher, he declared, was "bad enough," but not that bad. His brother Gil and Gil's wife Liz were probably continuing their campaign of revenge against Bill, hoping by one means or another to have him arrested again on the Red Bank affair.

When Walling told him that Gil and Bill Mosher had earlier spoken of a similar job and that there were other reasons for suspecting them, Westervelt listened intently. With his aid, Walling said, he believed he could restore the stolen boy. Was not Westervelt a father? Would he refuse to relieve the sufferings of the sorrowing parents in Philadelphia?

He reminded Westervelt of the reward posted in the case, a reward in which he was now inviting him to share. Westervelt asked whether officers were already watching for Mosher and Douglas. On being told they were, he expressed the view that with their involvement the reward shares would be too small. In that event, declared Walling, it might be arranged that the entire $20,000 would go to the informer if he were able to provide information leading to the apprehension of the criminals and the restoration of the child. When Westervelt continued to hesitate, the superintendent told him to think it over; he set a time for them to meet again the following day at Walling's home, 311 19th Street, just off Second Avenue.

The superintendent felt that the atmosphere of a private dwelling would be more conducive to the sort of rapport he wished to strike up with his man. To put him at his ease at their second meeting, he inquired about his family circumstances. Westervelt told him he had been married a little over ten years, after a wandering early life spent in San Francisco, New Orleans, New York, and New Jersey, where he was born. His parents had raised a family of twelve brothers and sisters of whom six were still alive. He had worked at various trades, starting off as a boilermaker, and had served in the army. His household consisted of his wife and two young children. They lived in two rooms on the top floor of a tenement at 298 Henry Street, renting their quarters for seven dollars a month.

At the moment things were very difficult. Often there was nothing to eat in the house. Westervelt was not regularly employed, but at times he got a day's work at the West Washington Market and occasionally he was called in as a substitute conductor on the Eighth Avenue line of horsecars. To help out, Mrs. Westervelt, an excellent seamstress, made dresses and other garments and sold them to friends or at neighborhood auctions. Westervelt's great hope was to be taken on full-time on the cars. The superintendent went to his desk and promptly scratched out a note to the head of the company, saying that he would appreciate any consideration given the bearer in the matter of permanent employment.

There was one other matter, Westervelt said as he accepted the note. He had been unjustly discharged from the police force of the city. He would be much more inclined to work on the Ross case if he were reinstated, and with official status he could be more effective. Would the superintendent help him by speaking to the commissioners? Walling said he would do all he could and report back as soon as he had any news. Meanwhile, could Westervelt give him any indication of the present whereabouts of Douglas and Mosher? He could not, declared Westervelt, for their relationship was such that he never knew their business or got in touch, but waited for them to contact him. He would try to find out what he could about them and he would assist Walling if one other condition was met: his role in the case must remain anonymous. Walling shook on this and handed Westervelt a five-dollar bill to tide him over his financial straits.

Left alone with his thoughts, the superintendent wondered whether he had made a wise move in taking into his confidence a man who had earlier been dismissed from his own force. Could he be trusted? Would the lure of the reward and the hope of reinstatement be sufficient inducement for him to betray his friends? Certainly it was worth trying, especially as all other avenues seemed to lead to dead ends.

No special watch was placed on Westervelt or his residence, but officers who patrolled the district were asked to be alert to his comings and goings and to events that occurred around his house.

More swiftly than anticipated, Walling received an apparent confirmation of his judgment. Before a week was out Westervelt came in with what looked like a valuable piece of information. He had it on good authority that Mosher and Douglas were heading toward Astoria. He remembered that they often took the Astoria Ferry at 92nd Street and the East River. If the superintendent had the ferry watched, he would probably catch them, since they were in the habit of crossing with rods and other gear on the pretense of going fishing. Westervelt described their mode of dress.

The superintendent sent for Officer James Moran, who had known Douglas nearly all his life, having grown up in the same neighborhood, and who, as one of the arresting officers in the Red Bank robbery also knew Mosher. Shortly before that episode, Mosher and Douglas had been appointed deputy marshals of Moran's district, the Thirteenth, where a few days before the municipal election they shot and wounded a man named Peter Wilmot. Moran had arrested them for felonious assault but through political influence they had managed to secure their release.

On receiving his assignment Moran hurried to the ferry, only to learn that men answering to the description of Mosher and Douglas had passed through a short time before. Moran continued his watch for a week. When his vigil produced no results, he was ordered to other duties. Two weeks later he was reassigned to the ferry, which he maintained under surveillance for almost a month. The net result was the same. He caught no sight of his men.

Discouraged, Walling nonetheless felt he had come close to apprehending the suspects and pursued his liaison with Westervelt. Another figure in the case decided to give up. The man who had advertised in the New York *Herald*, offering a reward of $20,000 for little Charley's recovery, repeated his offer for several weeks. Then, at his rope's end, he explained his plight:

To whom it may concern. I advertised on August 26 for the im-

mediate return to me of the boy Charley Ross, on certain conditions
and for a stated reason. This I did in good faith. I did not, nor do
not, propose to deal with second parties, police, detectives, or the
Ross family. I so stated, clearly. A full month has passed and I
am not in receipt of any direct information. As I now have good
grounds for doubting that any crime has been committed, and for
believing that this affair will be officially compounded, I hereby withdraw the reward. I will not be duped by any official combination.
As only detectives and confidence men have replied, I have no one
to thank.

The disillusioned author of the personal signed his name
for the last time as Arthur Purcell.

29

WITHIN HOURS of the time Officer Moran began his first watch
at the Astoria Ferry, the criminals mailed a letter in New
York addressed to Ross. It was received late in the evening
of August 21. Two and a half long weeks had passed since
the anonymous writers had last communicated, on August 4.
The authorities had ignored the letter, hoping by silence to
show the abductors that they would not deal with them on
their terms. This point was considered to have been won.

*New York, August 21. — Mr. Ros: we have heard nothing
from yu since we wrote yu about 3 weeks ago. we then told yu
if yu had anything to comunicate to us to do it through the
New York Herald personals. we have seen nothing but these
words (Christian K. Ross, 304 Market street). we know not
what to make of that. we have therefor come to the conclusion
that yu don't mean to redeem yu child on the conditions
which we proposed. yu must bear in mind we would never
agree to any other terms. the fact of yu saying the action*

must be symultainous is absolutely imposible. we would require at least a few ours to examine the mony and see if it were spurious or all marked up and then but a few ours more would be necessary to place yu child in yu possession for he is not so far off as yu may imagin. the folowing is the way we had intended to return him to yu. we was going to put a labill on his back and take him to a respectable house at night rouse them up. tell them to take this child as directed pay them for their trouble. this arrangement does not met with yu concent so there is no other alternitive left yu. now we demand yu anser yes or now as we are going to urope the 24 Sept and he has got to be disposed of one way or the other by that time. if you say redeem him it has got to be on our terms alone if yu do not answer we shall take it as granted that yu dont mean to pay yu money. we shall act accordingly. address (John New Herald *personals.) you are listing to old womans visions and dreams which wil never find yu child. we could have told yu it was useless to go to illinoise to look for charly but yu would not have believed us.*

As noted before, other people besides the abductors got in touch with Ross as the case became known. Many of them were well-meaning, ready to proffer information they hoped would be valuable. Others were extortionists and crackpots. Where there was an appearance of sincerity, Ross followed through by whatever means were requested. In answer to an anonymous letter, he had recently listed his name and address in a New York *Herald* personal. The abductors had taken note and were puzzled.

For their part, police continued to marvel at the boldness of the criminals, who had obviously left Philadelphia and a state where they were little known in order to come to New York, where many detectives on the force were acquainted with them.

The morning after the new letter was received, Captain Heins wrote New York police telling them of its contents. Two days later he received a reply.

New York, August 24, 1874

W. R. Heins, Captain Detectives. — Dear Sir — Yours of 22nd received. I am more confident than ever that the parties Clark and Mosher *alias* Johnson are the parties we want. I knew before receiving your letter that they were somewhere in this vicinity.

Some one has let them know that they are being looked after and that is the reason for their change of tone. They are frightened and would, I believe, make terms very moderate, provided they could be assured of safety. There is no danger of their going to Europe; they have no money, and Mosher's wife and children would keep him here. Of this you can assure Mr. Ross, providing I am right as to the parties, and I have no doubt of it. I think it would be well for Mr. Ross to keep in communication (if possible) with them.

You can assure Mr. Ross that I think there is no danger of their injuring the child, or of their taking him to Europe, always providing we are on the right track.

Yours in haste,

GEO. W. WALLING, Supt. of Police

Spurred on by the superintendent's suggestion, Philadelphia authorities placed another hard-line personal in the New York *Herald* on August 26, five days after receipt of the criminals' last letter: "John — did not answer because your proposition led my friends to doubt whether you ever had it. Write, giving better proof and name an attorney or other person through whom arrangements can be made."

A reply postmarked Rondout, New York, reached Philadelphia a day later. On the west bank of the Hudson, Rondout was some ninety miles north of New York City. For the police and for Ross it was maddening to observe that the kidnappers were apparently able to move about the countryside with impunity.

Albany, August 26. — Mr. Ros — your timely answer saved yu child. We had determined if yu did not care to save him we would not swerve one jot or tittle from the fate we had designed for him — not that we delight in blood but it was inevitable with our selves in order to carry out our plan of action yu ask for no more prof that we had him or that we have him — that is right — yu should have prof that we are the identical ones who kidnaped Charley — we thought that yu were well satisfied that we were the kidnapers — we wil first prove to yu we took Charley — ask Walter if one of the men did not hold him betwen his legs an partly on his knee with the cloth in front of him while Charley set behind us both entirely out of sight — ask him if he did not want to go up on main road to git fireworks an we told him we would first go to ant Susy's that she kep a shop where we could get them cheaper. ask him if we did not keep givin him pieces of candy as we rode along. ask him if we did not go from your house west to Morton street and then south instead of going towards the depot on Washington lane as it has been stated in the papers these remarks we think are suficient to prove to yu that we are the men who took him if yu have received any other letters headed other than Ros or Mr. Ros they are forgeries, we have sent you 8 or 10 letters in all, if you had accepted the proposition we made yu some four weeks ago yu would now without doubt have yu child safe in yu own house but yu rejected the offer and left us without the means to negotiate with yu. Mr. Ros if yu ever expect to recove yu child yu have got to in a measure rely on our faith. in dealing with us yu must be satisfied that yu child was taken for a ransom. we have set the price and asked the ransom of yu. do yu think if yu paid the ransom once that we would ever ask it the second time, no man would be foolish enough to pay ransom the second time for a thing he had paid for once and did not get. if we wanted more money from yu we would ask it

*now, instead of asking more we would rather throw off some.
but the public have interfered so much in this bisiness that we
are determined every dollar shall be paid or not one cent Yu
have asked that the action between us should be symultainous
Yu must know from the nature of this busines that is impossible — first we would have to give yu Charley when we receive the mony yu git yu child, We might git a bundle of
brown paper and a chain around our necks No sir Mr. Ros
We must have at least 4 or 5 hours to examine the money to
see if yu have delt faithfully with us what we mean is yu must
give the mony in good condition unscarified or not at all,
then yu have performed yu part in good faith When that is
done we have no further use for Charley he has answered the
whole end for which we got him and we as vile as we are
would be working against our own interests if we did not return him to yu as we promised we only wish it was posible
to effect the change symultaniously but as that cant be done
yu must accept the best we can offer yu, do yu open this
correspondence with the intention to pay yu money on our
terms and git yu child or is it the foolish advice of some of yu
friends again with the idea of entraping us. do you want to
daly along and keep your child month after month living in a
place where the strongest could not live over one year. we
would not let him unnecessarily sufer but this exteriordary
search has made it necessary to keep him where the light of
the sun has never shown upon him since the 2d day of July.
we have seen Charley about 4 days ago his whole cry is he
wants Walter to come see him and he is afraid he wil not go
to Atlantic City with his mother. don't think this is only an
appeal to your affection as a farther it is symply the words
that he used when we saw him last. Mr. Ros. One word more
— do you want to redeem Charley or not on our terms. if yu
do yu must make up you mind that the money must be paid in
good faith. don't deceive yu self that if the ransom is not paid*

that we will set yu child at liberty. we can never do that our whole plan would be frustrated at one blow and our work would come to naught. as yu deal with us so shal we deal with you in return. We saw yu personal in Herald *of 26. whatever answer yu have to make to this let it be in Albany* Argus *no put it in New York* herald *personals as we wil leave here to-day and drop this somewhere on* OUR WAY *to New York. we can see the New York* herald *any part of the United States.*

(Address as be for John.)

P. S. — yu acted wisely in refusing these letters until yu got yu child — if yu had published them, no doubt it would have been the means of sacrificing you child.

When Walter was asked the questions posed by the kidnappers — their manner of proving they were the actual abductors — his replies generally coincided with theirs. On setting out on the journey, he recalled, they drew up a dirty lapcover which nearly covered himself and Charley. He asked the men to take them to Main Street to get crackers, but one of them had said they would go to Aunt Susie's, where they could get a pocketful for five cents. The men gave them pieces of candy along the route and he still had a sizable cache in his pockets when he reached home. In the matter of the direction taken to leave Washington Lane, however, Walter stated very firmly that they did not turn west on Morton Street before reaching the railroad depot, as the kidnappers indicated, but instead the wagon had gone down Washington Lane past the depot without turning.

There was no doubt in the minds of Ross or the authorities that the anonymous writers had the boy in their possession. The police nevertheless took advantage of this discrepancy to lead the criminals on. In reply to the letter of August 26 they inserted a personal in the September 6 New York *Herald* which read: "John, He denies the directions you give. I re-

A woodcut of Austin Street's portrait of Charley Ross. The painting, based on a photograph of the boy at two and a half, was done with suggestions from the Ross family to show him as he was at four.

Frank Leslie's Illustrated Newspaper

The abduction scene was sketched by W. P. Snyder. The boys were

A facsimile of the first of twenty-three letters from the kidnappers.

Six-year-old Walter Ross was also abducted but was released the same day. This engraving of him was reproduced in Mr. Ross's book.

American vs. Italian Brigan

Christian K. Ross, father of Walter and Charley Ross, in an 1875 illustration.

ABDUCTION OF CHARLIE BREWSTER ROSS.

On July 1st, 1874, at about four o'clock, P. M., Charlie Brewster, and Walter, the latter about six years old, sons of Christian K. Ross, were taken from the side-walk in front of their father's residence, on Washington Lane, Germantown, Pa., by two men in a buggy. Walter was carried about five miles, and there left upon the street; but of Charlie no subsequent clue has been obtained; it is earnestly solicited that every one, who shall receive this circular, make diligent inquiry, and promptly furnish any information obtained, and if the child be found, cause the detention of the parties having him in custody.

This circular must not be posted up, and care must be exercised, that suspicious persons do not obtain access to it.

Members of the press are specially requested to refrain from publishing the interrogatories hereafter given, so that the parties having the child in custody may not obtain the means of training him regarding his answers thereto.

On the discovery of any child, who shall be suspected of being the lost one, a photograph should be immediately obtained, if possible, and forwarded; and photographs of the parents will be sent for identification by the child.

$20,000 REWARD has been offered for the recovery of the child, and conviction of the kidnappers; all claims to which, however, will be relinquished in favor of the parties giving the information which shall lead to this result.

The front page of a four-page circular prepared by the Pinkerton Detective Agency. The picture used was the only known photograph of Charley, showing him at age two and a half.

Mosher and Douglas were fatally shot while emerging from the cellar door of a Bay Ridge, Long Island, home they had been burglarizing.

Although witnesses spoke of the deformed nose of one of the kidnappers, this identification clue was ignored in a widely circulated reward proclamation. The artist who did this engraving of Bill Mosher obligingly built his nose up to handsome proportions.

American vs. Italian Brigandage

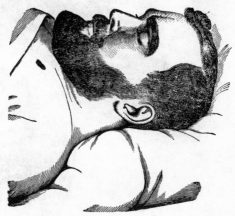

The same artist did this impression of Joseph Douglas as he looked in the Brooklyn Morgue.

American vs. Italian Brigandage

The Philadelphia Evening Star ran this sketch of Westervelt during his trial. The caption noted that "The face is strongly marked and is full of intelligence, and there is nothing in its profile indicative of a criminal nature." However, the jury convicted him of complicity in the abduction of Charley Ross.

In 1924, fifty years after the kidnapping, the Ladies' Home Journal *ran a cover story on little Charley which reproduced these engravings of his picture and home. "The house stands lonely and remote and melancholy," read the caption. "It is Philadelphia's house of sorrow."*

quire conclusive proof. Send clothing to any point that you please, and advise.''

The abductors had erroneously claimed to have sent only eight or ten letters to Ross. The seventeenth to bear the familiar handwriting arrived in reply to the personal. It was postmarked New York and dated September 6.

Mr. Ros we cannot see how yu can resist the proof that we have got him notwithstanding Walter's contradictory story, yu must admit he was taken by some one yu must admit he was taken for a ransom now if we have not got him who has got him — has any one else asked yu for a ransom we think not. mr. percell that benevlent man who offered to pay the ransom now says yu have never lost yu child — we know percell lies because we have positive that we have him and yu have positive proof that yu lost him. Mr. Ros in order to convince yu that we have him yu require some of his cloths sent yu. it was hinted some six weeks ago in one of the editorials to send yu some of Charly cloths in answer to that we said we would never do anything of the kind because we could give an irrestible proof without it — if we sent you any cloths we have got to expres them which we wil never do we don't know for certain wether his cloths have been saved up to the time we dont go near him often for we have nothing to do with guarding him though we have seen him three or four times since 2d of July we told you in one of our letters that Charley had never been in any way whatever disguised nor at that time he had not been but since then he has had his hair cut short and girls clothes put on him now wether they have kept his cloths or not we cannot say and we cannot send them if they have them the probability is they have destroyed them for every possible precautionary measure has been taken since we have seen what great efforts have been made to find his place of concealment we were surprised to think yu would

*make such efferts to find him when we told yu that to search
for him yu was only searching for his life and any approach
by a detective to his hiding place would be a certain sign for
his destruction yu either don't believe this or yu don't regard
the life of yu child where he is now confined wil be his tomb
unles yu bring him out with the ransom yu detectives can
never do it your friends who advise yu that we wil set him
free should you not ransom him wil be the worst advise yu
ever had. your friends yu say ask for more proof that we
ever had him they are as foolish as percell for he says you
never lost him. your detectives have never had the slightest
clue or trace of him since the our he was taken but in order
to convince these sceptical friends that we had him and have
him we will now give the detectives a small clue to work upon
but it will serve no other end only to convince these sceptical
friends or yours that we have him. on the night of 2d July
at 11 o'clock we passed through Trenton, N. J. Charley lay
in my arms asleep. after we had passed about 2 squares up
bridge st Charley's hat drop off and we did not notice it until
he woke up and asked for his hat we would not go back for it.
you can get this hat by advertising for it there if it is not
worn out. if it should be worn out you can find out who found
one that night or the next morning. now ask one of your
domestics or Mrs. Ros if charley did not have on the afternoon
of the first of July a narrow faded pink ribbin tied around
his head to keep the hear out of his eyes. if yu find this a fact
which we have no doubt yu wil and as it was never described
in the advertisement, we think no human being could mention
it but the party who took him. if this does not satsfy yu and
yu friends that we have him then yu must go unsatisfied.
this clue of the hat will end there when you find it and it wil
avail yu nothing more. let the detectives work it up much as
they please, the clue will end there we know or we would
not told of it. Mr. Ros we dont know wether yu ever mean*

*to ransom yu child yu certainly dont act much like it. but we
do know yu will never get him without it unless you are for-
tunate enough to ketch us knapping and take him by stratagem. there is not one chance in 10,000 of ever getting him
that way. yu must not delude yuself with the idea that if we
go to europe this month that we wil set yu child free or take
him with us and then will be the time to find him. that wil
never be Mr. Ros we have told yu befor if yu ever expect to
get yu child yu wil have to ransom him and to the full amount
we named. if you deal fair with us we wil deal fair with yu if
yu play any tricks with us we shall do likewise with yu. whatever you do with us we shall do likewise with yu. whatever
yu do with us yu must do it in good faith or not at all then
yu get yu child safe and sound. we shall not keep up this correspondence much longer, whatever yu mean to do must be
soon. we see the New York herald every day whatever yu
have to say we wil notice it. we are now in lansingburg above
Troy New York we dont know where we shall post this letter
yet we leave here to-day.*

As a result of this letter, the mayor of Trenton advertised
for the hat mentioned by the abductors and also sent men to
search the area where it had been reported lost. It was not
found. The faded pink ribbon had been accurately described.
Sarah Kerr, the nurse who dressed Charley on the day of the
abduction, had not thought to mention it earlier when she
gave a description of the boy's attire.

While this latest set of missives caused Ross severe anguish,
it seemed clear that the real kidnappers were known and that
there was a reasonable hope they would soon be apprehended.
As he went to conduct his Bible class at the First Methodist
Church of Germantown, he once more permitted himself to
wonder whether by the grace of God his little boy would soon
be returned home.

30

In New York, Superintendent Walling sent for Westervelt, who was brought to headquarters by a detective on the afternoon of September 11. His two prior meetings with Westervelt had been relatively fruitless, but on this occasion the interview elicited new facts.

Westervelt said he was concerned because he would be harming his own sister and her children if he betrayed her husband, Bill Mosher.

"I don't know that I can blame you so much for that," the understanding superintendent said. But after all, the main thing was to get information about the two men which might lead to the child. The arrest of the men was less the order of business than seeking out clues which might uncover little Charley. If Westervelt was reluctant to talk about Mosher, let him do what he could about Douglas. Westervelt reiterated that while he knew Mosher to be a man of very bad character, he doubted his having arranged the abduction.

"Still, if Mosher can be taken in some way accidentally, I have no objections," Westervelt said.

Entirely unsolicited by any question from Walling, he revealed that in June he had spent some time with Mosher and Douglas in Philadelphia. The circumstances involved his dismissal from the police force in early January and his subsequent efforts to earn a living. After his last monthly pay of one hundred dollars was gone, Westervelt had been forced to live on his occasional earnings and on his wife's dressmaking income. From time to time he sold stove blacking and other items door-to-door.

"In New York I was kind of ashamed to peddle and sell

around there, and sometimes when I would see a friend I would go a whole block out of my way to steer clear of him,'' he explained to Walling. When he heard that Bill Mosher was doing well in Philadelphia, he decided to take his family to the Quaker City with the hope of bettering his condition in a town where he was not known, where he could go to every house and sell.

In late January they made the move, taking a room on the second story of the frame house being rented by the Moshers at 235 Monroe Street, just off Third Street. In addition to the Mosher household, Joseph Douglas was also a tenant in the house. Mosher was using the alias of Henderson, while Douglas was going under the name of Clark.

''I did not hear anything while I was there between January and April of any crimes contemplated or in progress, or any theft, or anything wrong,'' Westervelt related. He admitted that he had seen some shawls and dress goods come to the house by express. He supposed these to have been stolen, but tactfully said nothing.

Disappointment had marked the Philadelphia venture. Mosher was not doing notably well. He had canvassed for pictures, window shades, Bibles and other books, earning a percentage on each sale. Not making enough, he opened a small stand on South and Second streets, selling pictures, frames, and other articles. When this business failed, the Moshers took the house on Monroe Street at fifteen dollars a month rent, furnished it and let out rooms. To supplement the thirty dollars monthly income this brought in, Mosher peddled a stove polish door-to-door along with the preparation he called Mothee. He also spent a great deal of time at Daley and Company, an auction store. Here he would buy second-hand furniture — a broken chair or a sofa with a missing leg — fix it up, and send it back to the auction store for resale.

Westervelt had picked up the traces of some of Mosher's

ventures, selling stove polish as well as Mothee, which cost two to three cents a pack to manufacture and sold for twenty-five cents a pack or two packs for thirty cents. On bad days, fifteen cents became the asking price. Income for a hard day's peddling could run as high as six dollars, but more often returns were as low as fifty cents. As a consequence, Westervelt explored other avenues. One day he worked on the docks during a strike of longshoremen. The job ended when the strike was settled. Several times he made trips to New York, hoping to find articles he might profitably resell in Philadelphia. He peddled a few gas burners which he had ordered sent down C.O.D., but again the income was small.

"After I came there, I done nothing of any account," he summed up for Walling. "I was seeking employment all the time I was there. I went to a great many places to look for work and answered many advertisements, but failed in every way."

In April he gave up and sent his family back to New York to the tenement at 298 Henry Street. A week later he followed them. His lot in New York was not much better. In May, while going through the Bowery, he ran into two old acquaintances, Thomas Richardson and Ike Morris, who had previously worked with Mosher in Philadelphia. The trio decided to form a loose partnership and manufacture their own moth preventative, following Mosher's formula. For a time they were fairly successful at selling Mothee in New York and the suburbs and also in Newark and Jersey City. When sales began to slacken in June, Westervelt determined to make another trip to Philadelphia, taking along two hundred packets of the moth powder.

On June 23, he took a cheap train which had what were known as emigrant cars on it. The fare on these cars was $2.00 whereas regular coaches cost $3.25. Westervelt boarded the train in New York at 7:00 P.M. and pulled into the West

Philadelphia depot at 10:30. He went straight to his sister's house. Mosher was there along with Douglas, who appeared unusually prosperous, dressed rather flashily in a new high hat, light pants, and a bright blue coat. They were all sitting out on the steps. Mosher played the harmonica. Westervelt would have liked to entertain the gathering with his banjo or his accordion, which he played each night when at home, but the instruments were back in New York.

"The morning following my arrival, I went down in the neighborhood of the Navy Yard," Westervelt continued. "I was not as successful as I expected to be. I took no dinner that day, but went into a grocery and got a lunch and sold part of the moth powder to the party there." At four or five in the afternoon he had returned to Monroe Street and again sat out in front with the family until bedtime.

Westervelt went out the next day selling moth powder in the direction of 15th Street below Chestnut and returned to Monroe Street in the late afternoon discouraged. He had sold only a few dollars' worth of his product after working hard all day. In an effort to provide distraction, Mosher beckoned to him and said, "Come and take a walk."

Together the two went a short distance and came to an old wooden building with large doors that served as a stable. Mosher proudly pointed out a dark bay horse which he said he had bought for sixty-five dollars. Westervelt was quite sure that Mosher earned his living less from selling Mothee than from petty thefts accomplished along the way. He suspected the horse was stolen, but gave no indication of his thoughts. He also noted an old-fashioned buggy in the stable. The next morning Westervelt took the train back to New York.

In answer to a question from Walling, Westervelt said he did not know Mosher's present whereabouts, but that he would report any new information he might receive. Again, he said that while he was unwilling to inform directly on

Mosher, he did not mind his being taken in some accidental way. Neither Mosher nor Douglas must ever know that he had had a part in apprehending them.

The new revelations elated Walling, who was increasingly convinced that Westervelt was innocent of complicity in the crime. How else would he dare give away so much in the way of valuable data? After eliciting further details, the superintendent wrote to Philadelphia.

New York, September 11, 1874

Captain W. R. Heins: — Dear Sir: — Since writing you this A.M., I have seen Westervelt; he says he knows nothing of the whereabouts of Mosher. He says Mosher lived in your city about four months ago at 235 Monroe Street, near 3rd Street, and that he had a stable between 3rd and 4th Streets, in some street not known, but the 3rd and 4th street from Monroe towards Washington Avenue. The stable was an old wooden building with very large doors, and near 3rd Street; that a wagon answering to the description you gave me was in said stable at that time, and may be there yet, but probably not; that they kept in said stable a dark bay horse; but he is confident the horse has been sold, but does not know to whom. I showed him the drawing of the wagon you gave to me, and he says he could not make a better one had he it before him, except that he thinks his would not be quite so much rounded at the top.

Yours in haste,

GEORGE W. WALLING, Superintendent

In a follow-up note, Walling cautioned Heins to give the new information neither to Ross nor to the committee of citizens. From them it might fall into the hands of a "private detective agency," an obvious reference to Pinkerton, with whom the metropolitan police often entered into professional rivalry. Heins abided by this admonition. He assigned two officers, Wood and Tryon, to "run this thing out." Neither they nor any of Heins's other men knew Mosher or Douglas. Among Pinkerton's corps there may well have been agents acquainted with the criminals and their habits. Due to Walling's professional jealousy, these men were denied the chance to follow up on the clues provided by Westervelt.

With the field to themselves, Wood and Tryon checked the former residence of Mosher and Douglas on Monroe Street. They then followed instructions which led them to a small street called Marriot's Lane, where an old stable had recently been torn down. Inquiries revealed that a man named Henderson had rented part of the stable several months earlier. After Henderson left, another tenant rented the stable and in turn sublet stall room to others. On July 1, the stable was under sublet to a man who did not know the former occupants, but only the present proprietor. When questioned by police he made no reference to Henderson or Clark, or to men answering their description. By this fluke a valuable lead was lost early in the case.

Further questioning of neighborhood residents showed that neither Mosher nor Douglas was seen at 235 Monroe Street after the abduction. Mrs. Mosher, alias Henderson, remained there for a time to give birth to her latest child. She had left with her family for New York on August 19. This information was relayed to Superintendent Walling.

31

WHEN HE RECEIVED the Philadelphia dispatch, a disturbed Walling sent for his informer, who was that day working on the horsecars. A detective escorted Westervelt to police headquarters. The superintendent's manner was less friendly than firm as he broke the news that Mrs. Mosher was in New York. Did Westervelt know she had removed to the city? Did he know where she was staying?

He did indeed. Westervelt calmly said his sister had recently come to the city and was living with her children in the Westervelt apartment at 298 Henry Street! Restraining his anger, Walling asked why he had not been told. The informer said that he thought he had made it clear he would assist in any way to apprehend Douglas, but that he could not find it in his heart to betray his sister's husband directly. If the police wanted to arrest Douglas, he thought he might furnish fresh information that could produce this result. Put squarely on the spot, the superintendent hesitated.

The Ross abduction was one of the most delicate and difficult cases Walling had ever handled. His plan for some time had been to find Mosher and Douglas, not with a view to immediate arrest, but with the thought of watching their movements and shadowing them to find a trail to the child. The kidnappers' letters had warned that if one of their band was taken, it would be the signal for the instant annihilation of little Charley. Walling sometimes feared that if his pursuit became too intense, one of them would murder the boy in order to wipe out all traces of the crime of abduction.

So cautious had he been that he had not had Westervelt trailed to his various appointments. From time to time, he sent men to see if he was working on the cars. While he had given orders to officers on the beat that Westervelt's residence was to be watched, these instructions were regarded as so routine that police were not even aware of Mrs. Mosher's arrival with her four children. Continuing his circumspect policy, Walling at this time did not give orders to have Mrs. Mosher placed under surveillance.

As a consequence of Westervelt's renewed offer to help apprehend Douglas, Walling asked Christian Ross to come to New York to discuss the matter. Did he, Walling asked, want Douglas arrested? If so, it could be arranged. Ross said he felt that the threats in the kidnappers' letters made it a grave risk to take Douglas without arresting Mosher at the same time.

"We will have them both," Walling replied confidently to this attitude of Ross's. "We know them and will pursue them until we find them."

His own view confirmed, Walling sent for his informer and said that while he wanted both Mosher and Douglas, he should in any event tell him where he could get Douglas. Westervelt readily offered the name of the restaurant-bar Mosher and Douglas liked best in the city, Smith and McNeal's, just opposite the Washington Market. Walling detailed Officer Moran to keep an eye on the place. Westervelt also told Walling that Mosher and Douglas were superstitious. In the past, they had frequented the establishment of the mother of Ike Morris, with whom Westervelt had entered into the Mothee business. Mrs. Morris, using the name Madame Morrow, operated as a fortuneteller at 134 East Houston Street. She had read Mosher's and Douglas's futures, assuring them that a bright and happy life awaited them and that they would die prosperous and rich. A detective was assigned to keep her premises under surveillance.

Westervelt in turn asked the superintendent whether he had made any progress in getting him reinstated to the police force. Walling said that he had made several inquiries, and would like Westervelt to meet one of the commissioners within the week. The appointment was set up and Westervelt left.

In addition to the "spotting" of Smith and McNeal's and Madame Morrow's, one of Walling's detectives reported that a noted receiver of goods operated out of a house on Baxter Street. Mosher was suspected of having disposed of his past plunder through this middleman. Walling ordered officers posted in a lager beer saloon which commanded a view of the premises.

At none of the sites under surveillance did policemen catch

any glimpse of Mosher or Douglas. After a time, Westervelt came to Walling and asked him if he had ordered Officers Doyle and Silleck to watch him. He had seen the two at Mott and Canal Streets, apparently keeping an eye on him. Westervelt declared in no uncertain terms that if he were being followed around the city like a thief, he wanted to withdraw from the entire arrangement. Although Walling had in effect instructed Doyle and Silleck to report to him any clues to the whereabouts of Mosher and Douglas, whom both knew by sight, he denied that the two had been detailed specifically to watch Westervelt. The informer added that he was under the impression that his house was being watched. This was completely useless, he said, since Mosher and Douglas would never come there. As a result of this conversation Walling withdrew instructions to have the Westervelt residence under observation.

After his interview with one of the police commissioners, Westervelt repeatedly asked Walling whether anything further had materialized. Walling had since learned that by law the present commissioners could not reverse an action of the previous incumbents, who had dismissed Westervelt. He tried to string Westervelt along, but eventually confessed that his efforts had come to naught and that he could not have him reinstated. The superintendent pondered whether the informer, with this incentive withdrawn, would continue to supply his valuable leads.

32

CHRISTIAN ROSS tried hard to follow each new report. During his fruitless journey to Albany he had contracted a fever from the malarial swamps of New Jersey which thereafter attacked him at unpredictable intervals. The slanders and calumnies cast upon his name and that of his wife took a severe toll. For more than two months he alternated between hope and fear. Finally something snapped. He became incoherent, his mind and body broken by strain, and was confined to his bed. Fearing for his life, the family physician removed him to Middletown, Pennsylvania, the home of his mother.

Henry Lewis, Mrs. Ross's brother, returned at this time from Europe. With Joseph Lewis, he maintained a place of business in the downtown area. As a result of Christian Ross's illness, the two brothers prepared to share the role he had previously played in the case. They were referred to Bullitt and McKean to learn all details of the public committee's activities, and to police authorities to ascertain the latest results of the search. Instructions were given that anonymous letters addressed to Christian Ross were to be delivered to them at their downtown office or at the main post office, should they call there.

The Lewises were advised that in reply to the kidnappers' last letter, sent from New York on September 6, a personal would be inserted in the New York *Herald* of September 14: "John — Hat not found. Am ready to pay sum demanded, but only through an attorney. He dare not betray you. Name one anywhere." When no reply was received, the personal was repeated on September 24.

On September 25 a response arrived from the criminals. It explained that they had been to New Brunswick, Canada, to see whether a simultaneous exchange could be arranged there, an idea first proposed by the resourceful Chris Wooster.

New Haven, Sept. 23. — Mr. Ros. — we did not see yu last answer til to day. we was in new brunswic british province and cold not see the New York herald we went there to se if the law would permit us to make a symultaneous change with yu but we find no such change can be efected with safety to our selves. you ask to transact the bisiness through an attorney this is to absurd to think of for one minute that man does not exist that we cold trust to receive that money but one of our own party and we are not wiling that one of our party shall become recognizable by any living person. as we now stand we can confront any one with impunity and are determined to keep so. if you be convinced that we have him and want to ransom him why did you not agree to our proposition. we have told yu if the money was lost in transit tu us it would be our los should yu folow our instructions and yu get yu child. Mr. Ros we cannot show the child to yu and we cannot give you any more proof than we have; yu must except this as the only alternitive left you to ransom him or murder him, for one or the other wil and shal take place before many days. Yu as his father have been mor cruel to him than we have. We told yu that his place of cencealment was such that no living being could find it and that it was not a fit place for any one to be in the length of time he has been there. We do not keep him there to punish him; your detectives have made it much worse for him than he would be had they not such a close search for him; he has kept his health wonderful considering his close confinement. We do not see him often or even hear from him. The last time we se him he had been ailing with pain from stoppage of urin he would go 24 and 30 ours without making water and then he would cry with pane when he would urinate, but his custodian got him som medicine which helped him. we tel you positively Mr. Ros his hiding place must be his tomb unless you bring him out with the ransom for we have a settled plan to act upon and we shal never digress from it and that is death or ransom. Yu will find we speak truth in this for once if yu compel us to put him to death yu shall receive a letter in 24 ours after, wher yu wil find his body. as soon as we cop another kid and it wil be a millionaire this time your child must die. we wil then see if he wil be so heartless as to let his child die. you detectives perhaps tel yu that yu wil pay yu money and get no child then but we dont do bisiness in that way we dont want him much longer neither dead or alive. if yu pay for him yu shall have him safe and sound. if not yu shal have him dead. so you can rest assured yu wil get him soon one way or the other. if die he must yu shal se that he has been dead but a few ours when yu git him then yu can thank yu friends for their kind advise. Ros this is the last advise we wil offer yu if yu reject it yu can make up yu mind that the day of grace is forever lost to save your child. Ros if yu want to save yu child yu must comply with our terms and yu yourself be our Attorney for we wil have no other and we are absolutely determined on that point. when yu see fit to change yu money for yu child in the way we direct yu can answer this through the herald *personal New York, we shall keep up this unnessary correspondence no longer your asking for more evidence that we have him looks to us as if it was a scheme of Mr. Haines to entrap us, but mr hains will never have that pleasure Mr Ros you must be convinced by this time that no reward however large can effect or influence our party we told yu this at the first and we told yu how hopelessly it was for yu to search for him when we had taken such great labor to find a suitable place to conceal him and the imposebility for any one to find him in our possession when we have it fixed so we can lanch him into eternity at an instant's warning, and yet yu consent that a reward shall be offered to induce some one who has no right to approach his hiding place but perhaps yu look upon this as romance or fiction yet fiction is sometimes more stranger than truth. Ros — yu should be your own counciler in getting yu child and then let the detectives council yu how to get us, take our advice for once and se if we do not give you the best council — that is get yu child at any price on any terms we*

*offer yu regardless of all other advise — we have told yu and
now repeat it that this thing is drawing to a final crises. Mr
Ros when yu conclude to act as our atty and meet us on our
terms then yu can answer this as directed we shal henceforth
notice nothing else from yu.*

The Lewises' greatest distress was occasioned by the letter's
revelation that little Charley had been ailing with stoppage
of urine, going for more than a day without making water
and suffering such pain that he would cry out. Mrs. Ross told
her brothers that little Charley had several times been afflicted
with this common childhood complaint. He had always re-
sponded to simple medication, niter supplied by the local
pharmacist.

In consultation with the Lewises, whose concern for the welfare of the boy reflected the mother's anxiety, authorities
placed a personal with a propitiatory tone in the New York
Herald of September 29: "John — your terms are accepted.
Name time between payment and delivery."

The criminals' reply, postmarked New Brunswick, New
Jersey, and dated September 30, was delivered to the Lewises'
place of business.

*New Brunswic, September 30. — Mr. Ros: yu have at length
agreed to our terms. how much better would it have been for
yu had yu complied at first. we told you at first there was no
other alternitive left you but to part with your mony or yu
child for one or the other yu must. we told yu before it shal
not exceed 10 ours from the time we receive the mony til yu
receive yu child and yet it may be a few ours longer. we must
have time to examine the money to see that yu have not got it
secretly marked up. we tel yu for your own interest not to
mark the notes in any way whatever for if you break the
terms of agreement with us we shal then break it with yu and*

*yu had much better keep your money for we tel yu positively
we would not keep our word. we would not liberate the child.
but on the other hand if yu come to us in good faith with the
intention of parting with yu money for the sake of getting yu
child and saving him from death then we pledge ourselves by
all the powers that be sacred in heaven and earth yu shall
have yu child saf and sound as soon as we can get him to yu
with safety to ourselves we think we told yu once how we
would return him tu yu. but this is the way we propose to do.
we will take him to some ministers house at night put a label
on him stating this is Charley Ros take him immediately to
304 Market st phil or washington lane germantown you will
find a sufficient sum in his pocket to pay yu for yu trouble
no reward will be paid. we have sent word to his parents
stating where he is. Mr. Ros we do not intend the party where
we leave him shall see us at all they will be perfect innocent
so you should not give them any trouble. we will send you
word immediately stating where he is left. but the probability
is he will be brought home long before yu get the letter but
this will make it perfectly safe and sure for yu to get him.
Mr. Ros it is true yu have got tu rely entirely on our honor
for the fulfilment of this part of the contract but you can rely
with implicit confidence. bad as we are and capable of the
blackest deeds yet we have some honer left. your large rewards have in a measure proved this there are 4 of us to
divide the $20,000 among and either one of the 4 could went
and got the whole amount to himself he had been without principal. how easy could any one of the 4 went on the sly and had
us all coped and revealed where the child was secreted but yu
see we have not done it. we have no fear of one another though
it were a million dollars. we have told yu for your own interest not tu mark the money which yu intend tu ransom
your child with. keep faith with us and we will keep faith
with yu and yu shal have yu child safe and sound in 10 or 12*

*ours. provide yourself with the amount in United States notes
from 1 tu 10 in denomination. not national bank notes when
yu are all prepared with this and are ready to meet us drop a
word in the* herald *New York yu can take as many of yu
friends as yu choose but do it quietly if yu want to get yu
child. Mr. Ros first get yu child then let the detectives assist
yu. yu see they have not the power to do anything. time has
proved this and if yu rely upon them so it will ever prove.
Mr Ros put yu child when yu get him on exhibition and yu
wil relize all your money back in 6 months for there is not a
mother in phila that will not pay a dollar to see him.*

In the New York *Herald* of October 7, authorities placed a
personal which read: "John — The money is ready. State
clearly and fully mode of payment and manner of delivery."
The kidnappers did not reply to this personal for some time.
Meanwhile, Joseph and Henry Lewis engaged in soul-search-
ing that was shortly to produce a drastic change in tactics.

33

THE LEWISES were kept informed of the many activities of
New York's energetic superintendent of police, whose enthusiastic reports were filtered to them through Captain Heins.
Walling had the feeling that he was just a step behind the
criminals, that their arrest was only a question of time. In
addition to Westervelt, he brought Old Gil Mosher back into
the picture. When he again asked Gil to produce a specimen
of his brother's handwriting, Gil said he was still unable to
find one. Westervelt likewise said he could find no sample of
the older abductor's script.

All his leads had come to naught, but before Walling could

register his disappointment, Westervelt gave him a new clue. He suspected that Mosher and Douglas were on a boat in the New York area. He said they had once owned a green clinker-built skiff with which they prowled up the East and North rivers and down to Staten Island. Their boat was a likely place to conceal the child.

Walling had long known that Mosher was a river thief. His detectives had recently brought him word of a new series of burglaries on the Long Island shores. The robbers had several times been sighted fleeing in a speedy black catboat. Each time they had escaped, presumably to hide out on one of the secluded islands along the shore.

A search of the rivers, shores, and islands of the New York area was obviously in order. Walling, well acquainted with the waters under his jurisdiction, rented a steam launch, and assigned officers Silleck and Moran to the project. William Westervelt was also induced to make the trip; and from Philadelphia Officer Wood arrived to assist in the maneuver.

The party steamed painstakingly through the localities suggested by Westervelt, exploring Long Island Sound, sailing up the East River, and up the Hudson as far as Newburgh. Each little bay and inlet was explored, each small creek and cove. The officers searched more than forty islands, ranging in size from five acres to a hundred, but found them unoccupied save for a few squatters. Small towns along the shore were investigated, as were occupied and unoccupied houses in the woods farther inland.

All eyes were peeled for both the type of boat described by Westervelt, a green skiff, and the black catboat seen by police after river robberies. The black boat had been described as drawing little water, hence able to navigate each quiet, shallow nook. The innumerable bays and watercourses about New York clearly provided the fullest opportunity for concealment, the party realized as the little launch plied its course.

The feeling was that possibly they had passed by the criminals' hiding place in the dusk. Several areas were searched a second time. After eleven days the detectives finally gave up and returned home. They had heard reports of burglaries along the shore but had not obtained the substantial clue that might lead them to the abductors of little Charley Ross.

Walling continued to have meetings with Gil Mosher and Westervelt. He had already seen the latter more than a dozen times. In addition to these two close relatives of Bill Mosher, a third man appeared on the scene. To Walling's office came Charles H. Stromberg, who said that he owned an eating saloon at 74 Mott Street. In the middle of June two men he knew to be of bad repute had paid a visit to his tavern. When they reappeared in July he heard from one of his bartenders, a young German named Henry Hartman, that they were suspected of being involved in the Ross case. He decided to keep a memorandum of their future visits.

"When I heard who they were and what they done that aroused my suspicions," he told Walling. "I allowed them to come there because I tried to catch them."

While they had been back twice — including a recent visit — Stromberg had not come to the police earlier because of fear the abductors might do him harm. From talk heard at the saloon he was under the impression they knew the police were after them. He had heard that they were eager to give up the child, that they would take anything they could get so long as they were assured of not being prosecuted.

As Stromberg sketched the physical characteristics of the two, Walling was certain they were Mosher and Douglas. He detailed detectives to keep a watch on the tavern. When the plainclothes officers arrived on the scene they learned that Mosher and Douglas had left an hour before.

One of the detectives watching the tavern later made an indiscreet inquiry about the two men. The watch was continued for a time, but Mosher and Douglas were never seen at Stromberg's by the officers on duty.

Stromberg told Walling on a subsequent visit that although they had not returned it might be of interest that on several of their previous visits they had conversed with a habitué of the saloon, a man named William Westervelt.

The irate Walling immediately ordered a detective to bring in the informer. Westervelt was hardly seated when Walling asked if he had seen Mosher and Douglas since their last meeting, a question he asked at each encounter. As usual, Westervelt said he had not. Jumping to his feet, the superintendent shouted that he had contradictory proof. To the blanching Westervelt he repeated Stromberg's story. His defenses punctured, Westervelt admitted that he had indeed made contact with the criminals.

His reluctant confession revealed that he had seen Mosher and Douglas not once but twice. The first time was at West Washington Market. They had chatted awhile and then stopped off at Stromberg's. A second time he had run into them on the street in the evening. On this occasion he attempted to follow them, but when they took a downtown stage at Broadway he lost track of them.

Why, demanded Walling, why had he not told him of these occasions so that he might have had the men arrested? Westervelt replied that both meetings were accidental and that there had been no opportunity to inform police. His relations with the two men had always been of the same nature. Mosher and Douglas were elusive and uncommunicative. Their activities could not be ascertained by asking them questions. It was possible he might hear from them in the not too distant future. If so, he would inform Walling immediately.

Walling asked one more question. In their conversations had Mosher and Douglas dropped any other hints that might show where little Charley was concealed? Westervelt said he was under the impression that the two men had recently traveled between New York and Philadelphia. Perhaps the child was secreted somewhere along this route, possibly near Trenton, New Jersey, since the name of that town had cropped up at one encounter.

Westervelt repeated that he still did not believe the two men were actually involved in the abduction. On the other hand, he knew their characters to be such that if they were the criminals, then to take them before the child was in safe hands would be a very risky business. It could lead either to the little boy's death or to his removal to another hiding place where he could not be found. He would therefore continue to make every effort to discover the child's whereabouts.

Walling gave Westervelt orders to remain in daily touch. He related details of the conversation to his detective force. To Captain Heins in Philadelphia he wrote in mid-October, "I am now positive that we are on the right track." Several days later, he followed up with a second dispatch:

William R. Heins, Esq.
Captain of Detectives
Philadelphia

Dear Sir —

I saw my informant last night; he says that we are surely on the right track, but they have hopes of getting the child redeemed, and he has not been able to find where it is. I think any arrangements made with the kidnappers for the restoration of the child would be a public calamity; no child would be safe hereafter if it had parents or friends who could raise money. I am confident that I shall get the guilty parties, and the child at some time not far distant, provided no compromise is made with them.

Very respectfully yours,
GEORGE W. WALLING, Superintendent

34

WHILE WALLING conveyed the impression that the kidnappers were moving about from place to place near New York City, the Lewises in Philadelphia received another letter from the anonymous correspondents. It had been mailed at Newburgh, New York, on October 15. It was received in Philadelphia the following day.

In answer to the authorities' personal of October 7, asking for a clear statement of the mode of payment and manner of delivery, the writers said this had already been explained.

October 11. — Mr. Ros: *you say the money is ready how is it then we can't come to a speedy compromise if yu was anxious to get yu child and wiling to pay yu money then there is no trouble about it we are anxious to give him up but only on the conditions we have before told yu you ask again how we are to deliver him to yu we told yu in our last letter plainly how we would return him to yu is not that way satisfactory yu don't want us surely to turn him loose on the road at the ded our of night we wil never bring him to you personaly nor wil we ever take him to any one you appoint but we will take him to a strange family where it is least expected and where you will be sure to get him if the way of delivering him is not satisfactory to yu then we cannot come to terms for we are determined in delivering him to yu that no person shal see our face when we do go with him we shal be completely disguised yu ask to state plainly how yu are to pay the money that will be told yu at the proper time so far as the money is concerned that is imaterial to yu what disposal is made of it so long as yu comply with our demands which you already know all you have to do now in order to have yu child restorded to yu is to make up yu mind that yu have got to part with so many dollars and it maters not to yu what becomes of the money so long as it satisfies our demand we return yu the child. yu may have a doubt that yu may not then get yu child. we cannot give yu the child before we get the money for then we part with every compulsion to make yu pay it. we cannot hand you the child as yu hand us the money for all the power and all the law is on your side. the thing is all embodied in a nutshell. the child is of no entrensic value to us whatever, any further than to compel yu to ransom him if yu pay the ransom and we do not give him up to yu would any one else give a dollar for their child when they would have no assurance whatever of getting him. yu certainly would not be fool enough to pay the ransom the second time when we had not kept faith with yu the first time but yu ask he might be dead and then we could not give him up — yes he might have been dead a dozzen times through your neglect to redeem him but as it hapens he has lived in spite of his close confinement again yu say we might hurried his death as we have threatened it so many times. That is true — we might but it has not come to that crisis yet so long as the inducement is held of geting the ransom he is in a measure safe but there wil be a time when the inducement wil exaust itself when this death takes place it wil be our policy and interest to make it known to yu at once that others may be wiser than yu — if yu should pay the ransom and then not get yu child would any one else have faith enough in us to pay a ransom when Ros did not get his child after paying for him — Mr. Ros you can rest assured with all confidence when yu pay yu mony yu wil get yu child but it wil be imposible unless you do. yu have ben living in hope of geting him without the ransom but the detectives in the case are powerless. yu get a clue every few days or rather a false clue. only a few days ago yu*

*child was seen in New Haven. i tel you positively and tu save
you trouble and anxiety that yu child has not been seen by
any human being since the third day of July other than the
party who have been in charge we could not take him five
miles without being arrested; when we return him to yu it
will be in the night time if at all when yu hear yu child is
seen here or there yu can have no faith in it. for he wil not
be seen by any one while we have him that yu can rest assured
of. yu say yu money is ready. are you ready to take a short
jonrney and have this thing settled. Mr. Ros this continual
correspondence looks to us as if it was but a ruse to get a clue
to our whereabouts. We tel yu positively should they succeed
in capturing one of us it would certainly prove death to yu
child. Do yu believe it or not — whether or not it wil not
alter our decree. If yu banish all hope of ever geting yu child
til yu ransom him and drop the detectives yu wil then take a
rational view of the thing and see it in its true light. We told
yu we were going to urope last month; part of us did go, but
we expect them back in few days and then we can settle the
business if yu are ready. We wil see the personals in the New
York herald.*

*October 15 — we had almost concluded after writing this
not to send it for you ask questions that answered planly —
but we wil see what you want now — if yu are ready to pay
we are ready to return the child to your satisfaction.*

Almost two weeks later, on October 28, authorities placed a
personal in the New York *Herald*: "John — Too sick to take
journey. Will relative answer?"

On October 31 a reply arrived. Having posted their letter
in Philadelphia, the criminals indicated that they had returned to that city.

Phila. Oct 31   Mr. Ros we told yu at the begining of this bisnes we would deal with none but you — the reason of this must be apparent to yu — the fate of yu child would depend entirely upon your actions in dealing with us — we know yu could not intentionaly sacrifice yu child in braking faith with us — we told yu in dealing with us yu must act in good faith and any breach of faith on your part would be meeted out in certain death on your child Mr Ros if you have any relative or friend that yu can delegate to transmit this important bisines then we are reddy to deal with him we care not who he may be if it be mr hines or the states attorney — we are wiling to negociate with him — but Mr Ros we want yu not to deceive youself in this bisines for we tell you plainly his acts will involve the life or death of your child — we shal regard him as your substitute in every particular and hold the life of yu child responsible for his actions. Mr Ros — from yu answers we understood yu agree to the terms we previously dictated — send your substitute to New York on tuesday 3rd november with the means to settle this bisines — remember the money must be in every particular as we directed for yu can accomplish nothing with us in using any stratagem for we will not release the child under any other circumstance than your carrying out the terms in good faith with us — it is unnecessary for us to pledge ourselves in anyway in regard to the child being immediately returned to you. all we can do or say is — it shall be our first move to restore the child after we see the money is all right. we shall spare no trouble or expense in returning the child to yu safely. though it cost us five thousand we would not hesitate to use it inorder to return the child. but it wil not cost us ten dollars and yu shal have him as safe and sound as he was on the 1 day of July last when he was playing in front of yu door with walter. your substitute on arriving in new york must put a personal in herald. *say — John — i am stoping at ——— hotel — with his name in full. Mr. Ros you say the*

*money is ready and yu substitute is ready. and we are ready
— then November the 3rd will prove or disprove the sincerity
of your actions. Mr. Ros — you see by this we have come
among you once more.*

Negotiations were clearly moving to a climax. The Lewises
and Mrs. Ross were increasingly inclined to heed the words of
the kidnappers and to prove the sincerity of their action. It
required all the persuasiveness of the police and the citizens'
committee to get them to accede to the personal which authorities inserted in the New York *Herald* on November 3: "John.
Change address of personal. Relative will not sign his name
in full."

The abductors' answer bore the same date.

*New Brunswick, November 3 — Mr. Ros. it looks very
strange to us that you should quible about the name to address
us. is your object to keep the detectives informed of our
whereabouts by having us writing you so often. it looks so but
time will prove all things. our advice is to you and it is better
than all the detectives combined can give you is to act
squarely in this bisnes if you have any regard for your child.
we think we have cautioned you enough on this point. we are
satisfied the detectives are working the thing up to their interest we know all about their doings and how they are bleeding you and Mr louis out of your money you will open your
eyes to their games. by the by we could tell you much about
them but our place is to keep mum and yours to investigate
before you give more money out. it makes us jealous to see you
pay out your mony foolishly when they can give you nothing
in return but a parcel of fabricated lies. we confes we are
bleeding you to — but we have an equivalent to give you in
return, if you child is any equivalent. you will find sooner or
later that there is no other earthly party in this world to deal*

*with than ourselves if you want to recover your child. Mr.
Ros why could not your relative give any name so that we
could have a name to address him? it matters not what the
name is we shall regard him as yourself in every sense of the
word so look to whom you appoint to transact this business for
you. we tell you positivey and absoluty that on his acts right
or rong square or crooked in dealing with us the life or death
of yu child shall hang now. Mr. Ros you may appoint any one
you please to transact the bisines with us but we want you to
bear in mind that his acts are your acts and it shall be con-
sumated just as you will it — and if you want your child
safe and sound this is the final day of salvation. we have
been at least under $15 a day expense since we had him but
that is our own affair. you may have been under five times
that expense for what we know. Mr Ross you must not be deceived from this because we are under expenses from keeping
him that we will turn him loose should you not meet our demands. we tell you positively we could not do it we would not
do it should it benefit us the whole amount of $20,000 than for
the redemption of your child. you may think from this should
you pay the demands. we might not then return your child.
Mr Ros when you have paid our demands in good faith you
have answered all we can ask of you and we tell you as we
have told you before that your child is not worth one cent to
us after that ony to return him to you and we would not fail
in any event to return him to you for $10,000. strange as this
may appear to you yet it is our interest to do so. should you
not come to our terms it is our interest that you never get him
and you may rely on it you never will alive. you may think
this is to cruel for any sivelized person to perpetrate but we
tell you positively it is the lot of one of us to perform it if
it comes to this crises. you will not be able by any quibbling to
stay the hand of fate much longer from him. we have kept
him over one hundred days longer than we expected. now it is*

for you alone to say whether he shal live or die. this is the last letter we shall we ever send you till we send you the final one revealing to you whether he is either alive or dead just as you will it to be. you need not ask more questions for they will not be noticed no answer will be returned. if you appoint any one to conduct this business for you let him come to New York make it known through personal with any address he choses. this address will do (John Johnathan is stopping at so and so. Johnathan or who he may be must not leave the hotel till he hears from us. if you mean square bisiness have your personal in Friday's Herald (N.Y.) and be in New York on Saturday morning. Mr. Ros bear in mind this is the last and final letter you ever receive from us unless you come to New York to close this bisiness.

Instead of complying with the demands of the anonymous writers, authorities inserted a completely variant message into the New York *Herald* of November 6: "John — You must change the name of 'John' for personals. It has become too well known."

The following reply was received in Philadelphia on Saturday, November 7.

Phila., Nov. 6. — Mr. Ros: *we told you in the last positively we would not write you any more. this dozing about puts us to no small amount of trouble we had left phila for New York thinking you were ready to close up the business. we told you positively procrastination is dangerous. had we accomplished what we have been fishing for the last three months your child would now have been dead but we have not yet caught the fish we wanted. yours is but a small item compared with something else. Walter said you owned the two new houses right opposite you or we should never troubled you. Mr. Ros you have asked to keep this negotiation a secret between ourselves it is a wise policy in your doings not that we fear being traped in our own game. This is positively the last from us. if you are sincere you would be anxious to settle this business if you regard the life of your child. we mean to fulfil every promise we made you in good faith. the result depends entirely with yourself whom you appoint to transact this business for yu we want at least two days notice before you come to New York for we may be 500 miles off and we ask for time to get there yu can say tuesday nov 10. Saul of Tarsus. (choose your own name say i will be stoping so and so all day. do not leave the hotel wherever you may be stoping for one minute during the day). this thing must come and shall come to a close in a few days.*

Advised that the Lewises were wavering in their determination not to compound the felony and were considering dealing in earnest with the kidnappers, Superintendent Walling sent an urgent dispatch to Captain Heins.

New York November 13, 1874

Captain William R. Heins: — Dear Sir: — Please see Mr. Lewis and say to him that I think it dangerous for parties to meet relative to any negotiations for the child, with a large amount of money, unless they have some officers within call, as the parties might be disguised, and in case the villains were to fail in making terms, they might take desperate chances to obtain the money.

GEORGE W. WALLING, Superintendent

Despite the warning, the Lewises held a strategy meeting with Mrs. Ross. Mrs. Ross related tearfully that the last word from Middletown indicated her husband was on the brink of death, and that each morning little Walter came downstairs and asked, "Has Charley come home, Mama? I prayed that he might come home last night, as you told me to do." How long must they continue to endure the suspense?

Finally the troubled family reached a decision. In the hope of saving Christian Ross's life and restoring Charley, they would pay the ransom. They would follow the instructions of the abductors in good faith, paying and taking the risk of having the child returned afterwards.

The authorities were duly informed of these conclusions and on Sunday, November 15, the called-for personal appeared in the New York *Herald*: "Saul of Tarsus — Fifth Avenue Hotel, Wednesday, 18th inst. all day. F. W. Lincoln."

On Tuesday evening, November 17, Frank Lewis and his father made the trip to New York, carrying with them a satchel containing $20,000 of unmarked bills in the designated denominations. They checked into the Fifth Avenue Hotel at 23rd Street and registered under the name of F. W. Lincoln. Unknown to them, Superintendent Walling had detectives strategically placed to watch the hotel.

On the eighteenth, the two Lewises remained in their room the entire day, waiting for the emissary of the kidnappers. Through the long evening and night they waited. The following morning, psychologically and physically exhausted, they checked out of the hotel. No one had come.

In the *Herald* of November 19 they placed a personal which read: "Saul of Tarsus — We have performed our part of the letter, you have again broken faith. We will have no more trifling; action must now be simultaneous."

At long last the family of the abducted boy had decided to heed the advice of the criminals, dealing with them directly, dismissing from their counsel the police and other authorities. The move had come too late. To the last two personals there was no reply. A correspondence unsurpassed in the annals of crime was at an end.

35

FRUSTRATED by his tireless but unavailing search, Superintendent Walling sent for William Westervelt. The two men went over the case. At one point Westervelt drew a memorandum pad from his pocket and pointed to a page on which he had written "Saul of Tarsus." The astonished Walling asked how he knew the code. Westervelt replied he had watched the personals since an earlier interview when the superintendent told him the kidnappers used them to correspond with Ross. The words "action must now be simultaneous" caught his attention. He thought they might have something to do with the case. Not satisfied with this explanation, Walling accused Westervelt of telling Mosher and Douglas that he, Walling, knew of the November 15 personal. This would account for the criminals' failure to appear at the Fifth Avenue Hotel rendezvous. Westervelt denied the allegation. He had voluntarily drawn forth the memo pad. If he had been implicated, why would he give himself away in this manner? After further discussion Walling came around to the same view of the matter, and as it was the dinner hour he invited Westervelt to dine with him at the House of Lords restaurant.

To Captain Heins in Philadelphia he reported on the meeting:

I . . . saw Westervelt and accused him of having played me false. He swears he has not, and says that he has seen Douglas and could get him for me, but does not know where Mosher is. I am certain that they are the parties, and am equally certain that they will not harm the boy.

I wish the boy's friends could make up their minds to defy the kidnappers; had they done so a month ago, I believe the child would now be at home with its mother. Nothing but the hope of gain and being able to make a bargain for their security, I am confident, causes them to keep possession of the child.

A little later he sent another note to Heins:

The parties are hard up and have come to the end of their tether. We are pushing them so hard that they dare not get out to do anything. I don't think Douglas will squeal unless we can get hold of him.

From one of his detectives the superintendent learned that the previous Monday night Douglas had gone to a waterfront saloon, one of his haunts, and found it closed. He had inquired for Westervelt. Less than an hour later Westervelt himself appeared at Walling's office and said that Douglas had been asking for him. Walling viewed the incident as proof that Westervelt was keeping faith with him and not double-dealing.

"I am satisfied that I could get Douglas, alias Clark, as I have heard from him several times, but he was always alone," the superintendent wrote Captain Heins, and then added a sentence which reflected his shifting attitude toward taking Douglas: "I do not want to get him without Mosher."

At Westervelt's suggestion the Morrises, old acquaintances of Mosher's, were put under surveillance. It was thought they might be the parties who were harboring the child. A check of their activities turned up no clue to the missing boy.

As the weeks passed, lead after lead was run down by detectives. The criminals appeared to be only a step ahead of the law. Yet that step was always there, and it did not appear to be growing shorter.

Only in one phase of the search was Superintendent Walling notably successful. By exercising extreme caution he managed to keep any knowledge of his pursuit of Douglas and Mosher from the metropolitan papers. Each day since putting his men on the trail he had feared that a news item might alert the abductors and spoil the department's plans. At one point the New York *Herald* was close to the scent. Several members of the Ross family, Walling, and detectives were about to hold a conference at the Metropolitan Hotel. A *Herald* reporter surprised the police chief in the lobby and asked pointedly if there was to be a meeting about the case that night. Walling denied it. Since the Ross contingent had already slipped upstairs to a private suite, the reporter was thrown off the track.

With little news about the abduction available to the papers other than recurrent stories of the missing boy's supposed discovery, the case drifted from the front pages to the inside sections of the papers. By December, journalists had turned their attention to other matters.

In the fall, thousands of White Leaguers under arms had overthrown the state government in Louisiana. "I will rout this party if I have to take the field in person," President Grant said at the time. Gradually order was restored and the elected government put back into the saddle.

The President had also made an appearance at the most dazzling social event of the season, the marriage in the nation's capital of Thomas William Fitch, a naval officer, to Mary Ewing Sherman, daughter of the famous Civil War general. Marching down the aisle, the bride leaned on the arm of her father, described by the New York *Herald* as bearing himself "like an uplifted lance" as he advanced with a slow tread toward the altar.

President Grant could not have been too happy about the November elections. Democrats made gains in many states, including Pennsylvania, where they squeaked by their opposition with a majority approximating five thousand votes. In New York, Samuel J. Tilden was the state's governor-elect, while Wickham was swept into office as New York City's new mayor, defeating the slate of Tammany Hall. The notorious Boss Tweed no longer ruled over his party, having been convicted of misusing public funds and sent to serve a prison term on Blackwell's Island.

The normal transfer of power in New York's main municipal office was hastened when the incumbent Mayor Havemayer died suddenly. He had been visiting Flushing, Long Island, on the afternoon of December 1, and when his return train broke down he was obliged to walk more than two miles against a strong wind. Shortly after arriving at his City Hall office he died of apoplexy.

While Boston's great literary event of the season was the public reading of a new book by Henry Wadsworth Longfellow, the entire nation erupted into literary controversy when an article in *Fraser's Magazine* audaciously asked if Bacon had written the works hitherto ascribed to Shakespeare.

"Was the Bard of Avon a genius, a plagiarist, or a Boucicault?" demanded one New York paper. Dion Boucicault, the reigning dramatist of the day, was asked his opinion, along with Bret Harte. Professor O'Leary of Manhattan College was quoted as saying: "As well might the pensive bird of Minerva warble forth the liquid notes of the lark as Bacon give life to Oberon or Puck."

Deeply involved in his own troubled case resulting from his parishioner's accusations, Henry Ward Beecher nonetheless found time to enter the fray, declaring that Bacon's intellect was deficient in the wit and fancy required for the writing of plays. Countering his view was the author of *Uncle Tom's Cabin*, Harriet Beecher Stowe, who said she found the Baconian theory ingenious.

Several stories of distant exotic places captured the imagination of the reading public as 1874 was drawing to a close. The New York *Herald* said it was sending Henry Stanley back to Africa on another mission, while from Greece came word that a German archaeologist, Dr. Heinrich Schliemann, had uncovered a city he declared to be ancient Troy.

Even more widely reported in the press was a story which told of the impending arrival of His Majesty, King Kalakaua, who had succeeded to the throne of the Sandwich Islands in 1873. His visit was designed to improve reciprocal trade between this country and Hawaii and the other islands.

At thirty-seven Kalakaua was said to have mental qualities which had won the respect of both American and European officialdom. One newspaper reported that the young king's policy since taking the throne "indicated a liberal and conservative spirit, tending to unite all classes and conflicting interests in his kingdom." The New York *World* took another view of the matter. "Did King Kalakaua Ever Eat a Missionary?" the paper headed its story, which relied heavily on the words of one Nauana, described as "a ragged old vagrant with an incurable passion for rum." Nauana had reportedly said, "If His Majesty does not know the taste of man-meat, it is simply because he has forgotten it."

Each stage of the king's visit, from his debarkation at San Francisco and his bilious attack in Chicago to his triumphal entry into Washington, D.C., received the full attention of the press. After December 13, however, a new development in the Ross case crowded the king into the back pages.

From Chester, Illinois, came word that a little boy who said his name was Charley Ross had been detained. He had been taken from the hands of a ruffian named Thomas Scott, who had brought him to the town. Scott, about fifty, was a heavy-set, medium-sized man with a game left leg. Curly black hair covered his head and a full beard adorned his face. He was shabbily dressed. He insisted the boy's name was Levi Scott.

His young charge gave not only the correct name and sur-
name of the missing boy, but the middle name, Brewster, as
well. Townspeople noted that he disliked Scott, his alleged
father. When a number of the ladies of Chester called to see
the child at the sheriff's home, a matron wearing a gold watch
and chain elicited the comment from the boy that his mother
also had a pretty gold watch and chain. He spoke a good deal
about his former house, the carpets, the piano, and other details of furnishing.

In appearance the youngster was almost identical with the
photo of Charley, declared the story in the New York *Times*,
save for the following qualifications:

Of course, five months of all manner of hardships, trudging
through the mud, heat, cold and rain; sleeping out in the open air
days and weeks together without being washed or combed, and
taught to beg, lie, and no doubt, to steal, and whipped until deep
scars and bruises mark his little back, as is the case with the boy
here, and every device used to alter appearances, hair cut short and
colored, etc., would necessarily make many changes.

The circular prepared by Pinkerton had listed a number
of tests for identification. Of the prayer, "Jesus loves me,
this I know, for the Bible tells me so," the detained boy knew
all but two words. A series of questions, posed by the sheriff,
drew further answers that indicated the missing Charley
might be before his interrogator:

"Where is your pa?"

"Do you want to know where my real pa is, or this papa
here?"

"I want to know where your real pa is."

"At home."

"Does your pa live in the country or in town?"

"Town."

"Is it a big town or a little town?"

"Not a very big town, but there is a big town close by."

"What is the name of the town where your pa lives?"

"I don't know."

"What does your mama do?"

"Oh, mama doesn't do anything much. She talks to ladies that come to see her, and reads the papers, and plays on the piano."

"What sort of a house do your papa and mama live in?"

"A big nice house, with lots of rooms in it."

"Where did this papa get you?"

"Me and brother were playing on the street, while papa and mama were eating supper and two men stole me away, and afterward let brother go, but would not let me go."

"Have you any uncles where you live?"

"Yes."

"What are their names?"

"I don't know."

"Have you an Uncle Joe?"

"Oh, yes."

"Where does your Uncle Joe live?"

"In the next house to our house."

"Did you ever go out riding with your mama?"

"Yes."

"What horse did your ma drive?"

"I don't know the name of the horse. I know, but I can't remember."

There were enough remarkable coincidences in the boy's answers to warrant one of the Ross family's making the trip to Chester. When Christian Ross's brother James arrived, he quickly ascertained that the boy was not little Charley. Lonely and abused, the child had evidently found escape in a fantasy identification with the lost boy of Germantown.

By now the townspeople had become so concerned over the child's welfare that plans were set afoot to remove him from the custody of Scott and to place him in kind hands for protection and care. Further, the citizen who was appointed his guardian wrote the police chiefs of all major cities asking that an account of the boy be printed in the metropolitan papers. When Henry Lachmueller of St. Louis read the published description, he saw points that made him think the boy was his son, who had mysteriously disappeared two and a half years earlier and for whom he had since conducted an intensive search.

Lachmueller made the trip to Chester and quickly recognized his son despite the fact that he had been shamefully disfigured, his back scarred, his face showing markings left by acid, his hair dyed an unnatural color. The father joyfully reclaimed the boy and returned to his home.

Before this emotion-ridden episode was fully cleared up, the most startling development yet reported in the Ross case broke upon an astonished public.

36

ON THE EASTERN SIDE of the Upper Bay of New York, the Long Island shore rose, in 1874, into an uneven and beautifully wooded bluff known as Bay Ridge. Along its sides and summit nestled gracious villas, summer houses of the wealthy, together with the year-round dwellings of the area's prosperous farmers. Residents could reach their homes from New York City in less than half an hour by catching a small steamboat which departed from the Wall Street Ferry.

On one of the headlands about a mile from the landing stood two mansions. One was a handsome modern frame structure surrounded by ample grounds and belonging to Judge Van Brunt of the Court of Common Pleas of New York. The other was an old-fashioned Victorian country house which belonged to his brother, Holmes Van Brunt, who farmed in the area. The houses were separated by a pleasant lawn.

A storm from the bay blew into shore on the night of December 13, 1874. It was pitch dark, cold, and wet with intermittent rain. Before closing his house for the season, the judge had furnished it with a burglar alarm system which signaled into the bedroom of his neighboring brother if there was the slightest interference with any door or window of the judge's house. Near two o'clock in the morning — it was now Monday, December 14 — this alarm bell rang with a sharp metallic clang. Holmes Van Brunt, for some time in ill health and sleeping fitfully, was instantly awakened. He called to his son, who occupied an upstairs bedroom, "Albert, go over and see what has sounded that alarm. I guess the wind has blown open one of those blinds again."

Albert, a young man in his early twenties, put a small revolver into his pocket as a precaution and walked some two hundred yards toward his uncle's shuttered house. Through the blinds of an upstairs window he noticed a soft flickering light. He returned to convey this intelligence to his father. Then he lit a lantern and went to awaken William Scott, the judge's gardener, who lived in a cottage at the rear of the two houses. Together Scott and young Van Brunt made another inspection of the disturbed premises. Peering through the blinds, they saw the shadows of two men.

"Father, there is someone in the judge's house," Albert said on his return.

"Get the shotguns, my son, and call up Herman Frank," the elder Van Brunt said, rising from his sickbed. While his father dressed, Albert went to awaken Frank, the hired man who slept on the premises. When the four men were gathered, the elder Van Brunt held a strategy conference.

"Now, boys, we have work to do, and we must understand

each other," he began. "We must capture these fellows if we can without killing them. But if they resist we'll defend ourselves. Albert, you and Scott stand before the front door. Frank and I will take the rear. And whatever happens afterwards, let us remain in the positions we take up, because if we move around we'll be certain to shoot each other in the dark instead of the enemy. Whichever way they come, let the two who meet them take care of them as best they can. If they come out and scatter both ways, then we'll all have a chance to work."

Their guns loaded and primed, the men went forth into the blustering cold, there to crouch uncomfortably in position while waiting for the burglars to make a move. Through the chinks of the shutters, they could see the two men wandering from room to room searching for booty. Dark lanterns flashed now and then, showing the faces of the burglars quite distinctly. At such moments they made ready targets, but the elder Van Brunt had given instructions not to kill except in self-defense.

The aged man, who had not left the house in two weeks, suffered from the cold and damp of the inclement night as the intruders methodically ransacked the house, emptying out drawers, tearing protective covers off statuary and clocks. Leaving the pantry, they went into the dining room, where a long delay ensued. Almost an hour had passed when Holmes Van Brunt decided to help matters along. "We must hunt them out. I cannot stay up much longer," he said. Standing guard before the rear door, he ordered the hired man to open it quickly. Frank obeyed, but in getting the key into its hole he made a perceptible rattling noise. Hearing the sound, the burglars quickly blew out their lanterns. Through the shutters one of them was seen to light a lucifer match and pass through the parlor, from which they hurriedly made their way into the basement.

The elder Van Brunt and Frank moved toward the cellar door. They saw it open with the body of one man protruding, followed by the head of another. Cautioning his son and the others to remain still, Van Brunt leveled his revolver at the foremost man, only a few feet away, and shouted, "Halt! Stop!"

In response two pistol shots flashed close to his face. Using the light from these shots to guide him, Van Brunt aimed at the first man and pulled the trigger. A vehement curse and a cry of agony followed. As both burglars turned to run up the alleyway at the left of the house, Van Brunt said, "They're coming. Give it to them."

The first of the criminals to emerge, already wounded, staggered near the wall of the house, firing wildly. The hired man gave him a blast from his shotgun. "I give up," the man gasped, and fell to the ground.

The second man ran to the front of the house and almost dashed into the arms of Albert Van Brunt, at whom he fired two shots, both missing. The criminal stood between the young man and the white wall of the house. When he raised his weapon for another shot, Albert hit him a savage blow with his shotgun, breaking his arm near the elbow and deflecting his gun. Shouting invective, the criminal prepared to fire once more, but young Van Brunt whipped out his revolver and sent a bullet into his chest. The man staggered, received another bullet in the head, and fell.

Suddenly all was silent. The two bandits were on the ground, the first near the spot where he had been shot by Frank and the second where young Albert's bullets had brought him down. The first made no sound. The second was breathing heavily.

From an upstairs window of Holmes Van Brunt's mansion, his wife and their daughter watched the whole affray and then came down. When the mangled burglar asked for whis-

key, Mrs. Van Brunt said, "Whiskey for him, for the man
who tried to kill my husband? Oh, no. I don't want him to
live. Let him die. At all events, he gets no whiskey from me."

A servant woman looked at the suffering housebreaker and
admonished him by saying, "It is just good for you."

"Oh, madam," the criminal replied, "I have been a very
wicked man."

Neighbors awakened by the shooting came running. A
young farmer named Theodore Bergen heard the wounded
man's request for alcohol and went to fetch a bottle. The
criminal put it to his lips, but after tasting pushed it aside
and asked for water. He drank deeply.

A light was produced and the elder Van Brunt bent over
him. "Young man, your time is pretty short now," he told
him. "If you have anything to say, you had better be about
it at once. Who are you? What is your name and where did
you come from?"

"Men, I won't lie to you. My name is Joseph Douglas,"
the wounded criminal began, speaking with great effort.
"That man lying over there is William Mosher, M-o-s-h-e-r.
Mosher lives in the city, and I have no home. I am a single
man and have no relatives except a brother and sister, whom I
have not seen for twelve or fifteen years. Mosher is a married
man and has five children. I have forty dollars in my pocket.
I wish to be buried with it. I made it honestly."

Asked if he had anything to add, the dying man raised
himself up and spoke in a hoarse whisper: "It's no use lying
now. Mosher and I stole Charley Ross from Germantown."

One of the astonished villagers, peering at the eerie scene,
asked why they had stolen the boy. "To make money," the
man replied. "And who has charge of the child now?" came
a further question.

"Mosher knows all about the child. Ask him," the criminal replied, pointing at the body of his partner, lying on the

ground some fifty feet away. Villagers raised Douglas so that he could see that his companion in guilt was dead.

"God help his poor wife and family," he said, looking over at the dead man.

Closing his eyes in pain, he begged that no more questions be asked of him, but the senior Van Brunt persisted. "Can you tell us where the child is?" he demanded.

"I don't know where he is. Mosher knows," came the weak reply.

Several times more the same question was put to him, but no further information was forthcoming. The bodies of the two burglars were taken to the porch of the Van Brunt home.

Writhing in agony, Douglas made his last remark: "Super-intendent Walling knows all about us, and was after us, and now he shall have us. Send him word." Almost inaudibly he added, "The child will be returned home safe and sound in a few days."

A doctor had been sent for. He arrived only minutes before Douglas expired, near five o'clock in the morning. In his last moments he had not spoken, had given no further clue to the whereabouts of little Charley Ross. As a drenching rain fell from the murky sky, the bodies of the two dead men were covered with a shroud that hid their faces from the world.

37

SUPERINTENDENT WALLING arrived at his office later in the morning of December 14 and found a telegram awaiting him:

TWO BURGLARS WILLIAM MOSHER AND JOSEPH DOUGLAS
WERE KILLED LAST NIGHT. DO YOU KNOW ABOUT THEM?
DOUGLAS DECLARED WHEN DYING THAT MOSHER KNEW
ABOUT CHARLEY ROSS.
                                         C. W. CHURCH

Church was a justice of Fort Hamilton, next door to Bay Ridge. Walling replied to him:

DOUGLAS TOLD THE TRUTH. I HAVE BEEN LOOKING FOR
THEM EVER SINCE THE BOY WAS STOLEN. WILL SEND AN
OFFICER WHO KNOWS THEM.

Following his chief's instructions, Detective Silleck arrived on the scene at ten o'clock and was taken to see the bodies of the two housebreakers. As the shroud was drawn back, the veteran officer recognized his men. "That is Bill Mosher, and that is Joe Douglas," he said. He pointed at the elder of the two and added, "Take the glove off that left hand and you'll find a withered finger." The glove was removed and revealed the little finger curled into the shape of an animal claw.

The criminals left behind two sets of burglars' tools, complete and well cared for. Each man had carried a revolving pistol and a large knife.

Moored in a breakwater about half a mile below the Van Brunt property was their boat, a black cat-rigged sailboat altered into a sloop. It bore no name. Inspection of the boat uncovered nothing except several copies of the New York *Herald* and one of the New York *Evening Telegram*.

Residents of Bay Ridge said the boat had come over from New York early the previous evening. At Winant's Hotel near the Bay Ridge dock, witnesses saw the men come in and drink several glasses of liquor. They carried on a short conversation in a low tone of voice.

They had left and apparently made their way up the ridge in search of a likely place to rob. Prior to the attempt on the judge's house there was a failure in another place. To the left of the Van Brunt property was a house occupied by a widow named Mrs. Chandler White. At one in the morning Mrs. White heard a noise downstairs and summoned her man-servant, who made a tour of the house and found a window forced from the outside. The intruders fled. They passed by Holmes Van Brunt's place, probably because he had a light in his sickroom, and on to the judge's dark house, entering by the cellar door.

For the farmers of Bay Ridge who had apprehended the criminals, Constable John Holland had a surprise in store. He ordered the Van Brunts, along with Frank and Scott, arrested and held pending an inquest. Holmes Van Brunt, eager to be done with the matter, demanded an immediate hearing, but the earliest date that could be fixed was Wednesday, December 16, at Kings County Courthouse in Brooklyn. These arrangements made, a coroner was called; he ordered two rough coffins from the Brooklyn Morgue. During the day a van from that institution arrived and took the bodies away.

Superintendent Walling sent a telegram to Philadelphia addressed to Henry Lewis:

> TELL CHRISTIAN K. ROSS QUIETLY THAT MOSHER AND DOUGLAS WERE KILLED LAST NIGHT WHILE COMMITTING A BURGLARY IN NEW YORK. DOUGLAS CONFESSED THAT THEY STOLE CHARLEY.

The message was relayed to the anxious father, who had passed through a crisis that brought him near death, and who was still recuperating at his mother's home in Middletown. Little Walter and Mrs. Ross, visiting him, received the news at the same time. In the hearts of the stricken family hope rose anew. Would their dear boy now at last be restored to them? Would they all be together again for the coming Christmas?

Captain Heins and William McKean of the citizens' committee hurried to New York for consultations with the chief of police and his detectives. Heins wired Frank D. Lewis:

SUPERINTENDENT SAYS THE BODIES ARE NOT DISFIGURED.
BRING WALTER OVER. HAVE HOPE OF FINDING WHERE
THE CHILD IS TONIGHT.

Joseph Lewis, Walter, and Peter Callahan, the gardener
who had observed the abductors in Washington Lane, took
the train to New York the next day. Walter was brought to
the morgue with no explanation of what he was to see. At the
sight of the two dead men, he became extremely agitated. He
stared at Mosher; his recognition was slow. "Oh, that's the
man," he finally said. "That's his nose. He gave me candies,
and Charley, too. And he wore goggles coming back behind
his ears."

Taken to see the body of the younger man, Walter's recognition was instant. "Oh, that's awful like him," he exclaimed. "He's the driver." Douglas had given him money
to buy firecrackers, and he had also given both boys candy.

Callahan was taken separately to view the corpses. He was
equally sure that Douglas was the driver. Although Mosher
had kept a handkerchief up to his face, he tentatively recognized him as the second of the abductors.

Following the identification, Walter, his uncle, and the
gardener were escorted back to their quarters at the Metropolitan Hotel. There they found that news of the Bay Ridge
shooting and Douglas's dying confession had been carried
across the country by the Associated Press. The metropolitan
dailies, which had had no inkling of the police pursuit of
Mosher and Douglas, spread the story over the front page and
let it spill over onto their editorial columns, with the following
a typical reaction:

There is a deep moral impressiveness in the circumstances of the
Bay Ridge tragedy which cannot fail to have a salutary effect on the
community and strike the criminal classes with mysterious awe.

When merited punishment overtakes deep guilt, the public sense of justice is satisfied; but when the punishment is astonishing and unexpected, and the sudden retribution which falls on one offense in the very act of commission, and which might seem greater than its wickedness deserves, reveals another and darker crime, which shows that the criminals had sinned up to the full measure of that fearful penalty, reverent minds cannot fail to recognize in so wonderful a coincidence the directing hand of Providence; and even the most thoughtless will be awakened to some dim sense of a moral Governor presiding over human affairs.

Most editorials considered that two well-known criminals had justly been shot down like dogs, their violent death having all the appearance of a startling act of poetic justice. "Vengeance is mine, saith the Lord, I will repay," was a Biblical excerpt much quoted. But while the villainy of the child-stealers was dwelt upon at length, the New York *Times* came to a more thoughtful evaluation of their character:

Mosher was evidently a superior strategist, but there is no evidence that he was either bloodthirsty or constitutionally cruel. The distress he was causing was simply to him a measure of the reward he would be likely to extract, and to that extent he affected what may fitly be called a heartless type of villainy. . . .

We shall not get any nearer the truth in this mysterious business by assuming the chief actors in it to have been monsters in human shape. . . . It seems probable that Mosher's connections lay rather among the class whom poverty and irregular occupation render unscrupulous about their mode of earning a living than among the class of habitual and professed criminals.

At another city desk the shooting down of the abductors provoked a crisis of conscience. After reviewing the circumstances of the case, including the paper's prior attacks on the character of the father, the *Herald* found that its role had been less than creditable. The Ross family had led a quiet, reserved life, and this very reserve, this distaste for playing any melodramatic role before the public had irritated the press and was the chief cause of the unjust aspersions cast upon them:

We feel it is but proper in this connection, as a concession largely due to the bereaved family of the stolen child, that the *Herald* should say that while its investigations of the matter carried on at a distance were meant simply to serve the public, they were in certain particulars erroneous in theory and facts. Our correspondent, acting upon false information, believed by him to be true, did the character of Mr. Ross gross injustice and we would not be wanting in the commoner feelings of humanity were we not thus to distinctly disavow his erroneous accusations and express our sincere sympathy for the afflicted family of the gentleman whom they affected.

After making amends for its slanderous treatment of Ross, the contentious paper could not resist an attack in another direction:

There is something exceedingly peculiar in the management of this case so far as the New York officers were concerned, something that would seem to invite investigation. There was awful bungling somewhere.

38

WHEN WORD of Bay Ridge reached Philadelphia, citizens swarmed once more to the Central Police Station and to bulletin boards of the various papers. Each bit of news elicited strong emotions. Sober looks at details of the shooting gave way to cheers when it was learned Douglas had said little Charley would soon be home.

Officer Wood, local veteran of the abduction case, gave his views in a press interview. He began by telling of how gallantly the officers of New York had entered into the cooperative search for the boy. The Philadelphia police view, he stated, was that four men were concerned in the affair. The abductors had early in the case taken the child away from the city, leaving Mosher's wife behind to ward off suspicion. They had probably settled in New York, sending back letters which she posted in Philadelphia. Some double-dealer had told the criminals that Superintendent Walling was after them. As a result they left New York, returning occasionally for a burglary that could replenish their dwindling finances, and then retreating again to a hideout on the Sound.

"Are you nearer the child now than before?" Wood was asked.

"I don't think they can now keep the child out of the way. Either the other two men have got it or Mosher's wife has it. I don't think she can keep out of the road. She has no means — neither have the other two men — for we know that the whole gang are reduced so low that they had to make forays into the town and commit house robberies."

"Is there any likelihood that they will kill the child?"

"No, no. I don't think that. They may 'drop' it."

"By that you mean set it down in some place where it may be picked up?"

"Yes, something of that kind."

Superintendent Walling was subjected to a similar interrogation by New York reporters:

"What effect will the death of Mosher and Douglas have on the Ross case? If the boy was in their care, may he not have been concealed in some place unknown to any other person and thus starve?"

"It is a pretty hard question to answer, whether the death of these men will have a good or a bad effect upon the case, whether it will facilitate Charley Ross's discovery if in the hands of other persons or not. My opinion is that it will be all right now. You see there is now no hope of reward. . . . And the boy will be a burden to his keepers, of no use to them, in fact. How easy it will be for them to set him afloat, put him out in the streets, with the knowledge that he would soon be taken up by the police as a lost child.''

''Do you think the boy is concealed in New York?''

''I do not think the boy is concealed in this city. To be frank with you, I never believed that he was concealed in this city. It is not for me to tell you all I know about the case in its present aspects, but I am of the opinion that we are still on the right track.''

''What about Mrs. Mosher?''

''I know she used to live in Philadelphia, and I know where she was last Saturday night. She has moved three times in a month, and unless she has moved since Saturday I know of her whereabouts. I would rather not say anything more about other parties who were somewhat connected with Mosher and Douglas in this Ross business. This woman may, in all probability, be able to do a great deal that will serve to unravel the mystery which now surrounds the fate of the lost child.''

''From the cautiously worded replies made by the superintendent to questions concerning the search for the missing lad, it is believed that within the next 24 hours the boy will be in the hands of his friends,'' reported the New York *Times*. ''Captain Heins of the Philadelphia detectives, and Mr. Lewis, a relative of the missing lad, remained in town all night in the hope of being able to take the boy with them when they returned to the Quaker City.''

On Tuesday evening, December 15, Walling asked Mrs. Mosher to call at his home on 19th Street. She arrived at the residence with her two eldest children and entered into a long discussion. At the end of the meeting she provided the police chief with a clue. She knew of an elderly man and woman who had been acquaintances of her husband's and who were the sort of people to whom he might have entrusted the stolen boy. As soon as she had left, Walling ordered Officer Silleck to investigate the couple. His report absolved them of any involvement in the case.

Earlier in the day, acting on another tip, Walling had sent Officers Doyle and Lawler to Westport, Connecticut. Their trail led them from that town to an island off the shore where a young, golden-haired boy was said to be in the hands of an old man and woman who refused to allow visitors to the island or to be questioned on their trips to the mainland. Detectives learned that the island was one they had searched on their steam launch journey. The couple's antisocial behavior resulted from their fear of chicken thieves. Doyle and Lawler returned to New York.

Gil Mosher was questioned, but apart from his view that Mrs. Mosher might know more than she was telling he had little to offer.

William Westervelt was sent for and once again provided amazing information which he said he was about to bring to the superintendent of his own accord. He had seen both Bill Mosher and Joseph Douglas on December 12, short hours before the fateful evening that ended with the killing at Bay Ridge. He had spent the night at a hotel with Douglas. To keep a record of the ensuing conversation, Walling called in Officer Wood, who had arrived from Philadelphia. Asked to begin at the beginning and leave out no details, Westervelt told the following tale.

Some weeks ago his sister, Mrs. Mosher, who had been staying with him and his family, had left. After several changes of address she had moved in with her friends the Morrises, and on Saturday, December 12, she asked the Westervelts to her new quarters. They had arrived at seven in the evening. Shortly thereafter Mosher and Douglas showed up quite unexpectedly. Mosher had chatted awhile and then gone off with his wife. Douglas left too, but asked Westervelt to meet him later at a corner of the graveyard on Second Street.

The two walked from the designated meeting place toward the Bowery, stopping for some oysters at Hunt's saloon. Near Bleecker Street they stopped again for coffee and a cigar before continuing down Catharine Street.

Along the way their talk was desultory — of old haunts in the Eighth Ward, where they were walking; of a house nearby where Douglas had once taken a furnished room and later kept a woman; and of other associations. When they reached Vandyke's hostelry opposite the Catharine Street Market, Westervelt began saying goodnight.

"If it was only morning, I would take a mess of fish home," he remarked. It was a Sunday morning custom for the Westervelts to eat seafood.

"Come on up and stop with me," Douglas had said. "It's late, and your door will be locked."

It was past midnight and Westervelt agreed to the suggestion. Douglas entered and registered as Day. Westervelt also used an alias. They shared a room with twin beds on the second floor, having instructed the counterman to call them at six in the morning.

Superintendent Walling interrupted at this point to ask the burning question, "Did he say anything about the missing boy?"

"I cannot say how he brought the subject up," Westervelt replied. "I think I broached the subject of the child to him. It might have been like this. I do not say in these words: 'I think you have got the child' or 'I think you are the parties,' but I cannot tell what it was. I cannot tell for certain whether the word 'child' was named that night. He commenced some way or other. Whether he or I started it I cannot say for certain, but I think he did. He got to asking what they could do with the money, in a braggadocio way. 'If they got us, they would have to prove it,' he said, 'and how could they prove it? They would have to find someone that saw us with it.' He might have said 'child,' but I do not know. They would have to see somebody who saw them take the child, but it would be all right. I think he said, 'with the plan.' They had changed their plans. Previous to this I had asked him how the devil could they get the money for it if the parties were willing? I cannot get the exact words, nor the answers. If it is not the exact words, it is the exact meaning. I suppose he suspected I knew something about it, and so let himself out in that way. I could not tell anything for a certainty. He said that he was going to London or Liverpool, that he was to hold a correspondence from there as if he had split from the others. That is about all. Then I was asking how in the devil he could get the money. He said that could easily be worked. One way, you could make an arrangement to meet him on the cars. They could stand on the rear platform of the car and jump the money to him, he said. They would not get the child to them for two or three days afterward. I asked him who would be fool enough to do such a thing as that. That is about all that he did say. He said that they had sent on a fearful letter — one that would make your hair stand — and if they could stand that they could stand anything. He never told me who wrote any of them. I judge Mosher wrote them. I was under the impression that Douglas could not write until I saw him sign his name at Vandyke's.''

The conversation had ended. The two men went to sleep. In the morning Douglas made an appointment to meet Westervelt one evening later in the week at the New England House. Then they parted.

Westervelt had not gone directly to Walling but was planning to do so the following day, he declared to the superintendent and Officer Wood. On Monday morning he read of the shooting at Bay Ridge and hurried to the Van Brunt property to see if the men were really Mosher and Douglas. He had seen the bodies of the criminals. The dead wagon had come and they had been put in their boxes and hauled away.

Westervelt swore that he planned to tell Walling of the meeting arranged with Douglas at the New England House so that he might be taken by the police, but the events at Bay Ridge had altered every scheme.

Westervelt now remembered that two of Mosher's associates were presently in Baltimore, where they might possibly have charge of the boy. Officer Wood immediately left to trace them down. He found that the two were thieves of a very low class, living in a squalid neighborhood. They begged to be let off, expressing at once the fear that they would be lynched. Officer Wood released them.

Numerous other clues were traced, but in each case they failed to lead to the missing boy. On Wednesday, Walling told reporters of these futile ventures and then went on to give some details of his interview with Mrs. Mosher. He had immediately asked her about little Charley.

"I wish I had him! How quickly he would be in your hands," she had said.

The superintendent then asked her if she had known of her husband's connection with the case before she came to New York. Her reply was lengthy and revealing:

"No, I did not. The first I knew of it was from some hints thrown out by my brother. I had heard things from him and others that made me suspect my husband had something to do with it. I said to him one day, 'Bill, can't you trust me? You ought to know by this time whether I would betray you or not.' He said, 'I'd trust you sooner than anyone else, and I know you would do nothing to hurt me. But suppose I had

anything to do with it — mind you I hadn't — but suppose
I had and I told you where the child was — I don't know, but
if I did — what good would that do? If I got arrested for
anything else, what would be the first thing you'd do to get
me out? Why, run to the police and tell where that child was.
They'd humbug you and pretend to make a bargain with you
to let me out. As soon as you told where the child was —
you'd tell in a minute to get me out of jail — and then where
would we be? That is, supposing I had anything to do with
it, but I hadn't and I don't know anything about the child.'
Then I said to him, 'If you tell me not to do that I wouldn't
do it, and I think I ought to be trusted as well as strangers.'
'Now, there you go again,' he'd answer, 'getting jealous of
strangers. They're telling you things on the outside and you
get believing them about me, when I'm telling you here to
mind me and look after your children. I don't know anything
about this case, anything at all, and if I did, I've given you
reasons enough why you should know nothing of it.' "

After relating that Mrs. Mosher had promised to do all she
could to help locate the missing boy, Walling delivered his
most recent view of the abduction:

"I don't think Douglas knew where the child was. I don't
think he ever knew where he was put. My idea is that when
they took the boy away, they put him into the buggy and
drove across country to Raritan Bay, New Jersey. When they
got to the water's side, Mosher took the boy out of the buggy
and put him into the boat waiting for them at the point where
they alighted. Mosher and the person — probably a woman —
in charge of the boat then rowed across the river with the boy
and left Douglas to get rid of the horse and wagon. Where or
how he managed this we have not yet been able to ascertain,
and now that he is dead it would not make any impression in
the case. If it was a woman who rowed that boat across the
water with Mosher, she is the one who has the child. And if

it was a man he was paid and sent about his business and the child was carried by Mosher on landing on the other side to where he knew concealment was well covered.

"Now that Mosher is dead the retention of the child takes a new feature, and I am of the opinion he will be turned out into the streets."

On Wednesday, December 16, the Brooklyn *Daily Eagle* proclaimed in banner headlines that little Charley Ross had been found. Policemen in the Bowery had seen a boy who bore a remarkable resemblance to the missing child. He was close to five years old, with long, curly, flaxen hair and brown eyes. He declared his name to be Charley. When he was taken to headquarters, the boy gave his father's name and address and an officer recognized him as a child brought in several times before as Charley Ross. On learning that its sensational story was unfounded, the *Eagle* dropped it from late editions.

In the same afternoon an overflow mob pushed its way into the Brooklyn courtroom where the inquest into Monday's Bay Ridge shooting was being held. After hearing the testimony of the various witnesses, the jury went out to deliberate. During its absence, the now famous farmers of Bay Ridge engaged in conversation with a party of their neighbors and seemed elated by the attention accorded them.

The jury found on its return that the defendants had killed in self-defense. "We commend the act of their defending their lives and property in such a courageous manner under such trying circumstances," the foreman said. The Van Brunts, their gardener Scott and hired man Frank were thereupon released from custody.

The public felt justice had triumphed in the criminals' bloody end. Unfortunately, death had sealed their lips. Their guilty secret went with them to the morgue and to the grave.

39

THE SIX MONTHS' manhunt for little Charley Ross had made his name known in virtually every American town and hamlet and in many English-speaking cities around the world. As word of the Bay Ridge shooting circulated, the abduction again became the chief topic of conversation in countless homes. The pages of imaginative fiction presented nothing more remarkable than the end of the two criminals: the chill darkness of a stormy December night enveloping the fatally wounded burglars and the voluntary confession which left the mystery of little Charley Ross yet unsolved.

The dramatic tale had been blazoned on the front pages of newspapers. It had drawn crowds to the trial of the Bay Ridge farmers and it had stimulated renewed efforts by police and private citizens to find the lost boy. Perhaps the most vivid of all testimonies to the public's absorption were the throngs who lined up in front of the Brooklyn Morgue to view the shattered bodies of the criminals.

Many of the visitors were ordinary curiosity-seekers; others were politicians. Members of the press kept a watchful eye on them, hoping to detect among the crowd members of the criminals' families.

The procedure for viewing the corpses was cumbersome. Mosher's body had been put on a refrigerated shell coffin and placed in an elevator used for hoisting bodies from the vaults below. To this gravedigger's dumbwaiter, visitors were led in slow file. A ghastly look lit the face, for the bluish-gray eyes were still wide open. While Mosher's hair was dark auburn, his sandy-gray mustache carried traces of white and was connected to side whiskers. He had a broad forehead and high cheekbones. It was noticeable that the cartilage between the bridge of his nose and the nostrils was absent. Many of those who gazed for a moment at the corpse recoiled in horror and left at once.

Others made their way down a narrow fifteen-foot stepladder which led to the vault where Douglas lay exposed. A cloth covered his body from the neck down, concealing the frightful wound in his stomach. Some drew back the cloth, but few could witness that grisly sight.

Employees of the morgue had searched the garments of the two criminals, going so far as to tear out the linings in the hope that some clue might be discovered which would aid in the recovery of the stolen boy. The ragged clothing, saturated with blood and perforated with shot and bullets, was heaped in a corner of the room. Even these unsightly remnants attracted earnest attention from the hordes who came to Brooklyn throughout each day.

Early on the afternoon of Tuesday, December 15, reporters were suddenly on the alert as they recognized Officer Lawler entering the morgue with two visitors. One was a heavy-faced woman about forty years of age, wearing a green and black striped dress with a black woolen shawl. The other was a refined-looking young woman of twenty or twenty-five, tastefully dressed in black cashmere, with a Paisley shawl and a fashionable black ostrich feather hat.

After speaking to the keeper, the young woman asked to see Coroner J. B. Jones, who had arrived for the postmortem. Stating that she was a friend of Douglas's who had known him in better days, she requested that his body be given up to her after the inquest. When the coroner said arrangements had been made to deliver both bodies to Long Island College Hospital for dissection, she begged that this not be done. Jones said he would have to know her connection with the dead man in order to establish her claim. The

woman then stated she was his wife. He had left her two
years ago. They had one child, a six-year-old boy, she said,
adding that she had not known of Douglas's bad antecedents
when she married him.

After the conference with the coroner, both women were led
to view the body of Mosher. The younger descended with the
keeper into the lower vault to look at Douglas. She returned
with a wild look. To a New York *Times* reporter she said that
she recognized both men, but that she knew nothing more, or
would rather not be asked to say anything further. She shiv-
ered in the cold of the place. When she was brought into the
keeper's office to warm herself at the stove, she manifested
such symptoms of uneasiness that her companion was soon
forced to lead her away.

Half an hour later a tall thin woman entered the building
alone. She inquired if two ladies had recently visited the
morgue. She suspected she knew who they were, she said,
because a neighbor told her two women had come by the house
on Monday while she was absent, planning to take her with
them to Bay Ridge. Hearing a description of the earlier
visitors, she established their identity.

"The younger woman was Mary Douglas, at least she went
by that name, and he said she was his sister. She is not his
sister, and she is not his wife. That's all I need to say. I knew
Douglas when I was a child. He was about my age, twenty-
nine years. Douglas used to live with Mary in Columbia
Street.

"The older woman, the person who was dressed in black, is
forty years of age and is Gilbert Mosher's wife. She and all
their connections are bad and I don't want to see them."

To reporters who inquired as to the woman's own identity,
she replied: "I am the sister-in-law of William Mosher. I am
the wife of Alfred Mosher, the youngest brother of the Mosher
family. We have five children. I have not seen William for

the last six years, for the reason that our family has not been on good terms with him. My husband knew of the disreputable course of life which he was leading and would not, therefore, recognize him in any way, shape, or form. He would not permit him to come to the house, as he did not wish to give cognizance to his discreditable career.''

Asked if she had any idea where the missing boy might be hidden, the woman said neither she nor her husband believed Bill Mosher to have been the abductor:

''In early life he was a decent fellow and as smart as there is in the country. The Moshers were born in New York, but their father and mother hailed from Little Neck, Long Island. The Mosher boys were boatbuilders by trade. Some years ago William was keeping an oyster saloon on Grand Street and would have got along there had he only been let alone by some parties. But he lost a child while there and business troubles beset him sorely.

''He could not have stolen anybody's child, as he was far too fond of his own offspring and of my first child to do such a thing as that, no matter what his faults may have been in other respects. He wouldn't harm a child, though he might kill a man. He was as good a man as walked the earth, but stealing was his fault, and everybody has his faults. William Mosher seldom or never drank liquor, never smoked or used profane or obscene language. He never had a fault but the one of wishing to acquire sudden riches, and he had a beautiful education. I have reason to think William provided his wife with plenty of money, but she was able to let all she could get slip through her hands as fast as she took it. That, I believe, is what hurried him into looking for money by some quicker way than the law allows. If some of those persons who have had so much to say about him would put their hand over their mouths, they would perhaps find more nearer home than they have had to say about him.''

After this defense of her family, the woman asked to see the bodies and demanded first to see Douglas. Returning to the ground floor, her glance fell on the face of the dead Mosher and she drew back with a shudder.

"This is a mournful visit indeed for me. Though we did not recognize him living for years, now that he is dead it is but right to pay some attention to the remains," she said. "I wish my husband had come with me but he does not want to know anything about it. He says he is almost glad William is out of the world, but he is sorry for the way he left it." Shivering from the cold, she made her way to the door and pushed through the crowd gathered outside waiting to enter.

For more than an hour the frustrated throng was forced to wait while Dr. A. W. Shepherd entered the vault to make a postmortem. He found that death had come to Mosher from a bullet which entered the left shoulder blade and passed through the heart. Douglas had died of bleeding. His abdomen was completely perforated with gunshot, the main wound above the navel extending over four and one-half inches.

As visitors continued to pour into the morgue on Wednesday afternoon, reporters saw a genteel young woman of about twenty-five, heavily veiled, enter the building. Excitement spread as it was learned that she was Martha Mosher, come by appointment to see the body of her dead husband. Accompanying her was a tall thin man with a black moustache.

Mrs. Mosher was pale and greatly excited as she went to the slab on which her husband's body rested. When the cover was removed from the dead man's face, she uttered a piercing scream and dropped to her knees at his side, imprinting kiss after kiss upon his brow.

The agony of the grief-stricken wife moved the attendants, who were daily witnesses to similar scenes. The poor woman was led away from the body with difficulty and taken to the office of the keeper. The man with her declared he was the dead man's elder brother, Gil Mosher, and that he would answer for her. He asked that the body be turned over to an undertaker named J. H. Munn, who would handle all arrangements for the funeral scheduled for Friday.

After regaining her composure, Mrs. Mosher granted an interview to a reporter from the New York *Herald*. She said she had first met her future husband when he came to visit his mother, who lived in the same house as her family. Although she was only fifteen at the time and he a little past forty, they had fallen deeply in love. When Mosher proposed marriage, her father asked her to wait a year before making a decision. She promised to do so, but when Mosher continued to pursue her, she gave in, marrying him at the Methodist Church on Willett Street. Her father thereafter stopped speaking to her.

William Mosher had worked at boatbuilding and at making bird cages. While he was industrious and attentive, he was subject to fits of melancholy when things went bad. They had six children, two of whom had died. She had only learned late in the marriage that her husband was a thief. Although she was now penniless, she still loved him.

"He was always kind and attentive to me, caring for me and his children first of all things, and whatever people may say of him and his life, I can't complain," she stated.

"He was a man who had no taste for amusement like other men. He never mixed in politics, or racing, or dogs, or the theaters, or anything that way. I don't think he ever belonged to a club in his life. He spent all the time he could with his children and me, and when he was at home it was the children all the time.

"He was one of the kindest-hearted men you could meet, and that is one reason that makes the present charge against him so extraordinary. I don't think he would hurt a dog. If he saw one in the street with a sore leg, he would take it up in his arms and carry it to some place where no one could injure it. When he came into the house, if he heard a child crying, whether it was his own or somebody else's, he would take it up and try to please it. He was very fond of children and thought the world of his own.''

While he was reticent about his business, Martha Mosher continued, her husband conversed freely with her on many other subjects. He was fond of reading, and though not a man who could write well or spell correctly, he was well informed, especially on mechanical facts. He delighted in explaining scientific matters, such as the law of gravity, to his wife.

Although he had read the Bible through and through and could argue and discuss it with experts, he did not think much of religion and was fond of comparing parsons to mechanics, saying the better they preached the more they got.

His only close companion during the years of their marriage was Douglas, whom he met, she believed, when the two were both at Sing Sing. Douglas, sent up for a robbery, had been in prison for some time before his mother, a very respectable woman, heard of it. The mother went to visit him and shortly after died of grief.

Mosher had been sent to Sing Sing with a five-year sentence for a crime of assault and battery he had committed before their marriage. Martha Mosher visited him regularly in prison and tried to get him pardoned. She went to see the man he had robbed and saw the governor three times. She visited the judge who sentenced him, the district attorney, and all the people who had come in contact with him in prison.

''He was the best-conducted, hardest-working man in the prison and earned the good opinion of all the people connected with it,'' she declared proudly.

She had finally drawn up a petition and even induced the

governor's daughters to sign it. These efforts brought about her husband's pardon.

"Yes, we were always poor, and if he was a bad man he never made much of it," she said of her later life with Mosher.

She repeated that her husband as she knew him was the last person one would expect to interfere with another man's child. Yet from what she now knew, it was apparent that he was one of those involved in the Ross abduction.

"Have you any idea where the child might be?" the reporter asked.

"I do not," Martha Mosher said with great feeling. "I would willingly give one of mine to restore Mrs. Ross her child, if that would do it."

After this lengthy talk, Mrs. Mosher prepared to leave. Gil Mosher asked her to go on ahead, saying he wanted to take a last look at his brother. He appeared deeply moved when he saw the face of William Mosher and came thoughtfully back to the keeper's room. There he was questioned by the *Herald* reporter and provided a footnote to the interview with Martha Mosher.

"She is a good woman, no better," he declared of his sister-in-law. "A kind mother and as true a wife as ever a man had. But she's not so innocent of Bill Mosher's doings as she pretends. That woman would do all Bill Mosher told her. Yes, and a lot of things he didn't tell her, to please him. She was all bound up in him from first to last. And she thought of nothing else in the world but him.

"She was always with him and never left him if she could help it. If he was in a boat and she could get to him, she'd be there. I don't think he did anything since he was married she didn't know about. Why, when he was up the river she was out there all the time. The keepers couldn't keep her out. She slept there at night when they would allow her."

"Do you think the missing boy will be found?" the reporter asked.

"Yes, I'm sure of it," Old Gil said emphatically. "I haven't the slightest doubt in the matter. Maybe Martha Mosher will find him, too. If she doesn't know where the child is, she knows those that do know."

Taking his leave, the eldest of the Mosher clan had a last word for the newspapermen: "You come to me when the boy is discovered and I'll tell you such a history as never was written. Take you a week to write it."

Throughout the week the crowds came to view the dead men. If other relatives appeared the reporters were not aware of it. At week's end they spoke to John Munn, the undertaker for Mosher, who had also been asked by Mary Douglas to inter the younger of the two abductors. Having received a permit to remove the bodies, Munn said that he would incur Douglas's burial expenses without thought of future remuneration. He had known Douglas in his young, innocent days, and Mrs. Munn had been present at his birth. Mary Douglas, who was now living with her mother, had tried without success to reform Joseph, who was much attached to her.

Munn knew very little of Mosher's family, who had promised him payment for his services on behalf of Bill Mosher.

On Friday afternoon, December 18, reporters watched Munn supervise the final services accorded the dead men. The shattered bodies were placed in caskets of imitation rosewood, ornamented on the lid and sides with silver-plated mountings. The one bore the inscription JOSEPH DOUGLAS, DIED DECEMBER 14, 1874, IN HIS 29TH YEAR; the other WILLIAM M. MOSHER, DIED DECEMBER 14, 1874, IN HIS 53RD YEAR.

A coarse blanket was put over the coffins, which were lifted into the undertaker's wagon and driven to Cypress Hills Cemetery in East New York. The bodies of the abductors of little Charley Ross were quietly interred. Present was a small assembly of family and friends, a modest testimonial to the fact that despite their errant ways the abductors of little Charley Ross did not go to their graves unmourned.

40

"HERE FOR THE INSTANCE were two notorious rogues in this city, whose faces were intimately known to the police, and there was twenty thousand dollars on their heads. Yet the police could not find them. Will this do? And the rogues were not lying hid either. They were active enough to organize a burglary on such a scale that a sloop entered into their combination." So ran a New York *Herald* editorial in the week after the Bay Ridge shooting. What were the police doing to find the missing boy? Were they bungling again?

In point of fact the optimism which had earlier welled up was rapidly turning to despair. It was increasingly apparent that the death of the criminals had removed the most likely path to the missing boy. Little Charley had not been set loose upon the street, as many hoped and expected he would be. Westervelt's clues had come to naught, along with Martha Mosher's.

It was theorized that Mosher had probably not told his wife who had the boy in charge. He had possibly not told even his accomplices. On one occasion a number of years ago when Douglas had been arrested, he had betrayed several of his comrades in order to obtain immunity for himself. Knowing of this, Mosher would certainly have hesitated to take him into his confidence. Police officers felt it was not unlikely that Mosher had put the boy in the hands of illiterate people who were in complete ignorance of the case.

Was the boy still alive? The question kept recurring in the minds of the authorities and the anxious public. Had the killing at Bay Ridge been the signal for his "instant annihilation," as the abductors had warned in their correspondence?

"I tell you what my candid opinion is," a respected police veteran told New York reporters. "If the boy is not forthcoming during the next ten days or so, we'll have to look for him up the river."

This gloomy forecast seemed to have been realized near the end of the week following the shooting. "The boy is dead," Superintendent Walling declared on Thursday, December 19. "I go to establish the fact, recover the body, and so put a sorrowful end to the suspense of the afflicted parents and the public, who so deeply sympathize with them."

Walling told reporters he had learned of an elderly woman who had known Mosher well. It was she who had set him up in the oyster saloon he had once run on Grand Street. This woman had recently disappeared from her residence in the city and had been trailed to New Britain, Connecticut. On arriving there she had had in her company a little boy exactly resembling little Charley Ross. Now the boy was suddenly and mysteriously dead and the woman's movements increasingly suspicious.

A day later Walling stated that his estimate of little Charley's death had been premature. He had gone to New Britain and found that the woman in question was living in dread of a visit from city officials. She was the owner of a tumbledown tenement which was in violation of city health requirements. This was the reason she refused to answer the door, expecting that her visitors might be officers with a summons.

On learning the purpose of Walling's visit, she had brought him a photo of the dead child, who he saw was not the missing boy. It was her niece's child, and he had died of membranous croup while attended by the leading physician of the town. The superintendent was able to verify these facts before returning to New York.

Another rumor of little Charley's death spread after the recovery of a drowned child's body from Newark Bay near Bayonne. When the corpse was examined, it was learned that the unknown boy was only twenty months old.

Superintendent Walling was constantly sending out detectives in all directions to investigate the reports and information of a varied character which he received. The sailboat used by the abductors was found to have been stolen from Samuel Wilmot, of Bridgeport, Connecticut, on September 29. Curiously enough, it had been made by Mosher himself. Some years earlier he had committed a crime and spent time in the local jail, where one of his assigned tasks was the building of two small sailboats. He named one of them the *Jail Bird*. It was later bought by Wilmot, who now claimed it only to learn that Mary Douglas viewed it as her property.

A report from Van Fleet's stables in Newark, New Jersey, intimated that the abductors' horse had finally turned up. Police investigated and learned that a well-dressed young man had brought in an animal which was in poor condition, with burrs knotting its mane and tail, and asked that it be held temporarily. When the young man did not return, a livery employee told police that certain characteristics of the horse showed it might be the one involved in the Ross abduction. Little Walter and one of his uncles made the journey to Newark. Walter immediately noted a spot of white some distance above the fetlock of the hind leg, a mark he had reported on the abductors' horse. There was also a white star on the forehead. When the animal turned its head, the underlip dropped and exposed the teeth in a gesture Walter had earlier described. "Look, didn't I tell you he laughed," he shouted, clapping his hands.

It was generally felt the identification was satisfactory, but the young man who brought in the horse was never traced, nor did the wagon turn up. An apparent clue again led nowhere.

After many months of searching, little Charley's hat, which in their letter of September 6 the kidnappers said had been lost in Trenton on the night of July 2, was finally found. Bit by bit the jigsaw mystery was clearing up.

Two days before Christmas one more piece fell into place when William McKean came to New York and spent long hours in the questioning of William Westervelt. It was McKean's distinct impression that the informer was evading questions and not telling the whole truth. He accused him of withholding facts and said that if he continued in the same manner the blood of Charley Ross would be on his hands. "God forbid!" cried Westervelt, jumping to his feet.

Further prodding elicited new information. Westervelt had always maintained that he knew of no extant sample of Mosher's handwriting. Now he remembered that in June, when he was with the Moshers in Philadelphia, Mosher had sent a letter to a Mrs. Murdock, who tended a lighthouse in Rondout, New York. Under an alias he had written to ask for a small sum due, giving Westervelt's New York address as his own. He had told Westervelt, who was broke, that on receipt he could keep the money. When Westervelt returned to New York the next day, he took the letter along and his wife had posted it on June 26.

Walling immediately sent Westervelt and Detective William Titus to Rondout. The two men returned a day later with the letter, to which Mrs. Murdock had never replied. The sprawling writing was easily identified. Beyond all doubt, Mosher had written the anonymous letters to Ross. Another piece had been found to fill out the puzzle. Only the key element in the case, the boy, was still missing.

Reports of youngsters who resembled the missing child

continued to turn up. Each investigation revealed a new case of mistaken identity. Seeing that current efforts to locate their Charley were failing, Mrs. Ross's brothers decided to try a new device. In the past, no reward had been offered for the restoration of the missing boy which was not conditional upon the arrest of the abductors. With their death, circumstances had changed radically. The Lewises reasoned that the people who had the child in charge might now be induced to give him up if they were promised a reward and told they need not explain how he had come into their possession. Accordingly, during Christmas week of 1874 the following advertisement appeared in newspapers of all the principal cities of the United States:

$5,000 REWARD

Five thousand dollars reward will be paid for the return,

WITHIN TEN DAYS

From this date, to any one of the addresses named below, of my son,

CHARLES BREWSTER ROSS,

Aged four years and seven months, who was taken from Germantown, July 1st, 1874.

Being entirely satisfied that his abductors were killed at Bay Ridge, L.I., on the 14th inst., I now offer the above sum for his return, or for information which shall lead thereto, promising to ask no questions.

CHRISTIAN K. ROSS

There was something curiously pathetic in this appeal. To George L. Harrison, Ross wrote a letter that conveyed his frame of mind:

My dear friend:

You have no doubt heard of the severe sickness through which I have passed, broken down both in body and mind, but through the kind Providence of God and the skill of my physician, with kind attentions of my family, I am raised up again. As soon as I gained strength enough by the pressure of my physicians as well as that of my family, I came here to my native village, where live my mother and two sisters, as well as my brother-in-law who is a physician. . . . I believe it was a good change for me, as I am much improved, but with the news of the last few days am anxious and awaiting to hear the result of this singular and inexplicable mystery.

Providence, or what I like better, God, seems to have foiled the efforts of man in the search for my little boy, but her own way lifted up the cloud which hung so heavily over us and brought to justice the perpetrators of the great crime committed not only against us, but against our whole nation, and while they have been called hastily into his presence, my heart says let the dead sleep.

My anxiety now centers itself on the one object. It is hard to remain here in quietness away from the excitement, but I believe it is the best and now anxiously await the telegram announcing that the end has come. No one but God knows, the suspense is terrible, but God, I know, can and will support me until I know how my dear little boy has been disposed of.

Please excuse the length of this letter, but I write with much nervousness and am unable just now to concentrate my thoughts.

Yours truly,
Christian K. Ross

"Charley Ross must be home for Christmas," said the Brooklyn *Daily Eagle*. "Then will the festival of Christianity and civilization be brighter in every American home than it ever was before. In the spirit of the season, rosemary will then be strewn on the kidnappers' graves for remembrance."

On December 25 the city church bells rang out, but there was no celebration in the Ross household. The first act of the drama of little Charley Ross had played itself out in Philadelphia, and in New York the second had ended with blighted hopes. A third and final act was about to begin.

Book Three

Book Three

41

As the new year 1875 dawned, the search for little Charley Ross continued unabated. The death of Mosher and Douglas had raised public hopes to wild heights. Newspaper readers waited in suspense for word that the little boy was found. When the five-thousand-dollar reward offer, which was limited to ten days, expired on January 2 with no result other than extortionist letters and misleading responses in personal columns, private citizens and authorities redoubled their efforts to find the boy.

Superintendent Walling requested the New York *Times* and other dailies to print descriptions of the abductors' horse and buggy. Because of the horse found in the Newark stable, New Jersey papers in particular were requested to comply.

Walling continued to conduct interviews with William Westervelt, Old Gil Mosher, and Mrs. William Mosher. At the Westervelt meetings, William McKean of the Philadelphia citizens' committee took an increasingly active role, often making the trip from Philadelphia to be present.

"It is confidently asserted by those who claim to know a great deal about the private history of the case that both Gil Mosher, the dead burglar's brother, and Westervelt, his brother-in-law, know where Charley Ross can be found, but have thus far been proof against every inducement that has been offered them to reveal the secret. They claim to know nothing, but it is believed that they are only playing fast and loose with the police and when the latter have dropped the case will at once open negotiations with the parents for the child,'' editorialized the New York *Times*.

In Philadelphia the police department, Pinkerton, the citizens' committee, and private individuals renewed the search for the missing boy. Near the end of January, Mayor Stokley supervised the preparation of a revised circular, which he ordered sent to justices of the peace in all towns and villages of Connecticut, Rhode Island, New Jersey, Long Island, and in New York counties bordering on the Hudson River. It was also sent to every Methodist minister in those areas and to Catholic clergymen in sections where that faith was dominant. Each recipient, most particularly clergymen whose duties included visits to secluded parts of the countryside, was requested to read it aloud to his congregation.

A photograph of little Charley occupied the upper margin of the circulars, which carried a full account of the abduction and a description of the missing boy with indications of how his appearance might have been altered. All clues provided by the anonymous letters were related, with the warning that they were derived entirely from the kidnappers' correspondence and might be wholly inaccurate.

''The object of this communication,'' the mayor's circular concluded, ''is to ask you personally to interest yourself in the search for the missing child, and to induce, if possible, the constables connected with your office to examine thoroughly all secluded places, caves, cabins, suspicious houses, vessels, canal boats, and any other localities in your jurisdiction where it might be possible to conceal a child.''

As the all-pervasive search continued, scores of boys continued to turn up. The state was rare indeed which did not wire Philadelphia or New York that it had found little Charley Ross. Resemblances were sometimes remote, sometimes striking, but the mystery of the boy's disappearance remained unsolved.

The wide publicity given the case led to an examination of Pennsylvania's laws on kidnapping. Current statutes defined the offense as a misdemeanor and provided punishment universally considered to be inadequate — a maximum of seven years' imprisonment and a thousand-dollar fine. Since no case of child-stealing for the object of extorting a large sum of money had ever occurred in the United States, such an act appeared never to have been anticipated.

A supplement was now added to previous legislation, making the crime a felony and imposing more severe penalties. For the abduction and concealment of any child under ten years of age, with intent to extort money, a fine not exceeding ten thousand dollars was to be imposed, with the criminal undergoing imprisonment by separate and solitary confinement for a period not to exceed twenty-five years. For accomplices not involved in the abduction, but found guilty of concealing, harboring, or detaining such a child, the fine was not to exceed five thousand dollars and imprisonment in solitary confinement was not to exceed fifteen years.

The law was passed unanimously by both branches of the state legislature and approved by the governor on February 25, 1875. In a special provision designed to encourage the restoration of little Charley to his home, it was stated that the present legislation would not apply to the detention or concealment of any child taken or carried away before the passage of the current act, where the person or persons now harboring or concealing the child surrendered it up to the nearest magistrate within thirty days, this immunity to expire officially on March 25, 1875.

The new law was publicized in newspapers of the principal cities of Pennsylvania, New York, and New Jersey, and copied by nearly every paper throughout the Middle and Eastern states. Christian Ross added a clause to its proclamation in which he declared he was satisfied that the two men killed at

Bay Ridge were the actual kidnappers. To the promised immunity from punishment he therefore offered the added inducement of a reward, "whatever sum is required, up to $5000, for expenses or otherwise in bringing about his restoration."

Every incentive had been offered for the recovery of the lost boy, and hope for his return was once again cautiously voiced. As the days passed, however, with still no Charley, the benumbed father was almost ready to abandon all hope of ever seeing him again. The continued concealment he considered "even more savagely wicked than the original crime itself."

Determined to leave no avenue unexplored, Ross told William McKean and Superintendent Walling that he would like to see Westervelt. He knew that the two men were having troubled second thoughts about the informer. At meetings Westervelt always maintained he knew of no messages going back and forth between Bill Mosher and his wife, nor was there, he said, any communication between Mosher and himself. His only contact had been Douglas. McKean continued to be skeptical. On one occasion he asked Westervelt to bring Mrs. Mosher to his suite at the Fifth Avenue Hotel.

The following day Westervelt escorted his sister to McKean's ground floor rooms near the 24th Street entrance. McKean asked him to wait outside. In a long intense interview with Martha Mosher, McKean elicited one telling piece of information. She remembered an instance where her husband had sent her fifty dollars through Ike Morris as intermediary. She was staying with the Westervelts at the time and her brother William had been there when Morris brought the money.

McKean dismissed Mrs. Mosher and asked Westervelt into his suite. Confronted with the evidence supplied by his sister, he said that he did, in fact, recall the day of Morris's arrival with fifty dollars. It had been absent from his consciousness until now. He could remember no other such interchanges between Mosher and his wife, or Mosher and himself.

Several days later McKean again made the trip from Philadelphia to New York to see Westervelt. The meeting lasted more than five hours, during which Westervelt corrected or altered several statements he had previously made. At one point McKean heatedly said that he suspected the informer of wearing goods stolen by the dead burglars. Westervelt admitted his studs were a gift from Douglas, but vehemently denied any knowledge that they had been stolen.

As McKean continued his driving interrogation, Westervelt broke down as he had so many times before and suddenly produced new information. He said he had seen Mosher and Douglas on several occasions other than those already known.

The two men had come to his house about August 13 or 14. He remembered the date because at the time he was actively seeking reinstatement to the police force. After they arrived he left to see his lawyer and learned that counsel fees would amount to fifty dollars if he wished to pursue the matter. Since he did not have the money, he returned home.

In the afternoon he mentioned to Mosher that Old Gil had come by several times inquiring for him. Clearly upset by this news, Mosher suggested that they go have a look at "the old bugger." When they arrived at the shipyard where Old Gil worked, Bill backed out. He waited for Douglas and Westervelt to bring his brother to a nearby saloon, where, he said, he could better face him.

Westervelt learned from a shipyard employee that Gil had not been at work for several days, but that he had been seen in the street with Officer Doyle. He conveyed this information to Mosher. All three men next went to a saloon at the corner of Allen and Houston. Douglas left to go over to Madame

Morrow's across the street and returned ten minutes later to report that Old Gil had been there and asked if Mrs. Morris had any letters or handwriting of Bill's.

An irate Bill Mosher hurried across the street. He returned a short time later with tears streaming down his face, voicing threats of what he would do to "the old bugger" if he saw him.

Back at Westervelt's house, Mosher started writing a letter to his brother, but was in such a nervous state that he could not control the pen. He had therefore dictated the note to Westervelt, saying that he did not understand what Gil wanted, and in any event had no time or money to spend on him.

Westervelt took the dictated note to Gil's wife and read it to her. Liz told him she thought the two brothers were together. Westervelt told her no, but did not reveal Bill Mosher's whereabouts. Liz then mentioned that detectives had come to her house inquiring about stolen silks. Taking Westervelt into a back room, she asked him in a confidential tone if she could trust him. If so, she knew a way they could "make a stake," she declared, and said that Bill Mosher and Douglas were suspected of being the abductors of little Charley Ross. She added that she had seen the boy's parents as well as Superintendent Walling. While Westervelt was there, Captain Hedden had come in. He had spoken briefly to Liz and departed, after which Westervelt also left, taking the letter with him.

When Westervelt returned home, he told Mosher and Douglas what Liz had said. In a fury, Bill Mosher tore up the letter he had dictated. Denying any part in the abduction, he said Gil and Liz were "trying to put up a job" on himself and Douglas.

His wife was about ready to leave Philadelphia and come back to New York, he told Westervelt. Would he help her prepare for the journey? When Westervelt agreed, having nothing else to do, Mosher gave him money for the trip. He also asked him to find out from Mrs. Mosher in Philadelphia whether anyone had been at the house making inquiries about him. If so, Westervelt was to place a personal in the New York *Herald* that said, "Napoleon — I have seen them and they are not well." If no one had inquired, the personal was to read instead, "Napoleon — I have seen them and they are well."

That same evening Westervelt had made the trip, only to learn that his sister was not yet ready to move. Westervelt took a train back to New York without having placed either personal in the paper. After selling most of her furniture at auction, Martha Mosher came to New York with her children a week later and moved in with the Westervelts.

The informer went on to tell the gaping McKean that he had also seen both Mosher and Douglas in late September. They had invited him to accompany them on a trip to Rondout at their expense. Out of work and with nothing better to do, he had again accepted. On the twenty-second Westervelt had taken a boat to Poughkeepsie, where a fair was in progress. There he had met Mosher and Douglas. They had gone together across the river to Rondout, two miles distant, where they stopped at an auction store before going on to dinner at a saloon.

"How would you like to take a walk here in the dark, Bill?" Mosher asked during the meal. Westervelt knew that in the language of the underworld he was being invited to participate in a burglary. When he demurred, the proposed crime — the store to be robbed had already been chosen — was not carried out. Together the three went to a fisherman's hut near which Mosher and Douglas had anchored a small boat. After they showed it to Westervelt they all slept in the hut.

The following morning they went to Poughkeepsie, then back to New York by steamboat. In the city they stopped at Smith and McNeal's on Washington Street to eat before parting. The same day, Westervelt said to McKean, he told Superintendent Walling the two men were up the river in a boat. He had also told Walling that they liked to eat at Smith and McNeal's.

"Did you discuss the Ross case while you were there?" McKean asked.

"I accused them of it," Westervelt replied. "Mosher told me, 'You ought to know better than that. Don't you know it was a job for to get us on that Red Bank affair?'"

"Do you remember Mosher writing a letter or mailing it at Rondout?"

"I do not."

When the authorities in New York and Philadelphia evaluated the continuing series of disclosures coming from Westervelt, they came to the conclusion that the informer had been an accomplice in the case, perhaps not in the actual abduction, but certainly in the later phases which involved the harboring and concealment of the child.

On April 13, 1875, Superintendent Walling sent Detective Silleck to bring Westervelt to his office. The officer went to 79 Montgomery Street, where the Westervelts had taken an attic room in February. Mrs. Westervelt told Silleck that her husband was at work at the Adams Express Company, employment which Walling had secured for him a few days after their move to the new address.

When Westervelt was brought before him, the superintendent told him that Ross and the people in Philadelphia wanted to see him. Westervelt agreed to make the trip but said he had no money. Walling handed him ten dollars.

"It is too much. It don't take all that," Westervelt said.

"Never mind, you may want something to eat," Walling answered.

Several hours later William Westervelt journeyed to Philadelphia, expecting to take the 3:00 P.M. return train the following day so that he would miss only two days of work. It was to be many years, however, before he would look upon the New York skyline again.

42

IN PHILADELPHIA a bench warrant was issued for Westervelt's arrest. When he appeared at the Central Police Station saying that Superintendent Walling had sent him, Captain Heins took him into custody. Heins then summoned a group that included Christian Ross, Henry Lewis, Detective Wood, and Robert W. Leslie from the editorial staff of the *Public Ledger*. These men questioned Westervelt at length. Leslie, who had had some training at shorthand, took notes. When the interrogation was resumed the next day a professional stenographer attended.

After these two sessions, Westervelt was taken to Moyamensing Prison. Ross, who had been functioning again since mid-January in the search for his boy, visited the prisoner but could elicit no further information. Mrs. Ross also made the trip to the county prison. After begging Westervelt to reveal any knowledge he might have of her lost boy, she knelt with him in prayer. Westervelt appeared deeply moved but said no more than before.

In an interview with the Philadelphia *Times,* Ross spoke both of the recurrent rumors of little Charley's recovery and of Westervelt:

"If my boy had been found, you may rest assured that the

press of Philadelphia and the country would know of it immediately. I feel too grateful for the deep interest they have, in common with the general public, manifested in his welfare and recovery to keep the tidings, whether good or bad, from them for an instant. From the peculiar circumstances of the case Charley has almost become public property. I do not want to be worried with any more unjust censures on my conduct. I have had enough sorrow on that score and can hardly understand why persons should be so wicked as to impugn the motive of myself and family while we are laboring under such a heavy load of grief. In ten days or a week I expect that Westervelt will be brought up for trial and then his connection with the case may be thoroughly ventilated. Westervelt says my boy was alive when his brother-in-law Mosher was killed, and this part of his story I believe. But he has told so many different stories about his connection with the matter that it is difficult to know which to credit. I feel satisfied that he was one of the parties interested. Charley's mother has abiding faith that her boy is in the land of the living and will be recovered. It would be a relief to me to know of his fate — whether dead or alive. We are constantly receiving reports, all of which we follow up.''

Studying all the records and information in the case, Furman Sheppard, the recently elected district attorney of Philadelphia, felt there was sufficient evidence to bring Westervelt to trial. In the docket index of the Quarter Sessions Court he had a clerk place his name with the notation: ''Sur charge kidnapping and conspiracy — committed to answer.''

In a five-count bill of indictment, Sheppard accused the prisoner of: (1) the abduction of the boy Charles Brewster Ross; (2) harboring the child after abduction; (3) conspiring to abduct; (4) conspiring to extort money from the father of the boy; and (5) conspiring to deprive the boy of his full and free liberty.

During the summer months of 1875 the district attorney put off the case in the hope that further light might be shed on it. When no break developed, he proceeded.

On the morning of August 30 a police van with Westervelt as sole occupant drove into the Quarter Sessions courthouse yard. The never-ceasing interest which the city's people took in the sad case had drawn a large crowd to the scene. The prisoner surveyed them with haggard features as bailiffs led him into the hot humid courtroom. After four months in close confinement in Moyamemsing he looked like a strong man worn down by constraint, his grizzled black beard contrasting with the pallor of his skin. To the low murmur of the crowd, he took his place in the dock.

Moments later a sudden commotion swept the room as the prisoner's wife, a pleasant-faced little woman in a faded black dress, came into the room accompanied by six-year-old Peter, and Mamie, a girl of eight. Mrs. Westervelt ran to the dock and threw herself into her husband's arms, bursting into tears and kissing him affectionately. The prisoner showed much emotion and caressed his wife and children. They were given seats in front of the dock.

The New York police were not as yet represented in the court, but Philadelphia's Chief Jones and his detectives, including Captain Heins, were all on hand. The principals of Bay Ridge had taken their seats at an early hour, together with other witnesses.

Reporters and spectators noted each arrival, but otherwise attention centered on the area where Christian Ross sat with little Walter at his side. Lines traced the father's forehead, reflecting the cares he had undergone. His eyes made a profound impression. There was about them a darting, roving quality as of one always on the watch, searching, searching.

At his side Walter sat gazing at everything in childlike fashion. Many noted his resemblance to the missing Charley, great save that his fine light hair was straight, in contrast to his brother's flaxen curls. When his glance wandered over to the prisoner's children, he looked as though he might like to get down and play with them.

At ten o'clock, Judge Elcock presiding, the crier arose and addressed the prisoner: "You are charged in this bill of indictment with kidnapping and conspiring to conceal for the purpose of extorting money. How say you, guilty or not guilty?"

"Not guilty," the prisoner answered in a firm voice.

Once Westervelt was arraigned, the securing of a jury was begun and a panel obtained without much difficulty, twelve men drawn from various walks of life, including tradespeople, manufacturers, and one juror listed simply as "a gentleman." This business done, the court adjourned until one o'clock, at which time Assistant District Attorney Henry S. Hagert opened the case for the Commonwealth:

"In July 1874, the citizens of Philadelphia were startled at the intelligence that an atrocious crime had been committed in their midst, one which to the criminal annals of the city prior to that time had been unknown. The intelligence of that crime spread far and wide over the country. In the Far West, in the East, in the North, and South, in large cities, in small hamlets, by the wayside, this story was talked of and carried with it sympathy and regret. The community was aroused and every man and woman became, as it were, detectives. I need not say that that crime was the abduction of Charles Brewster Ross."

Hagert said he would try to show that Westervelt had put himself in communication with the police and professed a desire to assist them in the recovery of the child, but that actually he was from that time until the end almost every day in the company of the criminals, giving them information of their pursuers' movements. As his first witness, he called

Christian Ross to the stand. Clearly broken down by the ordeal he had undergone and was still undergoing, the father of the missing boy was asked to relate the circumstances of the kidnapping, old ground for most of those present but necessary to the prosecution's presentation. He concluded by saying that only yesterday he had gone to New York to look at another child purported to be his boy, and that prospects continued to turn up in all the states, as well as one recent case in Scotland and still another in Germany. He then returned to his seat.

Later in the day Walter was called to the stand. He related his involvement in the abduction and also described his trip to New York to identify the bodies of the abductors. Although he spoke in a clear straightforward manner, a burly court officer standing at his side repeated his answers in a booming voice. Since the court had no stenographer, there was a pause after every sentence until it had been transcribed in longhand. Despite the extreme late summer heat and this cumbersome system, spectators were touched by the simple poignancy of Walter's narrative.

The second day's proceedings included testimony by workmen at the Boutilliers', across from the Ross house, who had seen the abductors on Washington Lane. Mary Kidder, the neighbor down the lane, was called to relate what she had seen of the men and their horse and buggy.

Hagert, a tall sallow man with a full gray beard and a sharp penetrating eye, appeared unhurried and took elaborate notes as the witnesses spoke. A shrewd lawyer, he occasionally permitted himself a subdued smile. For the defense, Joseph T. Ford and I. Newton Brown availed themselves of every technicality to make frequent objections, which Judge Elcock in most cases good-humoredly overruled.

Irritated by the heat and the slowness of the activity, the New York *Herald* correspondent wrote that as yet nothing had been introduced to show Westervelt's connection with the crime. "The proceedings are conducted with a clumsiness and deliberation which astonish a New Yorker," he declared. "Were criminal trials in New York allowed to drag their weary length along at this rate about fifteen prisons of the size of the Tombs would be necessary to hold the prisoners awaiting trial."

In an attempt to enliven matters a *Herald* man in New York called on Mrs. William Mosher at home. Conveying the impression that he was a nephew of Ross, he gained entrance. Mrs. Mosher, dressed in mourning, was reluctant to talk, but the persistent caller drew her out. She declared that she had consulted with her lawyers and would not go to Philadelphia to testify at the trial of Westervelt. Asked about the Murdock letter, she expressed great doubt that her husband had written it.

"I don't believe it. It can't be true," she stated. "Don't you suppose my husband would have been smart enough not to have written a letter? It would be too strong a clue."

"Do you think the missing boy is still alive?"

"I am sure he is living and will turn up before long. I know he is. My husband would not harm a hair of his head. I . . . I mean if he had anything to do with it. I am as sure that he is living as I am that I breathe. I would not believe him dead unless I should see his dead body before me."

"Do you think Westervelt had anything to do with the kidnapping?"

"He knows nothing at all about the case. He was just the same as kidnapped himself from New York to go there. He can tell nothing."

As the questioning continued, Martha Mosher became convinced she was dealing with a reporter and ordered the man out of the house, slamming the door behind him.

Not to be outdone, the New York *Times* stated it had received information "upon undoubted authority," information gained by an officer of the law, that if Westervelt was convicted, the boy would be returned home. The prosecution had withheld much material for reasons of prudence. It was expected, said the *Times,* that Westervelt would soon tell where the boy was.

As the third day's proceedings of the Court of Quarter Sessions began, the jury began to show signs of fatigue. One of their number, unused to the confinement of the jury box, had been sick during the night and unable to partake of breakfast.

A new face, that of Old Gil Mosher, appeared among the interested spectators, drawing the attention of reporters and public alike. Captain Hedden also showed up for the first time. During the early morning testimony of Henry Peacock, Superintendent Walling of New York entered. When Mary Westervelt pointed out his arrival to her husband, the prisoner straightened up and smiled, bowing nervously to Walling as the superintendent walked by the dock.

Farmer Theodore Bergen was among the morning's witnesses, along with his brother George. They were followed by Albert Van Brunt, and by Constable Holland and Officer Moran, all testifying to the events in Bay Ridge. The Bergens stated that Frank Lewis had said their expenses in coming to Philadelphia would be paid for. They said they also expected to be paid for their time. Van Brunt said his expenses were to be paid by Lewis, but that he did not expect to be paid for his time.

During the noonday break, copies of the New York *Herald* containing the interview with Mrs. Mosher were much in evidence. Asked if he credited the account, Ross said he had several times talked to Mrs. Mosher and she had said many of the same things to him. Consequently it was probably accurate.

In the afternoon an unfamiliar face appeared on the scene.
The perspiring but absorbed spectators listened attentively as
a middle-aged married woman, Mrs. Catharine Lyons, was
sworn in. Under questioning from Hagert she said that in
March 1874 she had moved from 237 Monroe Street, Philadelphia, next door to 235, where she had occupied the fourth-
story garret. The Moshers, known to her by the name of
Henderson, occupied the ground floor at the time, and the
man called Clark had been in and out of the house. She had
last seen Bill Mosher in the house in the middle of July.
Asked whether she had seen Westervelt, she replied:

"Yes, I saw him in the house a year ago last March. I saw
him about four or five times. He lived in that house until
about the latter part of March. I next saw him in July, about
the fifteenth. I saw him again later, on the Saturday before
his sister left for New York on the nineteenth of August."

At the end of Mrs. Lyons's testimony, Judge Elcock said
that due to the extreme heat and the illness of one juror he
would allow all the jurors to go to their homes for the night.
He cautioned them against holding conversations with anyone about the case, against reading the newspapers or doing
anything which might influence them to the slightest degree.

As the fourth day of proceedings began on Thursday, September 2, Hagert continued to conduct the case, while District
Attorney Sheppard observed and carefully took notes. After
the facts of the abduction had been established through Ross,
Walter, and other Philadelphia witnesses, the identity of the
child-stealers had been determined by the Bay Ridge farmers
and officials. Now Hagert and Sheppard appeared to be slowly
weaving a web around the prisoner, elaborating his relationship with the dead criminals.

In front of the prisoner's dock his children were quietly
playing, cutting paper dolls out of magazines and papers,
while Westervelt scribbled notes which he passed to his law-

yers. On the other side of the room, Walter alternated periods of listening with catnaps on his father's lap. The jurors, apparently refreshed by the night spent in their own homes and relieved by a drop in both the heat and the humidity, seemed in better spirits than on previous days.

In the morning the witness called was Robert W. Leslie of the *Ledger* editorial staff. Leslie recalled the meetings which had taken place the previous April 13 and 14, when Westervelt had been interrogated — with himself present to make notes — by Ross, Captain Heins, Detective Wood and Henry Lewis. Since Heins was somewhat deaf, many of the questions and answers had been repeated, giving Leslie ample time to make an adequate record.

The questioning of Westervelt had elicited responses which began with a biographical account of his life, telling of his economic plight, his dismissal from the police force, and his effort to improve himself by going to Philadelphia. It told of his visit to that city on June 25, when Mosher had shown him his horse and buggy. At a much later date, he had voluntarily informed Walling of this visit and of Douglas's and Mosher's having lived there, facts about which Superintendent Walling had not inquired. He swore he had not seen or heard of Mosher again until August 14.

Next he recounted the incidents of August 14, when he and Bill Mosher had tried to find Old Gil, and when he had written a letter dictated to him by Bill Mosher. This information he had communicated earlier in the year to William McKean when they had met in New York. He had also recounted the Rondout adventure to McKean. This he now repeated, stating that he had told Superintendent Walling the day after his return that the criminals might be taken at the Astoria Ferry.

In the latter part of October, Westervelt went on, he had met Mosher and Douglas in the street: "Douglas, Mosher and I went over towards Broadway, and I think it was on the corner of Bleecker Street and Broadway we went and had some oysters, and came out of there and walked to the river,'' read Leslie's transcribed notes. "I forget what streets we took. We went into a nigger church there somewhere along Bleecker. They were making a great time, and we went in and listened to them. I walked some more with them and then they left.''

It was on this occasion that Westervelt said he told Walling he thought the men lived up the river on a boat, because of hints they had dropped in their conversation and because in their walk they had tended in the direction of the river. He never asked them where they were going or where they lived because they were not the sort of men one could draw out in this fashion. The date of this walk he remembered as late October, and from that time until December 12 he had never seen or heard of them again.

Westervelt recounted again his last meeting with Mosher and Douglas, including the night spent at Vandyke's. He had intended to tell Walling of this, but had been delayed by news of the men's death. He had gone on his own to Bay Ridge and seen their bodies under the stoop at the Van Brunt house. This ended the transcription.

As the case went on the prosecution was marshaling evidence about Westervelt showing not so much his connection with the abduction as with a series of subsequent efforts at misleading the authorities. This became crystal-clear with the witness who opened the fifth day of proceedings on Friday, September 3. New York's superintendent of police was called to the stand before a jammed courtroom. All seats were taken. A goodly number of ladies, members of the Radical Society, occupied places in the female section. Several sober-faced divines were seen interspersed with the members of the bar.

The gruff-appearing but genial Walling testified that he had seen Westervelt more than twenty times, sometimes at his home, sometimes at his office. His interpretation of their relationship amounted to an accusation of guilt. On each occasion of their meeting he had asked the informer whether he had seen Mosher and Douglas, he related, and Westervelt had always denied having seen them, except once in early November.

Walling said that Westervelt never told him that he had met Douglas and Mosher on August 14. He said Westervelt never mentioned their coming to his house. He denied that Westervelt told him anything of the Rondout trip. He said Westervelt never mentioned Stromberg's tavern to him until questioned about it. He said Westervelt did not tell him of Morris's bringing fifty dollars to Mrs. Mosher. He said Westervelt did not tell him of walking with Douglas and Mosher to an oyster house at Bleecker and Broadway. He said the informant did not tell him when Mosher's wife moved in with Mrs. Morris. He said Westervelt told him nothing, until a detective brought him in, of Vandyke's or of a new appointment arranged with Douglas for the New England House later in the week of December 13.

Walling stated in unequivocal terms that he had at one point told Westervelt he was willing to take Douglas without Mosher. Yet Westervelt had never given him information leading to that result. All the information was either received too late, or must have been designed to mislead him.

The prosecution drew from Walling the following geographical information. From Allen and Houston streets it was less than a quarter of a mile to the nearest police station. Stromberg's saloon was only a quarter of a mile from the Sixth Precinct police station. Two station houses, the Second and the Sixth, were within a quarter of a mile of the Fulton Market. Vandyke's Hotel was no more than a quarter of a mile from the Fourth. The Fifteenth Precinct was not over four hundred yards from Bleecker and Broadway. Second

Street and Bowery was two blocks from a station house, as was Prince and Broadway.

At all these locations and others the informer had been with the abductors, said the prosecution. If Westervelt had been sincere in trying to apprehend Douglas and Mosher, it would have been an easy matter for him to do so.

Cross-examination of the superintendent did not shake him in his testimony, but it did reveal remarkable aspects of his mode of operation. Defense Attorney Brown began by inquiring whether Walling had asked the informant at the first interview where Mosher and Douglas had lived.

"I did not ask him at that time," the superintendent answered. "I did not ask him when he told me either. I did not ask him at any interview where they had lived."

"Then the first information the police authorities had of the residence in Philadelphia of these two men, and of the name under which they went in Philadelphia, and of the horse and wagon they had here were communicated to you by Westervelt long before the killing?"

"That is correct."

Turning to another matter, the defense attorney asked Walling whether he at any time had had positive knowledge of the whereabouts of Mosher and Douglas.

"The first that I learned was on the ninth of October that there was a place in New York City where they and Mr. Westervelt had met. That is the first and only place I learned to satisfy my mind on."

"Did you make any arrests then? If not, why not?"

"Because Mr. Westervelt saw the two men I had watching him and accused me of having him watched. I denied placing them there for that purpose. That was the place I watched for them until he accused me of watching for him."

"Why did you withdraw the watch?"

"Because I concluded they would not come."

"He was under police surveillance all the time?"

"No, sir, not all the time. At intervals he was, when I sent persons to see if he was at work."

"You found him at work?"

"Yes, sir. Sometimes and sometimes not. He worked whenever he had work. His was an extra car, not a regular. He was not at work several days."

"Why did you stop watching his house?"

"I withdrew the watch because I knew it was no use. Westervelt told me that they knew his house was watched and they wouldn't come there."

As the questioning continued Walling admitted that he was using various other means to locate the two abductors at this time, relying on Westervelt more for information which would lead to the child. The superintendent maintained, however, that after long debate he had told Westervelt he wanted Douglas.

"Did you know that men of this kind always travel in pairs?"

"No, sir. From my information I was of a contrary belief. From what Westervelt told me, all the information he got was from Douglas, and that he came around, but that we would have to wait, as Bill did not come around, and would not show up."

"Did Westervelt offer to turn in Douglas?"

"Yes, but I was afraid his arrest would frighten off Mosher."

"Do you not in New York have 'still' prisoners, such as Westervelt, who lay in jail in Philadelphia from April 13 to the trial opening without arraignment?"

"We used to have, but no more. We must take a man before a court if in session, to a magistrate if not. On taking him before a magistrate, notice of his arrest would be published. I recollect holding a prisoner twenty-four hours not long ago without sending him before a magistrate, and I was heavily fined for it.''

In an attempt to show that the defendant had actually been more than cooperative and had voluntarily offered valuable information to the police, Defense Attorney Brown asked Walling about the interview in which Westervelt had told him he suspected the men of being up the river in a boat.

"Did you ask him how he knew they were on the river in a boat?"

"I did not. However, I think he told me he had seen them somewhere in a boat."

"Did you ask when he had seen them?"

"I do not recollect asking him that."

"Do you mean to tell me that as the chief of the New York police force you did not ask the man when he had seen them?"

"No, sir. I do not recollect asking when he had seen them."

"You wanted to know?"

"Yes, sir, I did. I hired a little steam launch to learn if they were in the North or East River or around the bay near Staten Island."

"You did not ask him before starting the expedition where he had seen them?"

"I did not think it worthwhile. It was after they had gone away. It might have been two months, and even if it was a week he did not know where they were then."

As for Mrs. Westervelt, the defense attorney continued, he understood the superintendent had given her a letter to some parties to help her get work. Had Walling visited her?

"I did not."

"You knew where she lived?"

"I did not."

"You knew the condition she was in?"

"She said she was very badly off."

This exchange ended the cool, methodical questioning of

the executive head of New York's twenty-five hundred police-men. At its conclusion Superintendent Walling, who so often signed his letters "Yours in haste," hurried back to New York. The defense had tried to show that Westervelt had given much valuable information to Walling, indeed much more than had been asked for. The prosecution now countered with two witnesses whose testimony it hoped would produce a contrary impression.

At the Friday afternoon session of the court, Charles H. Stromberg was sworn in. In response to questions from the prosecutor, he stated that he owned a business at 74 Mott Street in New York, a drinking saloon. He had known Wes-tervelt about three years. In 1874 between mid-June and mid-October Westervelt had come in almost every day, except for several brief periods. Unemployed, he often arrived early in the day and was an unofficial helper about the place. Dur-ing the period indicated, Stromberg testified he had seen the prisoner five or six times with Mosher and Douglas.

On one occasion Westervelt had given him a letter to give to either Mosher or Douglas should they come in. When they did not, he returned the letter to Westervelt three days later. Westervelt himself had not appeared during this time. He said he had been on a clambake up the river.

In late September, Stromberg continued under questioning, he had encountered Westervelt on Christy Street one morning at about 2:00 A.M. He had said to Stromberg, "I can tell you confidentially that I can make from ten to fifteen thousand dollars, but by doing so I would have to give somebody away, which would send them to state prison for ten, fifteen, twenty years, or for life."

Stromberg saw the three men together for the last time in October. As usual, Westervelt arrived first. Mosher and Douglas took a drink, spoke to Westervelt, and left after about ten minutes.

Under cross-examination Stromberg revealed that Ross had paid his fare to Philadelphia and that he expected the state to pay for his time.

Officer Richard King of the New York detective squad followed Stromberg to the stand for the prosecution. King testified that he knew Mosher but not Douglas. He had seen Westervelt in January 1875 and told him that had he been on the case, he would have known how to capture the criminals. "How?" Westervelt had asked. "I would have placed a watch on your house," King had replied. "Then you would have got us," Westervelt had told him. On cross-examination, King repeated that he had not served on the Ross case, and that Superintendent Walling had not been aware that he knew Mosher. The use of the damaging word "us" by Westervelt was the key element in King's testimony.

Captain Hedden, in charge of a sixty-five-man New York detective squad, was sworn in and detailed his knowledge of the case, covering familiar ground. The matter of surveillance of Westervelt again came up.

"Were any of your men detailed to watch houses or him during that summer?" the witness was asked.

"Yes."

"How long a time?"

"I can't give the date. He was not watched, but his neighborhood. His house was watched by the policeman of the neighborhood. I don't know how it was. I did not give special orders how it was to be watched."

After a weekend respite, the trial of William Westervelt resumed on Monday, September 6, with the testimony of prosecution witness William Titus, a New York City detective. Titus was twenty-eight, and prior to joining the force had been a plumber and in the gas-fitting business. He had accompanied Westervelt to Rondout on December 24 to retrieve the letter Mosher had written to Mrs. Murdock. He had taken dinner with Westervelt, who said he could have gotten Mosher and Douglas and restored Charley Ross had he been re-appointed to the police force. Since he was not reinstated, why let somebody else take credit for it. Titus asked him whether on Westervelt's Rondout excursion with Mosher and Douglas little Charley had been there. "No, he was not with us at that time," Westervelt had told him. The prosecution asked the witness to repeat this last quotation, which he did.

After Titus left the stand, Gil Mosher was sworn in. His testimony added no new information on the case, and his presence was used by the prosecution principally to verify that the handwriting on the anonymous letters was that of his brother William.

The prosecution next called on Henry McDowell, who said that he owned a store in Germantown at Harris and Hancock streets. In late July or early August, he testified, the prisoner had come into his store and asked for a drink of water. He had spoken of Charley Ross's abduction from the area and showed great sympathy for the father, asking whether it was true he was failing in business. McDowell had told him he knew nothing about it but believed it was so. Westervelt had then asked whether Ross's brother-in-law was a rich man. McDowell had told him he thought so. After a half hour of conversation Westervelt left the store, having bought nothing.

The seventh day of proceedings brought Sarah Kerr, the missing boy's nurse, to the witness stand, to be followed by Officer James Moran of the New York police force, and William Heins, Philadelphia's captain of detectives. Joseph Lewis was also called. Each related his involvement in the case, reinforcing testimony by previous prosecution witnesses but adding nothing new of substance.

The key witness of Wednesday, September 8, was William McKean, manager and editor of the *Public Ledger* and close to the case since its beginning. McKean had recently been ill and spoke softly in a halting voice. He related his involvement with the citizens' committee and gave an account of his talks in New York with Westervelt.

On Thursday the prosecution played its trump card. It called to the stand a pleasant-faced, plump woman of about forty, Mrs. Lucretia Peers of Brooklyn. The witness was tastefully dressed in black, a pink bow at the throat, a blush rose in her hat. Her graying hair was brushed back tightly from a high forehead. From time to time she used a fan to cool herself. When she answered questions, Mrs. Peers appeared perfectly sure of her statements, closing her mouth decisively after every accusing sentence.

The substance of her testimony related to events of July 6, 1874. On that date she had taken a horsecar at City Hall, Brooklyn, to go uptown. Opposite her in the car sat a man and a child of about four with light curly hair and brown eyes wearing a brown linen suit and no hat.

"The child was crying," she told the hushed court. "The man never spoke to the child but once. He turned to it and said, 'Hush, hush!' The child seemed frightened of him and screamed. The man said, 'Go see Mama. Go see Mama.' The child stopped screaming then and the man took crackers out of his pocket and gave them to the child. The child ate the crackers and was quiet. When we came to North Fourth Street he left the car, carrying the child in his arms."

Mrs. Peers had continued on to the Williamsburg section of Brooklyn, but when she returned home she told her three children and husband about the incident. Later when she read about the abduction of little Charley Ross, she went to talk to Superintendent Walling.

"Was this the child in the car?" Mrs. Peers was asked, the prosecuting attorney handing her a photo of little Charley Ross.

"It is a good likeness," she declared.

"Is the man you saw with the child in this room today?"

Mrs. Peers unhesitatingly pointed a finger at the man in the prisoner's dock. "That is the man," she declared as spectators craned their necks. So loud was the commotion at her identification that Judge Elcock was forced to rap his gavel for order. In the dock William Westervelt had leaned forward for her answer, and when it came he appeared bewildered and stricken. With a look of anguish he buried his face in his hands.

"When did you next see the prisoner?" Hagert asked Mrs. Peers.

"I next saw the prisoner in June last in Moyamemsing Prison in this city. I went there at my own suggestion. I was shown to his cell and I gave him some tracts. I did not try to lead him to suppose that I was a philanthropist. I do not know what he thought. I said I would visit his family if he desired, and he said he wished me to do so. He gave me their address in New York. I went to see them and gave his wife periodicals and tracts."

Under cross-examination Mrs. Peers admitted that she had not actually seen a photo of little Charley Ross until Christmas of 1874, when Walling showed one to her at police headquarters. This was five months after the horsecar incident with the crying child.

After her visit to the prison in June 1875, she stated, she had informed Superintendent Walling that Westervelt was the man she had seen the previous July. She also said she had been to Walling's office about six times, always at her own instance.

Defense Counsel Brown tried to shake the witness's certainty of her identification of both the child and the prisoner, pointing out that Westervelt's appearance had greatly altered since he was in prison. Whereas he had worn only a mustache on the July date in question, his face became covered with a

dark beard in the period following his incarceration. Arguing
that identification under these circumstances was valueless,
the counsel for the defense said he himself was asserted to
look like a prominent politician, but that happily it was not
so, for the other man was notably bowlegged and he was not.
Laughter broke the tension of the courtroom, but when asked
to go over her earlier testimony, Mrs. Peers remained firm in
every statement she had made.

The day had provided the greatest excitement of the trial
to date. The presence of Westervelt in Brooklyn on July 6
in the company of a child could obviously be damning if
accepted. After the court had adjourned its morning session,
reporters spoke to Mrs. Westervelt about the witness. The
prisoner's wife declared that Mrs. Peers was a "crazy
woman." Superintendent Walling had long ago told her of
Mrs. Peers's frequent, unsolicited visits to his office, describing her as "crazy on this subject of Charley Ross." The
startling testimony was in the record, however, and at the
afternoon session of the court the prosecution put the last link
into its chain of evidence surrounding the prisoner.

Henry Hartman, the young bartender at Stromberg's saloon, was called to the stand. Describing himself as an intimate friend of Westervelt's, Hartman told how he had been
dismissed from the New York police force at the same time
as the prisoner and for the same reason. From July through
October of 1874 he had shared living quarters with Stromberg
in exchange for helping out as bartender in the saloon. Early
in July, Westervelt had brought two men into the tavern, in-
troducing one as Smith and the other as Anderson or Henderson. Smith, he had declared, was his brother-in-law, just
come to town from Philadelphia. Several days later Hartman
had seen Westervelt in the tavern talking to the younger of
the two men.

On one occasion, Hartman related, while reading a news-

paper account of the Ross abduction, Westervelt had remarked that he would bet two shillings he could tell who
stole the boy. This had been in early July. Later Westervelt
had told Hartman of a trip he had made up the Hudson.

"He was absent two days," the bartender testified. "I saw
him upon his return. He said that he was with Mosher and
Douglas. He told me they were up the river. He did not say
where on the river.

"Westervelt told me one morning, or evening rather, to let
him know whenever I saw a chalk mark over the cellar door
at No. 74 Mott Street, and that that was a signal that these
parties were in town, that he knew where to find them then.
This conversation was in the latter part of September or October 1874.

"I saw Westervelt next morning after the killing. I mean
Monday morning I went to Brooklyn with him. I had a
conversation with him on that trip about Charley Ross. He
told me that these two were the parties; also that if they
were arrested the child would not live three days. I asked him
then if he knew where it was, whether it was in a hut or cave
or somewhere. He said he'd never tell. He said that Mosher
had the child up the river somewhere, where he did not
know."

Hartman concluded his testimony by saying that while he
had been told in early July that Mosher and Douglas had
something to do with the abduction, he had done nothing
about it because he had been doubtful of their actual involvement in the case.

Late in the afternoon of September 9, Attorney Hagert
read to the jury the anonymous letters received by Ross and
had them entered in the record, this being the first time the
actual text of these documents had been made public. The
cold-blooded assurance of the correspondents had a powerful
effect on the courtroom. At the conclusion of the two-hour

reading the prosecution rested its case and the court adjourned.

On Friday the trial went into its tenth day with the beginning of the case for the defense. Counsel Brown announced that he would bring forth few witnesses, and at one time had contemplated using only the prisoner himself.

Three figures now made extremely brief appearances. A woman who gave her name as Kate Morgan stated that for a time in the summer of 1874 she had lived in the rear of 235 Monroe Street, Philadelphia. During the month of July she stated she had seen Henderson and Clark at the house, but not Westervelt. She had seen Westervelt on a Saturday morning in August just before Mrs. Henderson had left for New York. Mrs. Annie McElroy testified that she had also lived in the rear of 235 Monroe, but had not seen Westervelt at the house in July. Mrs. Mary O'Leary stated she had lived at 233 Monroe Street, and had not seen the defendant during the month of July.

The use of these three witnesses was an attempt to counter the damaging testimony of the prosecution witnesses who had reported seeing Westervelt in Philadelphia in July; to prove that Westervelt was not in Philadelphia on the date of the abduction or shortly after. To counter the even more dangerous testimony of Mrs. Peers, who said she had seen Westervelt in Brooklyn with a child on July 6, the defense called Mrs. Westervelt to the stand.

She raised her right hand and was sworn in. Reporters and spectators saw in her finely featured face a beauty which had been muted by care. So sympathetic was the impression she made that her appearance later led to the raising of a subscription fund for her and her two children.

After giving an account of her early married life, Mrs. Westervelt arrived at the crucial time surrounding the abduction. While in Philadelphia, she declared, her husband and

Mosher had not been companions. They had talked at the house, but never went anywhere together. Her husband at this time was a domestic man, spending most of his time at home.

As to his appearance, he had no hair on his face in 1874 except for a mustache. He had worn a little chin whisker some years earlier, what they called an imperial, but he had long ago shaved it off. So drastically had his appearance changed since she had last seen him in New York in April that on first entering the courtroom she had scarcely recognized him.

In June 1874, she testified, she and her children had sometimes lacked many of the necessities of life. During most of the month her husband had been at home, save for a trip to Philadelphia around June 25. He had returned to New York a day or two later, June 29, she recalled, the date being fixed in her mind because Westervelt had asked her what she was going to do about the next month's rent. She had suggested taking a brooch and pawning it, and had done so. When the money was not enough she had also pawned a small pocket watch, getting seven dollars for the pair.

Her husband, having no job, spent the first three days of July at home, Mrs. Westervelt went on. Sometimes he got up at two or three in the morning in order to be first in line for work at the Washington Market, but nothing had turned up. On the Fourth of July he tended bar at a picnic and returned home late in the evening with five dollars. During the day Mrs. Westervelt had been forced to confiscate forty cents her children had saved up to celebrate the holiday. She used the money to buy food. On July 5 her husband went off on another picnic, bringing home five dollars and a leftover ham. On July 6, tired from the previous day's work, he slept late and stayed home all day. It was her birthday. In the evening he played the harmonica, as was his custom. The rest of the month he was at home.

In August her husband went to Philadelphia for a brief
stay and brought his sister and her children back to stay with
them. He had not warned her of their arrival. Mrs. Westervelt had spent several weeks with Mrs. Mosher in 1873, and
thought her unexpected guests would make a similar stopover
this time. Although Mrs. Westervelt let her know she was
overstaying her leave, Mrs. Mosher continued on and even
went with the Westervelts in the summer to 363 Madison
Street. Not until late in the year did she finally go, moving in
with Mrs. Morris at 184 Houston Street. Two of her children
went with her, but two remained behind.

On the Saturday night before Mosher and Douglas were
killed, Mrs. Mosher asked Mrs. Westervelt to bring these two
to her new home, which she did. Then Mrs. Mosher said that
she was not yet ready for them, and the children went back
with Mrs. Westervelt to her house. This so annoyed her that
when Westervelt did not come home during the night, she did
not even ask where he had been. It was the only night, apart
from the Philadelphia trip of mid-August, that her husband
had not slept at home. A day later she learned he had spent
the night with Douglas. She was unaware during this time
that Mosher and Douglas had any connection with the Ross
case.

From December 12 to April 1875 she knew nothing of note
that had occurred in her family. When Westervelt left her on
April 13, the only money in the house was three dollars. She
had not seen her husband again until she saw him in court,
to which she had come voluntarily. Until Westervelt had gone
to Philadelphia, she had not known that he was in any way
suspected of complicity in the Ross abduction, nor did she
know that he was assisting Superintendent Walling until
Walling himself told her on April 18.

Cross-examination of Mrs. Westervelt occupied the court on
September 13, the eleventh day of the trial. On Tuesday, Sep-

tember 14, the defendant himself was called to the stand, which he then occupied for four days.

Spectators had been gathering for his appearance since dawn. When the doors of the courthouse opened, the first in line rushed in pell-mell, filling every available seat and clogging passageways. Many more were forced to wait outside. Women were in heavy attendance.

The questioning by the defense counsel had barely begun when it became apparent that the prisoner's line was to be firm and unswerving. His position was that he had co-operated in good faith with the New York police in an effort to apprehend the abductors and restore the child. He denied every charge against him save one — while he gave all his knowledge of the abduction and of Mosher and Douglas to Walling, he neglected to tell him they had come to his house after his sister's arrival from Philadelphia.

Of the period between June 25 and July 6, his version of his whereabouts coincided with his wife's. On July 6, his wife's birthday, he remembered having locked her up in the front room, merely for a joke. "This is your birthday and I'll give you twenty-seven slaps," he had told her.

"I was not in Brooklyn on the sixth day of July," he testified. "I didn't take a horsecar at the City Hall, Brooklyn, that day nor any other day. The only time I rode in a car with a child that age was in 1870 with my own little girl. The first time I saw Mrs. Peers was when she visited me in Moyamemsing Prison in June 1875."

Westervelt denied most emphatically that he was in Philadelphia in July of 1874. He declared that he had never been in Germantown in his life and did not so much as know the way to go there. Of testimony by McDowell, the grocer who had testified that he had come into his store and asked about Ross's wealth, Westervelt spoke unequivocally:

"It is as false as false can be. I never saw the man until I saw him on the witness stand."

As for Superintendent Walling, he had seen him on more than fifty occasions before the shooting at Bay Ridge. It was not true, as Walling had testified, that he had always denied having seen Mosher except on November 1. He had in fact told the superintendent on five different occasions before November 1 that he had seen Mosher and Douglas. During this period, Westervelt maintained, he had no reliable information that Mosher and Douglas were the abductors except from Walling. Ike Morris had laughingly suggested it at one time, and Gil Mosher's wife Liz had said they were suspected, but Westervelt had placed little faith in the word of either.

Questioned about Stromberg's saloon, Westervelt said, "I was in the habit of visiting there for want of a better place, I suppose. I was not working. I had no other place to go." He denied having conversed with Stromberg on Christy Street and saying he could make a stake of ten to twenty thousand dollars by turning someone in. Stromberg, Westervelt related, had had a quarrel with a stepbrother about the running of the saloon. Westervelt had testified in the case and Stromberg had told him he'd get even.

Westervelt denied seeing Henry Hartman on the Monday after the Bay Ridge killing. He had gone with Hartman on Wednesday or Thursday to check on Mosher's burial arrangements, at his sister's request. He denied telling Hartman that the child would not live three days if the men were arrested. "I will never tell," which Hartman quoted him as saying in answer to a question regarding the missing child, was a common byword at the time, but Westervelt did not remember using it. After the killing he had questioned his sister and given every scrap of information he had to Walling.

As Westervelt neared the end of his testimony he denied

incriminating statements of William McKean and those purportedly given by him on April 13 and 14 to McKean, Ross, Wood, and others. He denied ever having the conversation reported by Officer Titus. He said that the statements made by Officer King were the result of a misunderstanding — both witnesses had quoted Westervelt as using the pronoun "us" in situations which implicated him in the abduction. After the defense counsel elicited the information that Westervelt had never before been charged with a crime, he was asked the question which caused a hush to fall over the courtroom.

"William, under the solemn obligations which you have already taken, can you now furnish or could you at any time have furnished any clue to the facts connected with the abduction or place of abode of the child Charles Brewster Ross?"

"No, sir," Westervelt answered. "I wish to God I could." The words concluded his testimony on Friday, September 17, the fifteenth day of the trial.

Late in the day, District Attorney Furman Sheppard began his summation. He opened by asking the jury to take the acts of Westervelt and compare them with the acts of the conspirators. "If they tend to the same result," he said, "the jury will then have to infer from these facts if there was a conspiracy."

Walter's evidence, he stated, was sharp, discriminating, and clear, as was that of the father. The identity of the anonymous letter writers had been established. He recalled Mrs. Lyons's testimony, which brought Westervelt to Philadelphia on July 14 or 15 of 1874, and the testimony of McDowell, the Germantown grocer with whom Westervelt had conversed about Ross's finances.

Sheppard asked the jury to consider Westervelt's action in the instance where he had requested bartender Hartman to tell him when he saw chalk marks on the cellar door of Stromberg's saloon, saying this was a signal that Mosher and Douglas were in town. At this time, a letter to Ross from New Haven showed the conspirators were not in New York, a fact Westervelt obviously knew.

Westervelt had told Hartman that if either Mosher or Douglas were arrested the child would not live three days, that Mosher had the child somewhere up the river. The anonymous letters at this stage conveyed the same information. Where would Westervelt have got it except from Mosher and Douglas?

Mrs. Peers had testified to riding four miles in Brooklyn opposite Westervelt on the fifth day after the abduction. He had been with a child whose demeanor showed they were not father and son. The child had worn a linen suit and no hat. The abductors' letters indicated that on the night of July 2, passing through Trenton, little Charley's hat had fallen off. The boy's nurse had also told of his wearing a linen suit.

In trying to discredit Mrs. Westervelt's testimony, the district attorney said that it had obviously been given in order to locate Westervelt on the days immediately following the abduction. "Her object was to keep this man, who lounged in a saloon and had no work, at home for a week," Sheppard declared. While the wife's testimony was remarkably detailed for this period, especially for July 6, the day when Mrs. Peers had testified to seeing Westervelt in Brooklyn, for the prior period it was markedly sparse.

Mrs. Westervelt was either grossly deceived by her husband or lying, the prosecuting attorney continued. She professed not to know that he was constantly seeing Mosher and Douglas, or that he was acting with the police. She had not even known until considerably later that he had spent the night of December 12 with Douglas. Was Westervelt acting in good faith, doing the honest thing? If so, why deceive his wife? Why not tell her he was acting with the police? If on the other hand he was being dishonest, it was easy to see why he was deceiving her.

Westervelt knew that the police wanted a sample of Bill Mosher's handwriting. Why then had he written a letter which Mosher had dictated to him? Was it not a blatant attempt to foil the law? In all seriousness, was it possible to believe that a cool experienced criminal like Mosher would be too nervous to write his own letter?

Westervelt admitted withholding from Walling the fact of his sister's return from Philadelphia plus the fact that Mosher and Douglas were at his house shortly after. Also, from August 18 to September 11 he failed to tell Walling where the men had lived in Philadelphia. By the latter date they had left, and it was safe to tell the authorities. For that matter, the district attorney asked, would Mosher have been asinine enough to show the horse and buggy to anyone but an accomplice?

In the case of the trip to Rondout, had not Westervelt thrown police off the track by giving false information? Had he not said that Mosher and Douglas were on a green boat when in fact it turned out at Bay Ridge to be black? He knew the authorities were searching high and low for Mosher's handwriting, yet he did not tell of the Rondout letter until after the killing.

Westervelt said the last time he saw Mosher was in early November. The "Saul of Tarsus" personal appeared on November 15. From the correspondence, it was to be noted that on November 6 the abductors wrote that "Saul of Tarsus" could be used as a new code for personals. Since Westervelt admitted having seen Mosher and Douglas that week, he would have been privy to the new name. Why else would his attention have been drawn to it? Why would he have copied it?

Moving toward the end of his summation, Sheppard stated

the defense had produced only five witnesses. Mary O'Leary, Kate Morgan, and Mrs. McElroy had been produced simply to state that to their knowledge Westervelt was not in Philadelphia in July, as prosecution witnesses had testified, but this did not mean this was so. Mrs. Westervelt had been brought to the stand simply to show that her husband was at home in New York on the days following the abduction, including July 6. Her account and Westervelt's own testimony must be regarded in the light of the close scrutiny the prosecution had given them. Was not Westervelt actually the power behind the plot? Did he not constantly give either too little information, or give it too late? Or give information that was misleading?

"His part in the business was to control the police while the other two kept up their batteries upon the distressed father. He deceived Walling and decoyed him off on false trails."

Westervelt's guilt, the prosecutor concluded, was as great as that of the two abductors shot to death at Bay Ridge. He asked the jury to find him guilty on all five counts of the indictment.

On Saturday, September 18, the courtroom was so jammed that officials were compelled to enter by a side door. As Attorney Ford began his summation for the defense, his voice was loud and forcible and his remarks were listened to with the strictest attention.

He began by saying that he sympathized deeply with the grief-stricken father, and asked forgiveness if the testimony had wounded him. However, the manner of the defendant's being lured to Philadelphia was itself an act of kidnapping, Ford declared. On arrival, Westervelt had been taken to a station house where there was no bed or blanket. Sent to the county prison at Moyamemsing, he had been held for long months before being brought to trial and during the interim

was denied even the privilege of seeing his wife. This treatment, Ford said, was unlawful and brutal.

William McKean and Superintendent Walling had earlier
accused Westervelt of having stolen goods on his person. Yet
he had come to Philadelphia, clear proof of his innocence.

As for the facts of the case itself, both the prisoner and his
wife had accounted for his whereabouts in the period surrounding the abduction, the dates being impressed upon them
by Mrs. Westervelt's pawning articles to get food and pay
the rent, by the anniversary of her birth, and other significant events.

As for the later period, the jurors should remember that
conspiracy is an agreement to do something in the future.
The prisoner could not justly be held for those parts of a
conspiracy which took place before he became involved.

In point of fact, Ford continued, Westervelt was never a
conspirator. From August 18, 1874, until April 13, 1875, he
was in Walling's confidence and gave him substantially all the
information he asked for. Certain facts were held back because of Westervelt's feeling that the police were interested
in the Red Bank affair, in which he knew Mosher was implicated. It must also be remembered that the prisoner did not
believe Mosher to be the abductor of little Charley Ross. Although he had his suspicions aroused several times, he continued to believe Mosher innocent until December 12 when he
heard Douglas's revelations at Vandyke's Hotel.

Where discrepancies occurred between the testimony of
Superintendent Walling and that of Westervelt, Ford stated
that the probabilities were in favor of the account given by
the prisoner. It was surely not Westervelt's fault if Walling
didn't use the information he gave him, often voluntarily.
Walling's and Heins's failure to arrest Mosher and Douglas
was not a blunder, but a crime, inexplicable unless the officers
were seeking the reward for themselves, therefore delib-

erately relegating Westervelt's efforts to the background.

The evidence against Westervelt was all circumstantial, Ford continued. Mrs. Peers had seen a little boy in a horsecar in July 1874. Not until Christmas of that year, more than five months later, did she even see a photo of little Charley Ross in Superintendent Walling's office. Could this identification be treated as evidence? Westervelt was so changed since July 6, 1874, that his own wife had hardly recognized him in court. Could Mrs. Peers's identification of him be regarded with anything other then skepticism?

Finally the defense turned to the grim night of December 13 at Bay Ridge. There Douglas, Mosher's daily companion, had breathed his last. In his dying moments he could not reveal the whereabouts of the missing boy. Was it not preposterous to think that Westervelt, on much less intimate terms with Mosher, would know where the boy was? If he had been a party to the kidnapping, why had Douglas not mentioned him?

"If I were not convinced William Westervelt is innocent and persecuted, I would have prayed to God that my tongue cleave to the roof of my mouth and my right arm wither away before I would have raised my voice in his behalf," Defense Attorney Ford concluded. "When the parents' prayers, upborne on angels' wings, ascend to the throne of the Highest, they will be accompanied by the orisons of Westervelt and his wife for the restoration of the child."

Briefly, District Attorney Sheppard rebutted. He said the defense had not adequately explained the connection of Westervelt with Mosher and Douglas. They had said the evidence he had introduced in this regard was circumstantial, but this was not so. In any event, circumstantial evidence could not be thrown away. It was, in fact, "irrefragable, the strongest that can be procured." Did not the existence of the Supreme Being derive from circumstantial evidence?

Ford had taken almost the entire day in summing up for the defense. By the time Sheppard finished his rebuttal, it was past six in the evening. Despite the late hour and the fact that it was Saturday, Judge Elcock decided to keep the court in session and began his charge to the jury. Westervelt, whose head had been bowed during most of the day, looked up. His two children also seemed to recognize that something important was about to occur and stopped their silent play around the dock and nestled close to their mother.

"The abduction, concealment, and detention of the son of Christian K. and Sarah Ann Ross has been widely regarded as the worst crime of the century," Judge Elcock began. "The assassin's knife has created no such widespread horror. It has made every father and mother in the land tremble lest the grasp of some fiend in human shape, following this successful example — for successful crimes are often repeated — should carry away to a fate worse than death one of the children of their hearts. The whole people are indignant at the weakness of police authority and this country confines not the anxious hearts looking for the return of little Charley Ross, for his wrongs have traveled the seas to far lands."

It was true, the judge said, that the testimony against the prisoner had been largely circumstantial and inferential: his association with Douglas and Mosher, knowing them to be thieves; his being in Philadelphia with them; their meeting after his sister's return from Philadelphia, about which he had made a false statement; his association with them after knowing they were the abductors. Yet truth and justice could be reached by circumstantial as well as by direct evidence: "A chain of circumstances, each link founded in truth and tested by the rules of law, has ever been regarded as the strongest kind of proof."

A key point was that Westervelt denied being in Philadelphia in late July or early August, testimony in which two prosecution witnesses contradicted him. He denied taking a Brooklyn streetcar ride where he had been identified.

On the other hand, his strongest defense was his own and his wife's testimony. "If there is an honest, manly doubt as to the prisoner's guilt, entertain this doubt," the judge concluded his charge. "But do not be influenced by weakness or sympathy either for him or his family, for this is no hour for sympathy."

As the jury went out, the prisoner watched them closely. Spectators remained as the evening wore on, and the gas lamps burned brightly in the courtroom. The slow-falling rain beat against the window.

At nine-thirty the foreman of the jury returned to ask if they could acquit on one or two counts and convict on the rest. Judge Elcock told him yes, but that the sentence in either case would be the same. The foreman returned to the other jurors. When they were still deadlocked at ten-thirty, the judge adjourned court, confining the jury to quarters.

On Monday morning, when the court reconvened, an overflow crowd of reporters and spectators was on hand. After the sober-faced jurors had filed in, their foreman declared they were ready to deliver a verdict. "How say you?" asked the judge. "Do you find William H. Westervelt guilty or not guilty?"

"Guilty on the third, fourth, and fifth counts, not guilty on the first and second counts," the foreman replied.

As the reporters rushed for the exit, the prisoner drew a long deep breath, leaned forward to gaze around the courtroom as if looking for a friend, and then buried his head in his hands and wept.

"In finding Westervelt guilty of conspiring to extort money from the Ross family, but not guilty of kidnapping, the jury went quite as far as the evidence, even by great stretching, would justify," the New York *Tribune* reported the next day.

"No event that has occurred for a long period in our criminal court has occasioned a more profound feeling of satisfaction in the community than the conviction of Westervelt," said the Philadelphia *Evening Star*.

"The result, we need scarcely write, accords with general public sentiment," declared the *Public Ledger*. "No one who has watched this trial can fail to have seen how the evidence has shown his complicity — if not in the actual process of abduction, in the subsequent concealment, attempted extortion, and schemes to thwart the officers of the law.

"Justice may be tempered with mercy, and mercy can only be invoked by a genuine effort for the child's production. The prisoner has no hope but this, and his duty to himself, as well as to the law and the afflicted family, whose woes have been so heavy, should lead to a full confession."

One of the jurors told reporters that on Saturday night nine had been for conviction on the whole bill, three for acquittal. On Sunday morning this had shifted to ten to two. The elder members had been stern for conviction, the three for acquittal being younger men. By Monday morning a compromise had been worked out which found the prisoner not guilty of actual participation in the abduction but guilty of being a conspirator after the fact. While the testimony of Mrs. Peers and several other witnesses had been largely discounted, the prisoner's own statement had been the strongest evidence considered in the verdict of guilty.

"I pity Westervelt from the bottom of my heart, and if I have done him a wrong, I am sorry for it," another juror said. "I sympathize with his wife and children, but then there is the evidence, and Mr. Ross and his child."

Ross was interviewed by the press and said that he had talked to Westervelt and promised to do what he could for a pardon if he gave any information on the child, dead or alive. He had given none.

On October 9, Judge Elcock had the prisoner brought before him for sentencing. He said that he had carefully considered the reasons filed in support of a new trial, but since they embraced only objections to rulings of the court, rulings which had been fully discussed during the trial, he refused the motion. He asked the prisoner to stand.

"William Westervelt," he began, "a jury of unusual intelligence and character has found you guilty with William Mosher and Joseph Douglas and others, of harboring, concealing and detaining the child Charles Brewster Ross for the purpose of extorting money, and of consummating the aforesaid crime in pursuance of said conspiracy. It is a verdict I would have joined in had I been a juror.

"I had hoped ere this I should have been appealed to for a light sentence by some merciful cry revealing something of the fate of Charley Ross, but I have heard not even a whisper.

"By the act of April 5, 1790, all crimes not capital, for which by law then in force, burning of the hand, cutting off the ears, nailing the ear or ears to the pillory, whipping and imprisonment for life were inflicted as punishment, were changed to punishment by solitary confinement at hard labor for a time not exceeding two years.

"By act of Assembly, April 17, 1807, punishment in these cases was extended to imprisonment not exceeding seven years. By Supreme Court decision, punishment for conspiracy cannot exceed that for successful perpetration of the same offense. You are therefore punishable under the act last cited.

"I hereby sentence you to pay a fine of one dollar plus costs of prosecution, and to imprisonment at solitary confinement at labor in the Eastern Penitentiary for seven years."

Having pronounced sentence, Judge Elcock ordered that the prisoner be taken away.

"Now the experience of the Ross kidnappers will necessarily have the effect of deterring other villains from undertaking so dangerous and fruitless a crime," said the New York *Times*. And indeed the coming years did show that Christian Ross's sacrifice was not in vain. Kidnapping for ransom did not recur in the United States for many decades. Ironically, a half-century after the Ross kidnapping, the perpetrators of a shocking kidnap murder told psychiatrists they had studied the Ross case and had modeled much of their strategy after that of William Mosher and Joseph Douglas. The young criminals were students of the University of Chicago. Their names were Nathan Leopold and Richard Loeb, the killers of fourteen-year-old Bobbie Franks.

43

"OF ALL MY EXPERIENCES while connected with the police, I recall no case which gave me greater solicitude than the abduction of Charley Ross," Superintendent Walling was to write some years later in his memoirs. "I freely confess that Westervelt's entrance into the case was unfortunate. I well knew his relationship to Mosher. 'Set a thief to catch a thief' may be a good method, but I am forced to say it failed utterly in this case. I thought, as did many with whom I consulted, that Westervelt could be induced, by a share of the reward, to inform where the child was. I do not think Westervelt knew where Charley Ross was, but that he took some part in the abduction I feel positive to this day."

When Westervelt entered Eastern Penitentiary without having uttered a word as to the missing boy's whereabouts, the public consensus coincided with the superintendent's view. Many now believed the child had been killed when the abductors were shot at Bay Ridge. Others expressed the view that Mosher drowned him when he was afraid the police were near. Still others felt he must surely have died of grief and privation.

Every sort of theory was put forth. Perhaps the boy had been adopted by a distant family and taught to forget his home and parents. Perhaps he had been disguised in appearance and trained to beg, as had so many of the boys who turned up in the long search. Perhaps he was in the hands of ignorant backwoods people who knew nothing of the case.

In 1876 Christian Ross was prevailed upon to recount the history of the abduction, a task he undertook with the hope that Charley might himself somewhere see the book with his photo and that of his brother Walter, or that someone else might see it who would help to unravel the mystery of his disappearance.

"A fixed calamity abates with time," he wrote. "The sorrow of suspense grows intenser. The terrible anguish caused by this long suspense, to which the knowledge of the child's death would be a relief, it is impossible to describe."

The investigations of boys reported to be his son had given him constant employment, he said. At a great expense of time and money he continued to pursue each thread, and clues still came from every state, from Europe and South America, and even from the furthermost parts of Asia, a total already adding up to many hundreds.

"The children of continents whisper of their little lost brother in their play. The successful abduction and continued concealment of the infant child has caused the name of Charley Ross to be known in every household," the father wrote. "His form, his pretty features, his curling locks, his winsome expression are familiar to all, and in a measure he has become the child of the people."

Ross quoted *Mothers' Magazine,* which said that revolutions, catastrophes, crimes, and disorders of great magnitude had been forgotten, yet while matters lately regarded as of prime importance were scarcely referred to, the fate of a little child continued to awaken an absorbing and universal anxiety.

"Yet we are hopeful, believing that Providence, who so strangely suffered the abductors to be taken away without a sign, will further vindicate His righteous government, and not permit us always to remain in ignorance of what has become of our dear little Charley," Ross concluded his work.

In reviewing the book, entitled *The Father's Story of Charley Ross, the Kidnapped Child, Potter's American Monthly* described it as free from cant and void of all sensation: "The book at once makes the matter better and worse than it lay in one's mind before reading it."

Calling the treatment of Westervelt a farce, the reviewer said the anonymous letters had given Ross the best idea advanced in the case, to get the boy at any cost and then to go after the criminals. The ransom should have been paid. Had this been done, the child could have been secured within twenty-four hours and the abductors probably caught within another twenty-four.

"The scoundrels who stole this child were not all and only bad from head to foot, and from inmost center to the outmost atmosphere of the soul," the review went on. "Judging from their letters, they had a latent sense of truth, even of tender regard for outraged parental affection. Had they attained their only object, money, they would surely have restored the child."

Noting the familiar photo of the stolen boy used to open the book, the writer said, "Charley's face is what we would call an ordinary face, save for the mouth, that supreme and most exquisite utterance of the individuality, the character, and the soul."

And in the conclusion an estimate was given of the boy's fate: "Parental hope has a perfect right and much reason, from the evidence in the case, for supposing that the child is still alive."

The Father's Story became a best seller, but Ross's arrangements with his publisher were such that he made little profit during the first year. Income from his business had ceased as preoccupation with the search for his missing boy came to absorb all his time. Constant traveling to identify boys further deflated the family finances.

In one effort to help the afflicted man, Governor Hartranft tendered him the position of master warden of the port of Philadelphia. This position carried with it a salary of $2500 per annum. Ross accepted it as an expression of sympathy from the people of his state.

From the governor and the executive council of Massachusetts came a request to deliver a public lecture giving the facts of the famous abduction. Ross accepted with a humble note:

I have received and read with pleasure your kind letter. Believe me, the sympathy expressed and the interest shown by you are most endearing to me and will if possible stimulate me to greater effort in the seemingly hopeless search for my missing child. I do most heartily appreciate your kind offer, but am no public speaker, and can only undertake simply to tell the story of the abduction, and the efforts that have been made to recover my lost son, from a father's standpoint, as the facts are deeply burned in my heart.

Ross gave two lectures at Boston's Tremont Temple, hoping that additional exposure of the facts in New England, where his book had not yet been distributed, might uncover some new clue to little Charley. Newspapers reported that while Ross was not a finished public orator, the poignant subject left both the audience and the speaker much affected, several times reducing them to tears. Funds received went into the search for the lost boy.

From the New York *Times* came a plea for every parent who sympathized with the father to contribute twenty-five cents to cover the pecuniary loss he had sustained. When Ross heard of the subscription fund, he wrote a letter to the paper. He had just regained complete control of his book, a fact to which he alluded in his letter:

While it is not unpleasant to me to know that you and those who have contributed to the fund desire thus to express their appreciation of the sacrifice I truly believe I have made for the public good, yet the proposition does not accord with my feelings. I would, however, suggest that the object may be realized in a way more agreeable to me by directing the attention of the public to the book written by myself. I long with great anxiety for an extended circulation of it, as an advertisement of the loss of my little son, and as an incentive to each sympathizing reader to render me more or less aid in my search, which can never cease except with my life.

The *Times* printed this unaffected and touching letter, asking its readers to cease their contributions to the subscription fund and to address themselves instead to Ross, sending $1.50 for each copy of *The Father's Story of Charley Ross*.

Another proposed solution to Ross's financial dilemma came in a telegram from Bridgeport, Connecticut. IF YOU WILL MEET ME AT MY HOME HERE BEFORE MONDAY I WILL PAY YOUR EXPENSES BOTH WAYS. I WILL PAY A LARGE REWARD, AND THINK I CAN GET CHARLEY, IF ALIVE, the dispatch read. It was signed P. T. BARNUM.

Ross knew of Barnum's shrewdness. He remembered, too, that the abductors' boat had been stolen from Bridgeport, Barnum's home. Thinking that perhaps the renowned show-man had information on the case, Ross made the trip. At the Bridgeport railroad depot, he was met by a carriage and taken to the Barnum residence, no longer the fabulous Oriental pavilion named Iranistan, which had burned to the ground, but the more modest, more refined Windermere.

"You know I am a showman. That is my business," Barnum began. "It occurred to me that if we could find Charley, I might use him in such a manner as to reimburse me and at the same time to bring back to you all that you have spent in searching for him. I am known to everybody in the country, even to the lowest criminal classes. I am willing to offer a reward. If by this means the boy is secured, I wish to exhibit him in order to recoup my expenditure."

When the father expressed shock at the proposal, Barnum continued: "Mr. Ross, consider which is worse, to permit Charley to grow up among outcasts and criminals such as now have him, if he is alive at all, or to bring him under your own control, where you can watch over him and care for him?"

Unwilling to leave any avenue unexplored that might lead to his boy, Ross returned to Philadelphia to consult with his wife and brothers. A decision was made to accept Barnum's offer with one provision — if the boy were found it should be discretionary with the family to reimburse Barnum rather than to place him on exhibition. Barnum accepted this condition. The following announcement was prepared and widely printed in newspapers across the country:

$10,000 REWARD FOR CHARLEY ROSS

I will pay $10,000 for the delivery to me alive of the kidnapped child Charley Ross or for information that will lead to his recovery. I most solemnly and sacredly pledge my word of honor and my reputation as an upright businessman not to attempt for myself to discover the identity of the persons negotiating with me in this matter, nor to convey to any other person any hints or clues on which any accusation, or even suspicion, shall be directed against them. The parents of the child unite with me in this pledge, and agree, if their darling child is by this means returned to them, to abandon all at-

tempts to punish any person connected with his abduction or concealment; they agree never to appear against such parties, and with
myself will use every endeavor to shield them from exposure. For
the last three years these parents have suffered more than death,
and now that Mosher and Douglas, the real abductors, are dead, it is
hoped that the persons who have the child in custody will be willing
to accept this reward and immunity. The reward shall be paid in
current money as soon as the child is identified by its parents. As
an added security to the persons bringing him a reasonable time shall
elapse between his delivery and the public announcement of the fact
so that the parties delivering him shall have every opportunity to
avoid discovery.

P. T. BARNUM, Bridgeport, Conn.

I sanction the above arrangement for myself and wife.

CHRISTIAN K. ROSS

Springfield, May 18, 1877

The meeting with Barnum was not Ross's first encounter
with the entertainment world. The father had previously
learned of a scattered population living in a highland area of
New Jersey and along the quiet shores of Raritan Bay. Many
of these people, he was told, had little communication with
their neighbors, their isolation being such that a child brought
there could easily be concealed over a long period. Since two
of the abductors' letters had been posted in nearby New
Brunswick, Ross determined to make a trip through the area.

In the company of detectives he visited many secluded hamlets as well as individual houses set back in the woods. At
Red Bank he called on the man whose store Mosher and
Douglas had robbed four years before. Several suspicious-
looking households nearby were also investigated, but no
meaningful clue was developed.

During the course of the trip Ross heard of a circus and
menagerie company that included among its exhibits a wax

figure of Charley Ross. One evening, after dining in the small town where the circus was performing, the father mingled with the crowd and entered a tent which had been divided into two parts. In the front compartment were the representatives of what was called "The Intemperate Family," while in the back five members of "The Ross Family" were on display. The figure supposed to be little Charley was dressed in a brown linen suit. The face was a poor likeness, lacking the missing boy's roundness of features. The boy stood next to a little girl designated as his eldest sister. Also in the group was Mrs. Ross, dressed in a green silk dress and displaying a sad countenance, and the father. The figure of the latter showed a clean-shaven man of about thirty-five with a florid complexion and a large dark mustache. It bore no resemblance at all to the actual man.

"The Ross Family," read the placard. "I will give to any one who will restore to me the lost child, Charley Ross, or who will give me any information which will lead to his recovery, the sum of $2000." The signature was that of the circus proprietor. Making his way through the crowd, most dense around the Ross exhibit, the father spoke to this man, introducing himself by the name of Robinson. He was told that many persons who would not ordinarily go to a circus had come to see the wax figure of little Charley. The Ross exhibit was the most profitable on the premises.

"Are the representations of the Ross family accurate?" the incognito father asked.

"They are excellent," replied the proprietor. "I know Mr. and Mrs. Ross very well and I assure you they are almost perfect likenesses."

Good-humoredly the father revealed his true identity. The circus owner pumped his hand, deeply honored by the meeting.

"Well, Mr. Ross, I'll tell you, but I would not care to have it known," he confessed. "We used to have a representation of an intemperate and of a temperate family in that van, separated by a partition. When we got the figure of Charley, we let the intemperate family stand, and changed the label of the other from 'The Temperate Family' to 'The Ross Family,' and put the figure of Charley in front as you see it. That's the way we arranged it.''

While touring in Canada, the proprietor said, he had encountered two tramps with a child. He allowed them to travel with his circus because he felt the child might turn out to be the missing boy. It had been a case of mistaken identity, but to Ross the gesture showed the man's interest and sympathy, and he expressed his thanks.

As he was leaving, the proprietor had a final word: "Now, Mr. Ross, when that boy is found, I want you to let me have him to exhibit. He will draw better than anything I can get. I'll give you a thousand dollars a week for him thirty weeks.''

Numerous other circuses, Ross learned, had wax figures of little Charley Ross. Whenever his travels took him near a traveling company, the father visited such exhibits. In each case he found the wax figures of his boy the center of attention. The likenesses were always very poor.

44

The most popular little boy in the United States would be Charley Ross if he were ever found. He was long ago adopted into the affections of the nation, just as the little maiden in the opera became the daughter of the regiment. For him, thousands of fathers have mourned and hundreds of tenderhearted mothers have wept. All parents have suffered a vicarious loss in losing him, so powerful is the sympathy which binds humanity together. If he should ever be found, there will be personal joy in innumerable households, and until that day a shadow, vague and dim, yet deeply felt, must rest unremoved upon the domestic life of America. Thus a personal misfortune has been exalted into a national grief.

As the decade of the 1870's wore on, editorials such as this continued to draw attention to the celebrated case. Each month brought new stories of boys found near and far, reputed to be the lost child. Bold type would announce the news dispatch and the following Sunday supplement would recap the case, for the sad little boy of Washington Lane had become a classic to the American press.

The proliferation of boys who kept turning up never ceased to astonish the tireless Christian Ross. Early in the case, railroads had offered him the free use of their facilities. Western Union had placed its wires at his disposal so that he might by judicious questioning determine the identity of far-off boys without embarking on wearying and fruitless journeys. So familiar were the operatives of the telegraph offices with the facts involved that often they would investigate a case announced by the Associated Press and resolve a young boy's identity before Ross had even heard of it.

When asking questions for identification, Ross always began with the color of the eyes. Many children had a light complexion and hair, but few had little Charley's brown eyes to go with them, since light flaxen hair usually accompanied blue or bluish-gray eyes. Descriptions relayed to the father were often unreliable. While women were more accurate than men, they too sometimes changed their minds about the description of the child they had seen, conforming to the published characteristics in their eagerness to establish the child they had found as the missing boy.

After determining the eye color, Ross tried to find out as nearly as he could the age of each boy and the circumstances in which he had been found. If there was reasonable doubt, specific questions relating to the family were dispatched by telegraph. If the matter had still not been resolved, an attempt was made to secure a photo. Where even this was shadowy, Ross or one of his family made a journey to see the boy.

Ross's attention was often called to little boys whose playmates called them Charley Ross. In each case it was found that the boy had the long flaxen curls and full round face of the missing child, leading his companions to call him by this name. Often these children were brought to police stations by well-meaning citizens who thought they had discovered the lost boy.

On one occasion two little children, a boy and a girl who had wandered from their Philadelphia homes at night, were taken by an officer to the police station. There the boy stated his name to be Charley Ross. The little girl, not to be outdone, also gave her name as Charley Ross.

Increasingly hallucinatory was the way many boys answered identification questions with remarkable accuracy. So widespread had been the publicity of the case, so penetrating the distribution of circulars recounting its particulars, that questions and answers and points of detail had been gradually memorized. The fanciful imaginations of childhood were stimulated by the case, and youngsters invented the wildest tales to account for their presence in strange places.

Typical was the tale of a boy found traveling alone on a New England train. To the conductor he gave his name as Charley Ross and said long ago he had come from Philadelphia. His mother's name was Annie and he had lived in a handsome big house. One day when he was playing in the lane two men had come and taken him away in a covered wagon. After traveling some distance, the men tied their horse to a shed and all of them had boarded a steamship. They had sailed off to England and stayed there awhile. The men had stolen some watches and also another boy. They had gone to India and Asia, then back to New York and from there to California, where the men had robbed a bank. Their names, the boy related, were Mosher and Douglas.

In St. Albans, Vermont, the excitement over this tale was intense. Townspeople gathered at the home where the boy was held, and many pronounced him to be the exact image of the lost child. Newpapermen came, and Philadelphia was contacted. As the hours went on, the boy found ever more outlandish stories with which to regale his avid listeners.

The following morning the sheriff was notified that his little charge's name was Jimmy Blanchard of Milford, New York, and that his parents had ordered him sent home by express. The boy had often run away from home and worked on the sympathies and credulities of people by spinning remarkable tales, including one in which he was Charley Ross.

Despite this news, the sheriff refused to release the boy from custody, stubbornly waiting for a member of the family to make the identification. One of Ross's brothers came and saw that the boy was not the lost Charley. Confronted with his deception, the boy burst into tears, still insisting that he was the missing child, that his name was not Blanchard, that his mother was Annie Ross.

Having printed every detail of the episode, the New York *Times* now retreated and said the whole business was a silly story which could not endure the light of facts. It would be an act of kindness on the part of the newspapers to give no more publicity to false stories of discoveries of the missing boy.

"It is beginning to be apparent that as one of the results of the Charley Ross excitement we are to have a multiplication of seven-year-old liars," said the New York *Tribune*. "Every few weeks a precocious humbug in pinafore is discovered in some out-of-the-way village, who sets the telegraph working and detectives running in half the cities of the United

States with a tale of adventure that ought not to impose itself even upon the habitual reader of dime novels.''

While Ross traveled far to see boys reputed to be his Charley, other hopeful pretenders to the name often made their way to Philadelphia. In one instance the residents of Quincy, Illinois, were so sure they had the lost boy in their midst that they contributed money to send him to the Quaker City. When he arrived at the railroad depot, his resemblance to little Charley was immediately noticed. Police hurried him to the house on Washington Lane, where so many other boys had presented themselves.

To Ross and his wife, the boy told a pitiful tale which was clearly true. He said he had been stolen from a good home, and beaten and taught to beg by his abductors. In Quincy he had run away and subsequently been sent to Philadelphia, not at his own suggestion but at the request of Quincy's residents.

"Do you think you are my mother?" the boy asked, looking up into Mrs. Ross's face.

"My little man," Mrs. Ross answered, holding back tears, "your story is very interesting, but you are not my son."

"I am sure of that myself," Ross said.

With his wife, he accompanied the boy and detectives to the Central Police Station. Arrangements were made to lodge him temporarily in the Wayfarers' Home until a permanent guardian could be found. The suffering of Ross and his family had once more found a counterpoint in the relief of a child.

On another occasion two prominent ladies of Philadelphia, visiting one of the city's orphanages, noted a little boy they felt bore a striking resemblance to the photos they had seen of little Charley. They secured the permission of the institution's director to take the boy for a day's outing. The ladies proceeded toward Washington Lane, and at the Ross house they told the boy to go play while they secreted themselves in the shrubbery near the front gate. They watched with rising hopes as the little lad hurried to the porch of the Ross house, where he saw Walter and entered into play with him in the easy way of children.

Mrs. Ross came down the stairs at this moment. When she looked out the window and saw what appeared to be the familiar silhouette of her lost boy, she raced outside to the porch. The boy turned and she saw that it was a stranger, a homeless child who had once before been brought to the attention of the family. When the women came up to join the group, they heard the sad news and took their young charge back to his orphanage.

As the decade of the 1870's neared its end, the father made one more of his many journeys to check on a distant clue. He returned, sorrowful and empty-handed, to learn from his wife that a Southern lady had written another in a set of kind, sympathizing letters. His wife had been too upset by the continuing strain to reply, but to this gentlewoman in Charleston, South Carolina, Ross now addressed a letter that told of the family's continuing travail:

Philadelphia, June 22, 1879

Dear Madam:

Your kind letter of 4th inst, with newspaper cutting reached me this A.M. Mrs. Ross also received a letter from you a few months ago, and I recollect her saying at the time that she would reply to it. She spoke of it as one of the kindest of the many letters written to her by strangers since the cruel abduction of our dear little boy. I suppose in consequence of the many cares incident to her family duties, as well as the subject being a very sore one to her, she deferred writing. For some weeks she has been quite ill, and now is very much prostrated.

It is truly wonderful how well she has borne up under this long continued trial. For nearly five years she has been in a constant state of suspense and expectancy, but her faith has never wavered that God in his mercy would either restore our dear boy or that some way would be opened by which we would learn what has been done with the child, but the continued strain and frequent disappointment have at last been too much for her physical strength, and her nervous system has become shattered. This last trip to North Carolina referred to in the cutting you sent seems to have discouraged her more than any for a long time, or possibly it was the last feather added to the previous burden that prostrated her. It seems she built great hopes of a favorable result from it, why I cannot say, as I told her before leaving that I regarded it as only a possible chance, but on my return, after telling her the result, she manifested more disappointment than I had noticed for a long time, and soon took to her bed with nervous prostration. I may say here that the newspaper report of my object in going to North Carolina is not correct. I did not go to see a child there, but to investigate a matter remotely connected in the place to which I went. The matter is still undergoing investigation, and I cannot tell what may be the final result.

Truly the ways of Providence are mysterious and past finding out, yet I do not despair but that I will yet get some light by which the mystery will be made plain. To this end I zealously look into every circumstance that I hear of that is either directly or remotely connected with the child's concealment, believing that while it is a privilege to pray for light and aid, yet it is also a duty to use every means at my disposal to find out the truth concerning this dark subject. It does seem to me that the parties who still persist in keeping from us the facts of the case are even more heartless than the abductors themselves.

Mrs. Ross and myself would both be only too glad to know that our dear Charley is safe in heaven than to be tortured by the dread that he remains in the charge of people who may lead him into a life of misery or of crime. While we have suffered beyond what any mortal can understand, yet we have the comfort to know that many a little fellow has been rescued from misery through the search for our Charley, and we believe the public have reaped largely the benefit of the sacrifice we made, for had I compounded the crime, I feel certain we would have had our son long since; but declining to do so, I have suffered and the public have been benefited, for I do not think a child will be taken soon again for a ransom. I have written you a long letter, much more so than I intended, but you will please excuse me; when I get on this subject I don't know when or where to stop.

With many thanks for your interest and with the hope that your prayers, added to those of so many others, may avail with the God whom we all worship and with the Saviour on whom we all depend.

I am, very truly yours,

CHRISTIAN K. ROSS

45

ON JANUARY 18, 1881, William Westervelt was released from Eastern Penitentiary in Philadelphia, an institution whose progressive practices had placed it on the itinerary of distinguished foreign visitors like Alexis de Tocqueville and Charles Dickens, a champion of prison reform. Westervelt had been a model prisoner and won time off for good behavior. Leaving the prison, he announced that he would go to New York, where his wife had managed to keep their home together by her needlework. He firmly maintained his innocence.

"I had nothing whatever to do with it," he told a New York *Tribune* reporter. "Because I was Mosher's brother-in-law all the detectives thought I must have been concerned in the plot. I had upward of fifty interviews with Walling, and Pinkerton called on me and offered to take me into his detective agency, but I wouldn't go. I reported this to Walling and it caused bad feelings between them. We were working up every possible clue, and on April 12, 1875, Walling told me he would like me to go to Philadelphia and tell the committee of citizens what I knew about the case. This led to a meeting with Ross, Heins, Wood, and others in the mayor's office, with a shorthand reporter. When I was ready to leave they detained me.

"I was the first man who was got hold of in such a way as to make his trial seem to be demanded by the circumstances and what was seriously against me, the popular mind was excited against me by portions of the testimony which looked bad but which would have been found to have been the result of mistakes on the part of witnesses, or probably worse than mistakes, had they been coolly and carefully sifted and weighed.

"Mrs. Lyons testified to my being at my sister's house in Philadelphia in July. She admitted to me afterward with tears in her eyes that it was an error she had made, that it was June instead of July.

"In the evidence of Superintendent Walling he admitted that I gave him the information which I stated, but said that I always gave it to him too late to be of any use to him. I would ask concerning the information in relation to Mosher and Douglas being at Astoria, when he neglected for ten or twelve hours to send anyone there, and when they did get there they found that Mosher and Douglas had left there only some fifteen minutes before, if that was too late? And I would ask if the information was too late when I told him I was to meet Mosher and Douglas that night and wanted him to make the arrest. And all the other information which I gave him I gave it to him as promptly as it lay in my power to do so. If he did not, or could not, make use of it, that lay with himself.

"All that I can think of is that the officials thought by convicting me, that it would be the means of bringing out some information from Mrs. Mosher, who is my sister, or some friends of Mosher's who would not like to see me suffer innocently."

"So you think Charley Ross is still living?"

"Why should I think he is dead? No one has ever heard of his death, so far as known. If the people who first had him in charge were able to keep him for many months without his being found out, why couldn't they have kept him for years just as safely? Why, he might be in any of the foundling asylums in New York City, and who would be the wiser? The police have never searched there, and if they did they might not find him."

"What are your plans?"

"I shall first endeavor to go to work. If I can find the time, I will try and follow a certain clue that has never been properly worked up. If Mosher and Douglas did steal the boy, there must have been a third person who took care of him, and I have my suspicions as to who it was. I have no hard feelings against Mr. Ross because I would do anything to get possession of a child of mine, but I do blame him for allowing an innocent man to suffer all these years after he knew that I could not throw any light on the matter. If I could help him get his child I would cheerfully do so. I have thought over every possible clue quite as much as he has. Last May my sister came to see me, but I could not learn anything from her that is not already known. I will try every means to recover the child just for the satisfaction of clearing myself, and I have hopes that before long I shall be able to discover something."

If William Westervelt ever discovered a clue to the lost boy, the authorities never learned of it. After his release he dropped out of sight as completely as little Charley Ross himself.

As the 1880's wore on, the missing Charley was still not found, but a vigilant public continued to turn up substitutes. In Burlington, Vermont, an amateur sleuth masqueraded for days in female dress as he shadowed a suspicious-looking couple with a young boy. When he induced Christian Ross to make the trip to check on his find, that tired man once again saw that it was not his son.

Ross went to Poughkeepsie to check on a clue furnished by a man named Hester, who had seen Mosher and Douglas on their Rondout excursion with Westervelt. The clue led nowhere.

Excitement developed briefly in New York when a young boy was brought to police headquarters by people who thought he might be little Charley. The boy turned out to be the son of the woman who called herself alternately the wife and the sister of Joseph Douglas. He was released in her custody.

Police in Wisconsin heard of a woman traveling with a young boy who resembled the missing Charley. When the woman refused to answer questions, suspicion grew and she was taken into custody. It was eventually learned that the boy was illegitimate, that the mother, ashamed, had been afraid to inform her parents of his existence.

In Wurzburg, Germany, a child who had suddenly appeared in incongruous company was investigated by the American consul at Nuremberg.

A child was reported living with a female fortuneteller on the shores of the Bay of Fundy in Canada.

Similarly, a young boy who suddenly appeared among the Tuscarora Indians in Canada was investigated.

Detectives in England spent long months following two camps of gypsies, each reportedly harboring a mysterious boy.

A Boston man who called himself Uncle Sam wrote the Boston *Globe* that he had reason to believe Charley Ross had been concealed in that city. Superintendent Walling characterized his story as false. Uncle Sam, he declared, was known to him. It was the pseudonym of a man named Holmes who claimed to have received a communication from the spirit of the dead Bill Mosher to his wife, giving the place of concealment of the missing boy.

Walling used the occasion to inform the press that he had sent detectives to five different prisons, including Sing Sing, Auburn, and Eastern, where inmates told wardens they had information that could lead to the missing boy. In each instance detectives found that convicts were trying to use the case to gain pardons. "He holds the opinion that the boy is dead," the New York *Tribune* summed up Walling's current attitude.

In Philadelphia, a mulatto known as George suddenly appeared on the scene claiming to know the missing boy's place of confinement and offering to help restore him. Ross interviewed the man and after a lengthy conversation concluded that his object was simply to procure a few dollars. The episode was only one of countless extortion and blackmail attempts. Monomaniacs, crackpots, amateur detectives, and genuine sympathizers continued to abound in the case. Though it seemed to many, as it did to the New York *Tribune* many years after the abduction, that it was time "the farce were ended," the farce was far from finished.

Even Superintendent Walling felt hopeful once more when he heard a story of a boy recently brought to Baltimore from Demerara County in British Guiana, where he had been taken from a mulatto woman who had him in charge. During the time the boy had been in Baltimore his skin had been steadily bleaching and it was said that day by day his resemblance to the missing Charley was growing.

"You need not laugh and say it is another case of mistaken identity," the superintendent said in an interview at his office. "I know Charley Ross has been found all over the United States and elsewhere for that matter, but I am strongly inclined to believe that the Demerara boy, now in Baltimore, is the missing boy.

"There is a little piece of secret history connected with the Ross case, which I am not averse to giving you now, and from it you will see why I place some reliance on the story that Charley Ross has really been found in Baltimore. When Mosher and Douglas, his abductors, were in Brooklyn, a peddler was often seen with them. This man was a suspicious character. He lived with a mulatto woman. When Mosher and Douglas were killed the peddler disappeared, but we finally got a clue to him in Boston, where he and the mulatto woman were living with a little white boy who had never before been seen with them. I communicated with the Boston chief of police and went to the peddler's house to arrest the inmates, but found that they had fled a few hours before. The peddler's stock, consisting of hatracks, his clothing, the woman's clothing, and other things were left behind, showing that their flight was sudden. The woman and child, who we supposed was Charley Ross, were never afterward seen, but now this mulatto woman turns up in Demerara with a child that is evidently not her own and is probably the Ross boy. . . . The child seems to remember about a man stealing him, and gives a description resembling Mosher. Now all these facts seem to tally, and the developments of the next few days will show whether they will weave into one story and prove that Charley Ross has at last been recovered.''

In Philadelphia Christian Ross also spoke to the press about the boy: ''I am going down to Baltimore to settle the question definitely because numbers of people think I am indifferent in the case. But I tell you I have had between five hundred and six hundred cases brought to my attention, and had I become enthusiastic over every one I would have been in Kirkbride's [a Philadelphia insane asylum] long ago. In regard to the little prayer which this boy makes, it is different from the one my wife teaches my children.''

Superintendent Walling's optimism had been premature. When the father reached Baltimore, he saw that the Demerara child was not his son. ''I suppose I shall continue to see boys until I die," Ross said sadly. "but I no longer expect to find Charley in any of them."

The boys were growing older now, this unending string of youngsters who thought they were, or hoped they might be, Charley Ross.

In 1885 Arthur Jackson Searing, seventeen, called a newspaperman to his home in Brooklyn. "Hush, they might hear us," he whispered, referring to his "parents." "I will meet you in five minutes on Flatbush Avenue near Fourth Avenue and I will tell you all about it."

At the designated rendezvous the young man confided that years ago, while playing with the children of the family he was with, they had told him he was not their brother but adopted.

"When the woman who claims to be my mother heard this, she looked at them in a peculiar way, but said nothing. I read a description of Charley Ross a year ago, and as I don't know any other boy that is missing, I suppose I am Charley."

Solemnly, the young man produced a photograph of himself as a child which bore a marked resemblance to the photos of little Charley Ross. He also recollected awakening many years ago in a stable and finding the man and woman who claimed to be his parents standing over him.

After listening to the not uncommon fantasy of this adolescent who firmly believed his avowed parents were not really his own, the reporter researched his background and found that he could not have been the missing Charley.

"Charley Ross, if living, is old enough to find himself and make his way back to his father," wrote the New York *Times*. "Accordingly, we may expect that every young fellow of sixteen or eighteen years of age who has no ostensible father, and who thinks that a father might be made useful, will begin to have vague recollections of having been stolen from a

Philadelphia home, and will make his way to Philadelphia and try to throw himself into Mr. Ross's arms.''

And truly, the boys kept coming. And when a respite occurred in their appearances, stories would find their way to Philadelphia of young men in other cities who might be the lost boy.

So in New York in 1890, reporters and detectives were put on the trail of the young son of John McChristie, a milk dealer whose wife was the widow of the dead burglar, Bill Mosher. Close to twenty years old, Charles McChristie was reported by an anonymous informant to be the missing Charley. Investigation established his real identity as Charles Mosher, the third child of Martha Westervelt and William Mosher. He had taken the name of his stepfather. In 1892, when young McChristie died under mysterious circumstances, the newspapers said they suspected foul play, unrelated, however, to the long-ago kidnapping.

A more prominent figure in the Ross abduction case, Holmes Van Brunt, died not many years later, on September 27, 1896. After the shooting at Bay Ridge, he had become the hero of his locality, especially among the young people.

A gradually failing Ross read of the death of the man who had been the prime mover on that memorable night at Bay Ridge when his son's abductors had been shot without revealing his place of concealment. In recent years the search for his missing boy had become an ever more painful obsession, and the once spry, wiry father snatched at the slightest information which he imagined could afford a clue to his Charley.

Through eight state administrations, including several changes of political party, Pennsylvania governors reappointed him master warden of the port of Philadelphia. Ross took his post seriously, maintaining an office downtown in the Merchants Exchange Building. Here he compiled a volume which found its way into the municipal library and archives: *A Digest of the Laws, Decisions, and Rules relating to the Board of Wardens for the Port of Philadelphia. Compiled and Arranged by Christian K. Ross, Master Warden.* The volume was published in 1895 by the printer for the state.

"Christian Ross Dead" read the headline for the story which the New York *Times* ran on its front page of June 22, 1897. "Death of the man who aroused the world to search for his lost child," said the subhead: "The abduction of Charley Ross, who was a beautiful child, practically wrecked the life of his father, and from the time the boy was stolen, nearly twenty-three years ago, life seemed a burden to the once bustling businessman."

After an illness of three weeks, Christian Ross died peacefully in his sleep. Although he had no record of heart trouble, it was that organ, understandably, which finally gave out.

46

A MONTH AFTER the father's death, a New York City evening paper printed an interview with Ellsworth Mosher, the son of Old Gil and a nephew of the abductor, William Mosher. An honest and industrious laborer, according to his employer and neighbors, Ellsworth declared he was ready to reveal a confidence which his father had told him to keep secret until after Christian Ross's death.

Sixteen years ago workmen had torn down a building at 55 Grand Street; from the basement of this building Gil Mosher's wife had once run a restaurant. Secreted in the walls workmen had found the skeleton of a boy's body. This body, Old Gil had told Ellsworth shortly before his death some years before, was all that was left of little Charley Ross. The ailing Gil had provided no further details, had not provided the background for his remarks.

Whether the story was spurious or true was never ascertained, but Sarah Ross, who had survived several near fatal illnesses, continued the search which her husband had abandoned only with his death. Many years ago, police and well-meaning citizens had brought to her home the little boys they believed to be her missing Charley. Later, adolescents had taken trains, and hitchhiked, and walked to the elm-shaded house on Washington Lane to be identified. Now middle-aged men began to make their appearance, and Mrs. Ross continued to see them, still daring to dream that she would find her lost boy.

"Is William Van Hodge really Charley Ross?" "Charley Ross Claimant: Family to Inquire," "Charley Ross Here Again," said typical headings in the New York *Times* as the quest carried into the twentieth century. When Mrs. Ross grew too old to make journeys to check out clues, her brothers and her husband's surviving brothers took her place. Each helped to carry on a correspondence which apparently had no end.

The search seemed to keep Mrs. Ross alive. Those hours which were not devoted to it were spent in activities on behalf of Philadelphia's charities. It was to attend a planning session for one of her projects that she made her way to the parsonage of her church in Germantown on December 13, 1912. She had hardly entered when she fell forward and died. As with her husband, it was the heart which had failed.

Two years before her death Mrs. Ross revealed that most of the letters she still received came from cranks. The task of investigating the cases which continued to present themselves now fell to her surviving children, sons Henry (Harry, in adulthood, used the more formal name) and Walter, and daughters Sophia, Marian, and Anne. Walter had become a prominent businessman of the city, a member for his firm of the New York Stock Exchange. It was he who spoke for the family on July 1, 1924, from his home in Chestnut Hill, just beyond Germantown:

"It is the fiftieth anniversary of a great sorrow to us. We have long since despaired. We are constantly in receipt of letters and visits from people claiming to be my brother. Of course, we have never given up all hope that some day he may return, but each of these incidents has only opened the wounds of our sorrow, recalling a tragedy that has hung over our family for these long years."

In the *Ladies' Home Journal* of July 1924, the cover story was entitled "Charley Ross: The Unforgotten Lost Boy." Its author, Clarence McCartney, opened his account by saying that when his friends from abroad came to town they seemed to know little of Philadelphia's shrines, but each one asked immediately about the story of little Charley Ross of Washington Lane.

"Never was there a child hunt like that for Charley Ross," the New York *Times* stated in its anniversary treatment of the case. "All America was spaded up. Every child of 1874 shuddered at strangers and thrilled, half envious, at Charley Ross. Parents used the name of the boy as a bugaboo and he is better known even now than men who have been president. Whatever happened to him, he yet lives, for he has become a legend and his name is known to the very youngsters of today."

For some years the Ross house on Washington Lane was rented by the Cliveden Presbyterian Church, to which Mrs. Ross had sold it at practically half its assessed value because it was to be used as a house of worship. Its porch sagging, its window sills awry, the old mansion seemed to stare at the world through vacant eyes. When increasing attendance and a growing congregation brought with them the need for a larger structure, trustees decided to tear down the once handsome but now gloomy relic of the unsolved kidnapping. In 1926 the house was razed and in its place rose a new church, an appropriate use for the property which Christian and Sarah Ross had long ago made a home of the spirit.

47

INTRIGUING AND COMPLEX figures had entered the famous abduction case at various stages. Now, near the end of the saga of little Charley Ross — if an end there is to be — one more participant came center stage. On February 5, 1939, a carpenter in Phoenix, Arizona, announced his intention of filing suit to establish his identity as Charley Ross. The man's name was Gustav Blair. He was sixty-nine years old.

Named as defendants were Walter, Sophia, Marian, and Anne Ross. Alleging that they refused to recognize him as their brother, Blair stated he did not seek a judgment to determine inheritance or property rights, as all that had long since been barred by time. He wanted only the right to bear his correct name and would prove his claim to that right in court.

"If my elder brother, Walter, lives for five years, he'll seek me out and admit our kinship," Blair declared. "I have been ignored by Walter and other members of my family despite the fact that they knew my claims were justified. My wife and I sacrificed our home and in some instances have gone hungry to prove my birthright."

Armed with documents amassed over a long period, for he had begun his legal fight many years earlier, Blair appeared in Superior Court on May 8 before Judge G. A. Rodgers and a jury assembled to hear his claim. The story he told was one to match the most imaginative that had been spawned during the long years.

In addition to Mosher and Douglas, there had been another accomplice in the abduction, Blair maintained. His name was John Hawks, an Illinois farm youth who had been mixed up with the Mosher gang. Hawks had taken possession of little Charley Ross after the abduction and, disguising him as a girl, had driven him across the country in a peddler's wagon. The wagon had stopped at the backwoods cabin of Rinear Miller, in Lee County, Illinois. When Hawks said he wanted to take Miller's son Lincoln, then eleven, back to Pennsylvania with him as a companion for what he called his sister's child, the elder Miller agreed to this. Hawks left the abducted boy for a few days with Miller and his wife, who had never heard of the kidnapping. While he was gone, they read of the case and when he came to get the boy, they refused to turn him over. Hawks was killed in the quarrel that ensued. Miller, fearing that he would be linked with the abduction if he revealed the boy's identity, reared him as his own in a cave. Just before the elder Miller died he confessed to his foster son that he was Charley Ross. The boy, now a young man, wished to preserve the good name of his foster father and determined to say nothing. But the desire to use his own name eventually came to the fore and he had now brought suit.

As his key witness, Blair produced Lincoln C. Miller, his "foster brother," who was seriously ill but came into court in a wheelchair. Miller testified that he had helped guard the young boy in a cave and that his father had told him Blair was the kidnapped child from Germantown.

Since no member of the Ross family appeared, Judge Rodgers entered a default judgment against them. After hearing the brief uncontested testimony, a Superior Court jury decided in eight minutes that Gustav Blair was Charley

Ross and legally entitled to bear the name. The jurisdiction of the court was limited, however, to the county in which it was situated.

Hardly had the Phoenix tribunal ruled when Blair — or, as the court would have it, Ross — announced that he would sue in Philadelphia to obtain a share in a supposed $460,000 family trust fund. He said he planned to leave with his wife for the Quaker City and on July 1, the anniversary of the abduction, he would be remarried in Germantown under the name of Ross.

From the Reverend Harold Melcher of the Cliveden Presbyterian Church of East Washington Lane, on the site of the old Ross mansion, came word that he had refused Blair's request to marry him: "The ceremony would have given some semiofficial recognition to the claim, which was thoroughly investigated some years ago and turned down for lack of sufficient evidence."

"Charley Ross Lost Again" said a Philadelphia paper when Blair failed to appear in the city for the marriage. On September 26, 1939, Blair went through with the ceremony in Phoenix. He announced that his second honeymoon would be passed in Hollywood, where his life story was to be written and, he hoped, filmed.

The elderly carpenter did make the trip to Hollywood and appeared on a number of radio and television programs, but his authenticity was not widely recognized. The Ross family continued to deny it insistently until the time of his death in the early 1940's.

"This thing has been going on for a number of years," said Walter Ross. "There are men all over the country claiming they are Charley Ross. This man's claims were entirely unfounded and we intend to ignore the action of the Arizona court." Incredible as it might sound, Walter added, over the long years more than five thousand applicants had come forward to show they were Charles Brewster Ross. None had been able to prove his point.

In 1943 Walter Ross died, the last of the principals in the greatest kidnapping mystery of the century. Within months of his death a familiar item appeared in the papers. Said the Germantown *Courier*: "Philadelphia police this week, for the thousandth time, were given a tip which may turn out to be a valuable clue in the search for Charley Ross, who was kidnapped from his Germantown home many years ago." And so the search for the lost boy was not yet over.

48

"MY SOUL PRAYS to God for thee that thou mayest stand in the day of trial, that thy children may be blest and thy people saved by His power."

So read William Penn's prayer for Philadelphia, composed in 1684. Almost two centuries later, a little boy of four, with flaxen ringlets that fell to his shoulders and a quaint manner that reminded his parents of the city's founder, was stolen from his home in Germantown. There had been a George Ross among the signers of the Declaration of Independence, and the home of Betsy Ross, the seamstress whose agile needle fashioned the new nation's first flag, was still much visited by citizens close to Philadelphia's traditions. Christian Ross, the stolen boy's father, was not unmindful of tradition and the demands society could place on its citizens, and when he was asked not to compound the felony of child-stealing he obeyed his friends and the authorities with heavy heart. Refusing to pay the ransom demanded by the kidnappers, he sought to retrieve his child in every way left open to him.

So fantastic was the drama that followed, so grotesque, so

bittersweet in its alternation of hope and despair, so ultimately unfathomable, that it became a legendary tragedy. The father's tireless search found an echo in the hearts of Philadelphians, as graves were opened and babes in their mothers' arms were awakened to see whether they had the brown eyes of the lost boy. From a grieving city the sad tale was spread far and wide. Little Charley Ross became a nation's obsession.

What in essence was it about the boy from Washington Lane — who never reappeared after his abduction and yet was never absent — that turned a nation into one searching party? What was it that permeated the spirit so profoundly that even madmen in insane asylums would cry out, "I am Charley Ross! I am Charley Ross!" After all, other boys had been stolen. Other fathers had searched the country over for them. They had not, it was true, been taken for the purpose of extorting a large sum of money, and therein lay one strong reason for the hold the case had taken on an entire people. Another, surely, lay in the charm and beauty of the child himself. Many obvious factors were there, but also one more: a charisma which attaches to but few figures in history. Perhaps in little Charley Ross the multitudes saw an incarnation of their own lost youth. Perhaps, finally, in that sadly sweet round face they came to see their own lost innocence, to find a fragment of their own elusive identity. For which one was not himself, in some sense, a child lost in the wood? And who would not wish to be found?

Acknowledgments

I AM PARTICULARLY GRATEFUL to the directors and staffs of the following institutions for so graciously making their materials and resources available to me: the Library Company of Philadelphia, the Historical Society of Pennsylvania, the New York Historical Society, and the New York Public Library.

Newspapers which furnished the most useful data in their day-to-day coverage of the Charley Ross kidnapping include the following: in Philadelphia, the *Public Ledger, Illustrated New Age, Evening Star, Evening Bulletin, Record, Inquirer, North American and United States Gazette,* and *Times,* as well as, in Germantown, the *Telegraph* and *Courier;* in New York, the *Herald, Times, Tribune, World,* and *Sun,* and the Brooklyn *Daily Eagle.*

Also consulted were *Harper's Weekly, Frank Leslie's Illustrated Newspaper, Potter's American Monthly,* and the *Chambers Journal of Popular Literature, Science, and the Arts.* The *Ladies' Home Journal* fiftieth anniversary review of the case, to which I refer in the text, appeared in the July 1924 issue of that magazine.

American vs. Italian Brigandage, an account of the trial and conviction of William H. Westervelt, was published by Barclay and Company, Philadelphia, in 1875. The following year *The Father's Story of Charley Ross, the Kidnapped Child,* by Christian K. Ross, was published by John E. Potter and Company, Philadelphia. George Washington Walling's *Recollections of a New York Chief of Police* appeared in 1887 under the imprint of Caxton Book Concern, Limited, New York.

Brief analyses of the Ross case can be found in a number of volumes, the most valuable to me being those in *Celebrated Criminal Cases of America,* by Thomas S. Duke, Captain of Police, San Francisco, 1910, and *Mysteries of the Missing,* by Edward H. Smith, Dial Press, 1927.

Finally, a special word of thanks to my friend Rita Senf for her scrupulous editing of several stages of the manuscript prior to submission to the publisher, and to another friend, Marguerite Young, who first evoked in my mind the haunting picture of little Charley Ross which led to my writing this account of his travail.

NORMAN ZIEROLD

New York City